W9-CIN-260

WILLIAM T. PORTER
AND THE
SPIRIT OF THE TIMES

This is a volume in the Arno Press collection

INTERNATIONAL FOLKLORE

Advisory Editor
Richard M. Dorson

Editorial Board
Issachar Ben Ami
Vilmos Voigt

*See last pages of this volume
for a complete list of titles*

WILLIAM T. PORTER

AND THE

Spirit of the Times

NORRIS W. YATES

ARNO PRESS

A New York Times Company

New York / 1977

Editorial Supervision: LUCILLE MAIORCA

———◆———

Reprint Edition 1977 by Arno Press Inc.

Copyright © 1957 by The Louisiana State
   University Press

Reprinted by permission of The Louisiana
   State University Press

Reprinted from a copy in
   The University of Illinois Library

INTERNATIONAL FOLKLORE
ISBN for complete set: 0-405-10077-9
See last pages of this volume for titles.

Manufactured in the United States of America

———◆———

Library of Congress Cataloging in Publication Data

Yates, Norris Wilson.
   William T. Porter and the Spirit of the times.

   (International folklore)
   Reprint of the ed. published by Louisiana State
University Press, Baton Rouge.
   Bibliography: p.
   Includes index.
   1. Porter, William Trotter, 1809-1858.
2. Journalists--United States--Biography. 3. Spir-
it of the times. 4. American wit and humor--His-
tory and criticism. I. Series.
[PN4874.P59Y3 1977]   070.4'092'4 [B]   77-70630
ISBN 0-405-10134-1

WILLIAM T. PORTER

AND THE

Spirit of the Times

WILLIAM T. PORTER

 AND THE

Spirit of the Times

A Study of the BIG BEAR School
of Humor

By NORRIS W. YATES

LOUISIANA STATE UNIVERSITY PRESS
Baton Rouge

To My Parents

Preface

TO weave a net of definition that will contain and reveal a subject as shapeless, heterogeneous, and complex as the background, contents, and influence of the *Spirit of the Times* is as hard as to catch fish by scooping up the river with a bucket. Yet, as the reader will see, this kind of fishing may bring results, under the right conditions. We have used a very small bucket and a very critical eye in dipping into the teeming pool of material offered by the *Spirit;* even so, we have come up with quite a haul. The magazine was subtitled *A Chronicle of the Turf, Agriculture, Field Sports, Literature and the Stage,* and we have thrown back, as it were, most specimens of the first three and the fifth categories. Thus, sporting writers like Henry William Herbert ("Frank Forester") and Charles E. Whitehead, writers on farming and stock-breeding like Solon Robinson, and men primarily connected with the drama like O. E. Durivage have been rejected as being of the wrong kind and "shape" except when their contributions have interest for the student of literary history and local color.

Our main topic, then, is, briefly, the part played by the "Tall Son of York," as Porter came to be called, and by the *Spirit* in promoting the regional writing of the Old Southwest and assisting the comic realists of this area to reach a national public. It is hoped that the material presented or paraphrased in these pages will clarify the role of the *Spirit* by illustration and also have intrinsic interest for the reader who enjoys a good story. Should these tales and sketches also lead the reader to hunt up the nearest file of the magazine for himself, incomplete though it probably is, or to peruse Porter's two volumes of sketches collected from the *Spirit* (*The Big Bear of Arkansas* and *A Quarter Race in Kentucky*), the author will be pleased. And so, he is sure, will the amiable ghost of the Tall Son. The stream is far from being fished out. A number of good yarns we have had to leave unreprinted and undiscussed, and many of these will repay further study.

Greater than the debt owed by the southwestern yarn-spinners to Porter and his periodical is that owed by the author to Professor James Davidson of North Texas State College and to Dr. Abe C. Ravitz of Pennsylvania State University for reading the manuscript of this study and for their many helpful and stimulating suggestions. The author is even now troubled at not having followed quite all of them. His general indebtedness to Professor Nelson F. Adkins of New York University is also heavy. In addition, he is grateful to Professor Sherwood E. Cummings of the University of South Dakota for moral support as well as for several timely comments and to Dr. Milton Rickels of George Pepperdine College for information about Thomas Bangs Thorpe; also to Mr. Franklin J. Meine of Chicago for his hospitality and generous counsel.

Space does not permit individual expressions of gratitude to all of the many persons and institutions that have helped the writer. However he would like to cite especially the staff members of the New York Public Library, the American Antiquarian Society, the Yale University Library, and the New York Historical Society, and to indicate his thanks to the various university libraries and historical societies of the South for the patience, helpfulness, and courtesy shown by their staffs. Further acknowledgments are made in the course of this study.

NORRIS W. YATES

January, 1957

Table of Contents

Illustrations

WILLIAM T. PORTER

AND THE

Spirit of the Times

CHAPTER ONE

Porter, the Man, and His Magazine

I

THAT sharp-tongued critic of American life, Mrs. Frances Trollope, complained that periodicals in this country were a debasing influence on literary taste. She made one small exception in favor of the *American Quarterly Review*, remarking that to the "eye of the body" it looked exactly like the English *Quarterly Review*.[1] This bit of condescension must have infuriated many a tobacco-chewing country editor even more than the English lady's many comments on which the barbs were open rather than concealed. Yet it is a commonplace that most American magazines and newspapers were modeled on those of the British Isles and continued to borrow their formats, steal their news, and pirate their well-known authors while waving the Stars and Stripes and emitting eagle-like screams at the strictures of Mrs. Trollope, Basil Hall, Frederick Marryat, and other critical Britishers. Consistency, foolish or otherwise, has rarely been a hobgoblin of the American editor.

Nor did this specter bother William T. Porter, who had founded a weekly sporting magazine in New York City in the closing days of 1831, the year before Mrs. Trollope's *Domestic Manners of the Americans* hit the bookstalls. Porter announced that his periodical was modeled on *Bell's Life in London*, a leading sporting journal of that city. But in its thirty years of life,

[1] *Domestic Manners of the Americans* (New York, 1927), 77, 85, 268. Cf. Alexis de Tocqueville, *Democracy in America*, tr. by Henry Reeve (2 vols.; New York, 1898), I, 230–41; Harriet Martineau, *Society in America* (2 vols.; New York, 1837), I, 109–15, 237; G. W. Featherstonhaugh, *Excursion Through the Slave States* (2 vols.; London, 1844), II, 49–51; Frederick Marryat, *A Diary in America . . . Part Second* (3 vols.; London, 1839), I, 163–94.

Porter's magazine, the *Spirit of the Times,* drew most of its readers and reputation from the geographical areas and social groups which have often been regarded, rightly or wrongly, as those most distinctly American. Moreover, this paper gave an important boost to the writing of literature about just those shock-headed, one-gallused, tobacco-spitting, whisky-guzzling coonskin republicans of the back country whose lack of domestic manners horrified Mrs. Trollope. And thereby hangs our tale.

History may never repeat itself exactly, but certain historical phenomena seem to have a familiar ring. One hundred and twenty odd years ago a good many people then as now believed that the road to success was any highway that led to New York City. This feeling was strong in New England, which was losing ground commercially to the island city in the decade that included the opening of the Erie Canal (1825). New York was the source of an especial itch among various alert, ambitious young men who found the commercial, journalistic, or literary circles of Boston, New Haven, or Hartford too small, and the rigorous morality of the descendants of the Puritans too cramping to suit their talents and personalities. Born in Maine, Nathaniel Parker Willis had come to New York from Connecticut; so had Fitz-Greene Halleck. This Knickerbocker wit and poet may well have met Porter when glasses were raised and stories were traded by the "Barclay Street guards," a convivial gang that used to gather at Frank Monteverde's restaurant, a popular rendezvous of the New York literati.[2]

In 1825 the more sober-sided William Cullen Bryant came to the mushrooming city to edit the *New York Review and Athenaeum Magazine* and eventually to forsake literature as a profession while he edited the *Evening Post.* About five years later two other young journalists followed independently from the rocky backlands of Vermont and New Hampshire. Each of this pair had served an apprenticeship in upcountry composing rooms; each was to cut a wide swath in his own journalistic field. These two young

[2] Francis Brinley, *Life of William T. Porter* (New York, 1860), 86–100; Stephen C. Massett, *"Drifting About," or What "Jeems Pipes of Pipesville" Saw-and-Did* (New York, 1863), 56; Nelson F. Adkins, *Fitz-Greene Halleck, an Early Knickerbocker Wit and Poet* (New Haven, 1930), 252n.

hopefuls were the twenty-year-old Horace Greeley and his fellow journeyman printer, two years older, William Trotter Porter.

It is worth mentioning that by no means all the Yankees who joined this exodus to New York were would-be writers or journalists. The stream also included Daniel Drew and P. T. Barnum. But Porter, never much of a hand at turning an honest or a dishonest penny, surely had less of the acquisitive drive that impelled the migration of such sharp operators. It was the bleak and crabbed aspects of New England morality, its academic garb, its rigid dogmatism and harsh judgments on human nature that seem to have driven forth this genial son of a Vermont lawyer. Fourteen years after leaving his boyhood home for the last time he remembered with repulsion having to "battle it with the Moral Philosophy prof about 'Edwards on the Will.' The logic of the old divine was too subtle for young minds, and admitting his reasonable premises, he would straightway hurry you into conclusions, accurately deduced therefrom, which revolted your moral sense, though you could discover no way of escape from them." [3] When he wrote this, Porter was comparing Edwards' argumentation with that of a sporting correspondent of the *Spirit of the Times* in order to refute this gentleman's stand on the proper placement of bets for a horse race. *O, tempora!* . . .

However, Porter's background had never been strictly Puritan. His family, though of the oldest New England stock, were Episcopalians. Samuel Porter, the first of his line in America, had emigrated to Plymouth in 1622. William hardly ever mentions his family tree in his extant letters and writings, but his brother-in-law, Francis Brinley, becomes defensive about the fact that William's grandfather, Asa Porter, was a Tory and had fled to Canada during the Revolution. Brinley asserts that "at any rate he was ever faithful and loyal to the new government." [4]

Several elements in William T. Porter's early background are undoubtedly reflected in his magazine and in the "Big Bear school" of writing of which he was editorial foster-father. [5] Old

---

[3] *Spirit of the Times*, IX (1839), 99, hereinafter referred to as the *Spirit*.

[4] Brinley, *Life of William T. Porter*, 1–5.

[5] This term seems to have been first used by Bernard DeVoto, "Frontier America," *Saturday Review of Literature*, V (June 1, 1929), 1067–68.

Asa Porter had received from the British Crown in return for his sufferings at the hands of the patriots a large grant of land in Broome Township, Canada. His total estate, including several large tracts in Vermont, is said to have encompassed 100,000 acres, and he had a passion for fine horses, as did his grandson. Benjamin, William's father and apparently one of Asa's several sons, was described to Brinley by an old acquaintance as definitely a gentleman and of open-handed and genial tendencies. He seems to have passed these tendencies on to at least two of his five sons, William and the oldest, Dr. Thomas Olcott Porter.

Too, Benjamin was a friend of Daniel Webster in his youth, and off and on for over ten years Webster visited the Porter home at Newbury, Vermont, where William had been born.[6] Benjamin Porter died in 1818, when William was nine years old, and it is not impossible that the editor may have cherished youthful memories of the great Whig politician. Anyhow, throughout Porter's editorial career, flashes of Whig fire occasionally sparked his pages, rare exceptions to the rule of "no politics" to which much of his success as an editor must surely be attributed. And upon Webster's death in 1852 Porter devoted nearly the whole of a front page with black-leaded borders to a glowing obituary tribute well garnished with anecdotes.[7] Not even Henry Clay, the idol of border-state Whiggery, rated so much space and attention.

Two other figures, closely associated, stand out as representatives of the opposing forces whose conflict helped to shape the personality of young William. One was his remarkable old nurse, Sally Kinnicum (or Kinnikum), whose exploits Porter fondly recalled two years before his death, in one of his few personal editorials. Sally "gave us our first lessons in bare-back riding," Porter affirmed. He reverted to horse-racing cant to call her "the choicest bit of blood and bottom we remember to have seen . . . . the old girl was straight as a javelin, tough as a pine knot, with a laugh like a whole band of music," and had long, free-flowing white hair. She was a fast runner, and would assist young William to escape from the other figure, Master Clark, the tutor, "whose

[6] Brinley, *Life of William T. Porter*, 13–14.
[7] *Spirit*, XXII (1852), 433.

dingy black tights, we remember, were so shiny, as to afford us the benefit of a pocket mirror whenever we had occasion to take a rapid survey of our person." She went fishing with William, climbed trees and explored the woods with him, and on one unforgettable occasion she hoisted him to her back and raced three village boys for the prize of "a half dollar, and a prime lot of fish-hooks." When she stopped, William sailed over her head, "lighting directly on our countenance, and striking daylight through our under lip—the scar of that memorable wound bearing evidence to this day." [8] Thus did Porter make his first acquaintance with the steeplechase.

One must turn the searchlight of doubt on this rhapsodic reminiscence in view of the fact that Porter confessed that "we were then in our third summer." Truly he had a remarkable memory! But the editorial is valuable in revealing how little some of Porter's earlier tastes had changed later in life, and his dislike of Master Clark certainly resembles his later distaste for his preceptor at Moore's Indian Charity School, which he attended from the ages of twelve to fourteen. After his father's death his mother had moved with the family to Hanover, New Hampshire, and at Moore's school, which was connected with Dartmouth College and open to whites for a small fee, William suffered under an autocrat with a heavy ferule and the schoolmasterish name of Archelaus F. Putnam. Putnam may have been the professor of Moral Philosophy who tried to cram "Edwards on the Will" down the throat of a young fellow who much preferred Walton's *Compleat Angler*—thus exhibiting a lifelong tendency. His sister Sarah declared in later years that William had done well in school, but he pleaded to be let out and was finally apprenticed to a printing firm in Andover, Massachusetts. Ironically, theological works were the specialty of this firm, and no doubt young Porter had to pore over these as he learned the layout of the type case. [9]

In 1822, perhaps while William was still in school, his oldest brother, Dr. Thomas O. Porter, went to the South, where he

[8] "Sally Kinnicum . . . A Youthful Reminiscence," by "the Editor," *Porter's Spirit of the Times,* I (1856), 106–107, hereinafter designated as *Porter's Spirit.*
[9] Brinley, *Life of William T. Porter,* 18–24.

knocked about for two years as an itinerant teacher. His younger brothers are said to have read and reread his letters. While in Georgia, Thomas became friends with the amazing Mirabeau Bonaparte Lamar, later president of the Republic of Texas, with whom he carried on a long correspondence after his return North. During the thirties and forties the Doctor and William, in fact all five of the brothers, formed an affectionate, close-knit group united "by almost hourly intercourse," and the durable friendship between his brother and Lamar could have been the first of William's many contacts with the great southern plantation families. Undoubtedly this friendship lies behind the puff for Lamar in the *Spirit* which appeared shortly after the battle of San Jacinto.[10]

Thus among the elements of Porter's early life and background we find the open-handed ways and liking for fine horses which one often associates with country gentlemen, a love of companionship, a dislike of academic routine and Calvinistic morality, a fondness for sport and the literature of sporting, and possibly an interest in things "Southron." These elements may or may not have directly influenced his mature life and work, but notice of them may at least help us to understand more readily the career of Porter and the *Spirit*.

II

Porter grew into a tall, gangling fellow of six feet, four inches, and his long arms and legs must have just about filled some of the cramped country print shops in which he seems to have served his apprenticeship and worked as a journeyman between 1822 and 1831. By 1829 he was doing editorial work as well on small-town Vermont newspapers; in that year he edited the *Farmer's Herald* at St. Johnsbury, Vermont. But before he settled into the printing trade for good he may have tried his hand at teaching.[11]

Whatever the case, Porter came to New York in 1830 or 1831 and in the latter year he was foreman in John T. West's shop at 85 Chatham Street. In this capacity he gave the verdant country youth Horace Greeley his first job in New York, and at once assigned him a passage from the New Testament to set in very small

[10] *Ibid.*, 31, 74, 78–79; "Mirabeau B. Lamar," *Spirit*, VI (1836), 172.
[11] Brinley, *Life of William T. Porter*, 32–33.

type—a test that the young typesetter passed with flying colors. Porter and Greeley evidently became good friends, although they eventually went widely separate ways. Greeley remembered his old boss as "a tall, comely youth, of about twenty-five, very urbane and kind toward those younger and less favored than himself, and a capital workman." [12]

Within a year Greeley was working with Porter on the new *Spirit of the Times*. Just when Porter got the idea of founding a weekly paper of interest primarily to travelers, sportsmen, and lovers of humor we do not know, but on December 10, 1831, Porter and James Howe, another young printer, published the first issue of the paper in a chill, dreary little attic print shop overlooking Fulton Street. According to Greeley, "It was a moderate sized sheet of indifferent paper, with an atrocious wood-cut for the head—about as uncomely a specimen of the 'fine arts' as our 'native talent' has produced." [13]

A digression—the foreman of the composing room was probably Francis V. Story. Story used the proximity of the office to Wall Street to get acquainted with businessmen who shortly thereafter backed him in starting the *Morning Post*, the first penny paper in the city. The *Morning Post* (not to be confused with Bryant's *Evening Post*) soon failed, but let it be remembered that in later years the penny press, which an early *Spirit* employee helped to start, probably hastened by its ruthless competition the downfall of the far more expensive *Spirit*.[14]

By no means are all of the files of the magazine for its first five years (1831–1836) available for study. Brinley himself, working in 1859 or 1860, complained that the early numbers were not to be found, and until quite recently only a few scattered issues for these years had been brought to light by scholars and collectors. These incomplete early files, together with Greeley's letters and memoirs plus a few scraps of miscellaneous detail from other sources, furnish what we know of the history of the *Spirit* before

---

[12] Greeley to Brinley, reprinted in Brinley, *Life of William T. Porter*, 32–33; Don C. Seitz, *Horace Greeley* (Indianapolis, 1926), 41–42.

[13] James Parton, *The Life of Horace Greeley* (Boston, 1872), 100.

[14] *Ibid.*, 108; Horace Greeley, *Recollections of a Busy Life* (New York, 1873), 88, 91–92; James Melvin Lee, *History of American Journalism* (rev. ed.; Boston, 1923), 186–87.

1836. Most of this information has been compiled elsewhere in a thornily bibliographical article; it is enough to say that the running title varied, that Porter sold out, that he worked briefly for two other humorous papers, the *New-Yorker* and the *Constellation*, that he went to work for two of the subsequent owners as sporting editor of the organ which he had founded, that he edited two other papers for brief times, and that he repurchased the *Spirit*, perhaps with partners, by January 3, 1835. At that date he was editor-in-chief, a post which he held uninterruptedly until 1856, although he lost the ownership in 1842.[15]

It suffices also to say that the two young editors needed every bit of that optimism which marked Porter's approach to problems all his life. The little four-page weekly was born into a world of stiff competition; New York City already had thirty-one weeklies and eleven semiweeklies. Small wonder that in this crowded pool the *Spirit* was soon gobbled up by rivals and merged with at least two other journals and that two other papers which Porter edited during this five-year period were shortly devoured or expired for lack of pecuniary nourishment. Although the *Spirit* within a year stoutly proclaimed a circulation of 3,000 (and some writers even credit it with 6,000), it was rather costly at three dollars per year and was shortly beset by more than strictly financial difficulties. Howe soon withdrew his assistance, and that first summer of the magazine, 1832, was the season New York long remembered as the time of the cholera. Circulation must have fallen off, and Porter found it difficult even to pay his help. Greeley stuck with him through most of that dreary summer, left for a short while, returned, and finally quit for good in September, 1832. Six years later he was still dunning Porter for back wages in a letter headed effusively "Old Friend." [16]

William Harlan Hale, a practicing journalist himself, has

---

[15] Norris Yates, "The *Spirit of the Times*: Its Early History and Some of Its Contributors," *Papers of the Bibliographical Society of America*, XLVIII (Second Quarter, 1954), 117–48. This article is supplemented by Clarence S. Brigham, "Letter to the Editor," *Papers of the Bibliographical Society of America*, XLVIII (Third Quarter, 1954), 300–301.

[16] Lee, *History of American Journalism*, 196; *Spirit*, II (August 10, 1833); Jennette Tandy, *Crackerbox Philosophers in American Humor and Satire* (New York, 1925), 71–74; Greeley, *Recollections of a Busy Life*, 88–91; Brinley, *Life*

written that "The average four-page paper of 1830 was a dingy, ill-printed sheet, made up of a jumble of market and ship-movement items, 'Foreign Intelligence' paragraphs often lifted from other papers which in turn had lifted them from European journals, speech extracts or sermons, all this being livened up with a column or two of the editor's thickest vitriol and padded with Poets' Corners, Local Gleanings, and Miscellany." Except for the sermons and the vitriol, this description well fits the *Spirit* of the early 1830's. Most of the items named by Hale may be found in the sample issue of March 30, 1833. Only in a few articles about horse breaking, game laws, and coon hunts, and in a few notices of horse races and Jockey Club meetings may one see that the editors were trying to follow a specialty and create a sporting paper. The sporting articles make up less than one fourth of the total space in this number.[17]

Clearly if the paper was to become a success as a sporting journal, Porter and his associates had to fulfill certain requirements. First, they must print news items that breeders, trainers, and racers of horses, as well as hunters and fishermen, would find indispensable. In order to print such news Porter had to establish coverage of races and meetings of jockey clubs in the various states, particularly in the South, where racing flourished on a grand scale under the auspices of the well-to-do proprietors of large plantations. Paid correspondents were unknown in those days, and Porter had therefore to rely on the good will of these gentlemen and their friends in obtaining reports and notices of races past, present, and to come. In an early issue of the *Spirit* the editors laid their cards on the desk and pleaded for such amateur correspondents, saying flatly that "the extensive circulation of our paper through the Southern and Western States, makes it an important object with us to notice the results of matches in those States as early as our situation admits." [18]

One way to get correspondents was to make as many personal

of *William T. Porter*, 32–33; Horace Greeley to William T. Porter, June 1, 1839, in Greeley Papers, Manuscript Room, New York Public Library.

[17] Horace Greeley, *Voice of the People* (New York, 1950), 21; *Spirit*, II (1833).

[18] *Spirit*, I (October 20, 1832). Most of the numbers in Volumes I–IV have no pagination.

contacts as possible among the sporting fraternity and among one's fellow writers and editors. Designedly or otherwise, Porter had begun to make such contacts early, when he edited the two short-lived comic weeklies the *New-Yorker* and the *Constellation*, the latter founded by his early friend Asa Greene, a humorist who himself showed a lively interest in the South by writing a mild satire on southern hotheadedness and northern abolitionism entitled *A Yankee Among the Nullifiers*. We know that Porter was good at making and keeping friends; Alban S. Payne, a pugnacious New York doctor who wrote for the *Spirit* as "Nicholas Spicer," declared of the Tall Son "His personal popularity and genial magnetism exceeded that of any man I ever knew." James Oakes, another of Porter's earlier contacts, became a fast friend and a regular *Spirit* correspondent for over twenty-five years, habitually using the *nom de plume* "Acorn." More significant was Porter's contact with George Wilkins Kendall. Kendall, like Porter, had spent his youth in New Hampshire. We do not know whether he and Porter had known each other before both came to New York, but in the big city the two used to go bowling together, and Kendall in middle age recalled in a letter, ripe with affection, the good times he and Porter had had knocking down the pins at Holt's, next door to the old Park Theatre, in 1832, the cholera year. In the summer of 1839 Kendall met Porter again in Kentucky and they took in the races there. From time to time Kendall also saw him in New York, where they would hoist a few and swap yarns at Monteverde's with such literati and personalities as Halleck, Lewis Gaylord Clark, and Colonel Albert Pike when he was in the city. Porter and Kendall may also have visited their respective boyhood homes together. Kendall further kept the friendship alive by sending Porter various gifts during his wanderings in the Southwest and in France. Later, two of William's brothers, George and Frank, worked for awhile on the New Orleans *Picayune*, Kendall's paper.[19]

But most of this came later. When Kendall and Porter were

[19] The *Constellation*, IV (April 20, 1833), 252, and IV (August 31, 1833), 401; "William T. Porter" [obituary], *Porter's Spirit*, IV (1858), 328; Brinley, *Life of William T. Porter*, 33, 199; Frank Luther Mott, *A History of American Magazines 1741–1850* (Cambridge, Massachusetts, 1939), 480; Asa Greene,

hobnobbing in New York in 1832, Kendall's great days as editor of the *Picayune* and as "the first thorough and graphic war correspondent" were still unforeseen. Kendall was also to make the "Pic" one of the leading publishers of backwoods humor for a limited regional public, and probably more yarns and sketches were reprinted in the *Spirit* from the *Picayune* than from any other exchange source, with the possible exception of the St. Louis *Reveille*. For Porter, Kendall was to prove not only a lifelong crony, but a bonanza of back country humor.[20]

III

And yet Porter's original intent was to found a journal that would be primarily sporting, not humorous. In the earliest surviving copy of the *Spirit* a house ad (an advertisement for the paper itself) announces that this paper is to be a sporting magazine "on the Model of *Bell's Life in London*." It is one of the ironies inherent in the career of the *Spirit* that, had its editor been completely successful in this first intention, literary historians would not now care much whether its files survived, or decayed in grandpa's old trunk. Porter's decision to copy *Bell's Life* and to record the turf news of England as well as of America was thoroughly conventional; most journalists were then English-minded. For instance, one of Porter's own sporting writers, Henry William Herbert, not only was of English birth but once proposed to Evert A. Duyckinck that the two of them start a literary journal "on the plan of the English magazines." But Porter soon showed

---

A Yankee Among the Nullifiers: an Auto-Biography by Elnathan Elmwood, Esq. (New York, 1833), conceived as an answer to Thomas Cooper's *Memoirs of a Nullifier;* Fred E. Pond, *Life and Adventures of "Ned Buntline"* (New York, 1919), 34–43; "Reminiscences of the 'Spirit' Family," by "Nicholas Spicer," *Spirit*, XXIX (1859), 27–28; "William T. Porter," by "Acorn," *Spirit*, XXVIII (1858), 289; Fayette Copeland, *Kendall of the Picayune* (Norman, Oklahoma, 1943), 16, 35, 142–43; 264; *Spirit*, XXIX (1859), 123–24 (see also note 2 above); XIII (1843), 235–36.

[20] Allan Nevins, *The Evening Post, a Century of Journalism* (New York, 1922), 183–84; Franklin J. Meine (ed.), *Tall Tales of the Southwest . . . 1830–1860* (New York, 1930), xxix; Carle Brooks Spotts, "The Development of Fiction on the Missouri Frontier," [fourth installment] *Missouri Historical Review*, XXIX (January, 1935), 100–108.

his main interest in American sport and strove to acquire correspondents in the South and West.[21] "Trammelled by circumstances," he reminisced later, "retarded by inexperience, we groped our way slowly into those Southern and Western regions of our country where the sports we advocate were more generally appreciated and more liberally encouraged." By 1837 he was praising Kendall, Oakes, and many others, some of whose pseudonyms were: "N., Index, A Looker-On in Venice, A Virginia Turfman, D. Q., J. L., O'Kelly . . . . And what can we say of our thousand and one private correspondents scattered over the Union, the Canadas, and from beyond the seas?" In 1849 he claimed that the number of correspondents had "doubled within the last eighteen months." [22]

In addition to lining up these amateur contributors Porter tried in other ways to make his paper an indispensable clearing-house of turf news. He printed a great many notices of past, present, and future race meetings, gave much space to discussions of problems of training, clocking, and betting, and printed detailed lists every year of the winners of races in all parts of the country. Porter also maintained an "Alphabetical List of Stallions . . . Compiled Expressly for the New York Spirit of the Times," which usually occupied a full page, as in the sample issue of March 8, 1836. In addition this number includes notices of Jockey Club races at Trenton, New Jersey; Washington, D.C.; Mobile, Alabama; and Natchez, Mississippi; as well as a table of "American Races to Come—1836" in which every state is represented, with New York, New Jersey, and the South predominating. One also finds in this issue a survey entitled "Prospects of the Northern Turf Campaign," and a miscellany under the standing head "Turf Register." The American turf news is supplemented by several columns of reprinted news of the British turf and by advertisements for individual stallions, veterinarians, gunsmiths, musical-

[21] *Spirit*, I (April 5, 1832); Henry William Herbert to Evert Duyckinck, May 13, 1847, in the Duyckinck Collection, Manuscript Room, New York Public Library. Duyckinck, with Osgood and Company, subsequently founded the influential *Literary World* minus the help of Herbert.
[22] *Spirit*, VIII (1838), 4; VII (1837), 4; XIX (1849), 1. Cf. *Spirit*, XXI (1851), 1.

instrument makers, and patent medicines for horse and man. Clearly Porter was thorough in his desire to please the American sportsman, particularly the horse fancier.

Despite his conviviality, the Tall Son of York was a hard worker. As we shall see later, he had his finger in all sorts of editorial pies, and in the thirties he seems to have shouldered most of the day-to-day burden of answering correspondents and writing articles, especially what modern editors call dope stories, or sporting forecasts. He did get some help from his brothers, and in 1838 his job was no doubt made easier by Richard Hays, who joined the staff in that year and remained continuously with the magazine until 1860. During another boom time, in 1846, when Porter was overwhelmed with work, he was lucky enough to acquire the services of Edward E. Jones, whom a mutual friend of both, Fred E. Pond, called a "genial Southern gentleman of the old school" and "an entertaining and informing writer on turf topics." [23] Jones not only stayed with the paper for the rest of its natural life, but he acquired sole ownership in its last months and went down with his Confederate colors flying.

But Porter did not simply slant his paper toward anyone who liked to run horses. As we examine the *Spirit*, we gradually feel a certain inconsistency in his policy. He definitely catered to the well-to-do classes among the sporting fraternity. In 1835 Porter stated flatly that "our course will be among the refinements, the luxuries, and the enjoyments of society," and two years later he declared that the *Spirit* "is designed to promote the views and interests of but an infinitesimal division of those classes of society composing the great mass . . . . we are addressing ourselves to gentlemen of standing, wealth and intelligence—the very corinthian columns of the community." [24] Porter did not come down off this high horse of snobbery for years, if ever. Yet frontier and backwoods humor is supposed to be democratic, or at least democratizing in its influence. Why, then, did Porter have such a pronounced upper-class bias? And having such a bias, how did he ever become the father of the Big Bear school of writing?

[23] Fred E. Pond, "Foreword" to Ben. Perley Poore, *Biographical Sketch of John Stuart Skinner* (n.p. 1854), 2–3.

[24] *Spirit*, V (1835), 1; VII (1837), 4. Cf. *Spirit*, IX (1839), 1.

We shall suggest some answers to these questions as we go along. We have already hinted at one answer, namely, that Porter had set out to establish a sporting paper. Organized sport in America at that time meant principally the turf and the chase, and horse racing on a big scale has always been the sport of kings and such favored persons as possess incomes approaching the level of royal revenue. Then, too, the turf and the hunt flourished primarily in the more thinly settled, agrarian South and West. In consequence the most active horse fanciers and breeders tended to live on the plantations of the slave states.

Up to the time of the embargo and nonimportation acts (1807–1809), the center of breeding for the turf in America had been among the tidewater planters of Virginia and Maryland. Mr. Fairfax Harrison feels that the embargo eliminated these planters from the leadership in raising blood stock and that a sort of interregnum lasted until about 1820. After that date new leaders developed from the Roanoke Valley of North Carolina and Southside Virginia and from the still newer areas of Kentucky and Tennessee, liberally supported by commercial cities of the Atlantic Coast such as New York, Baltimore, and Charleston. The Roanoke Valley seems to have lost its supremacy as a breeding ground around 1840. The generally westward movement of turf activity and the influence of John Stuart Skinner and his *American Turf Register* and *American Farmer* were probably bound up with the rise of racing to the status of a sport conducted on a national scale, a rise which took place largely during the 1830's. It is worthy of note that Porter edited the *American Turf Register* from 1839 to 1844.

In the South a good many plebeians also practiced the sport of their alleged betters. Thus the important Pharsalia Race Course at Natchez, Mississippi, was the scene of "dozens of sprint races," most often for a quarter mile. These races were arranged and conducted by the less well-to-do horse owners, who were thereby enabled to feel that they too were participants in the royal pastime. One must continually recall the existence of this quarter-race crowd, with their dirks and whisky flasks, to get the full savor of a large **class** of racing yarns in the *Spirit*.

To make this journal a success, however, Porter had to cater to the wealthy slaveholding sportsmen and their friends and allies, who "ruled" racing in that they developed the thoroughbreds, supported the big tracks, and determined the code to be followed in the judging of races, the awarding of prizes, and the placing of bets. Their formal and psychological dominance continued even after the actual racing activity of these gentry waned following the panic of 1837. And there is never any sign that Porter regretted this dominance; in fact there are many signs that he shared the ethical, social, and political views of what we may loosely term the southern gentleman. We are entitled to suspect that his background may have predisposed him to the views of this open-handed rural sporting class. Whatever the causes, we know that among his personal friends were such men as Colonel Wade Hampton, owner of one of the country's largest racing stables and a veritable colossus of plantation wealth.[25]

But what about the second of our two questions? With his bias toward the southern aristocracy, how did Porter move from publishing the sports of gentlemen to printing the rough-hewn native humor of the southern frontier? A partial answer may be that social and economic changes forced racing in the grand style from Porter's pages and helped to usher the rude, crude humor of the backwoods into its place. Somewhat earlier Porter had promised to "mingle the amusements with the realities—the sarcastic with the beautiful—the tart with the humorous, so that whoever takes up our sheet shall lay it down with a smile on his face and in charity with humanity." And how does he propose to do all this? Why, by means of "the choicest selections from the highest class of English *Belles-Lettres.*"[26] In other words, what was not sporting material was to be merely reprinted stuff, preferably borrowed from English magazines.

[25] "The Late Col. Wade Hampton, By the Senior Editor" [William T. Porter], *Porter's Spirit*, IV (1858), 5; Carvel Collins, *The American Sporting Gallery . . .* (Cambridge, Massachusetts, 1949), 7; Brinley, *Life of William T. Porter*, 266–67. Much of the background material in the three preceding paragraphs was drawn from Fairfax Harrison, *Early American Turf Stock 1730–1830* (2 vols.; Richmond, Virginia, 1934), I, 31–33, and Edwin Adams Davis and William Ransom Hogan, *The Barber of Natchez* (Baton Rouge, 1954), 202–13.

[26] *Spirit*, VII (1837), 4.

Thus Porter was doing just what would make his paper un-distinctive. Every editor of a magazine for genteel folk did the same thing—padded his columns with news and articles cribbed from *Blackwood's Magazine,* the *Quarterly Review,* and other European journals of quality. Allan Nevins writes: "It was usual, whenever a packet arrived with a fresh batch, to cut the domestic news to a few paragraphs, stop any series of editorial articles in hand, and for several days fill the columns with extracts and sum-maries." Porter in the middle thirties illustrated this generaliza-tion perfectly. A standing feature of the *Spirit* during these years was a two- or three-column chunk of matter headed "The Letter-Bag of the Great Western." The *Great Western* was one of the crack London packets with which Porter seems to have had an arrangement whereby he received the latest English magazines promptly and regularly whenever the ship docked in New York. In an early editorial, "An Original Touch," Porter boasts that this week's *Spirit* is made up almost entirely of the writings of original native correspondents. Why? Because the *Great Western* was late—so "we placed original matter, instead of selected, as usual upon those pages of our paper first printed." [27]

To the end of his career Porter reprinted such popular Eng-lish novelists as Dickens, Thackeray, Charles Lever, and Robert Surtees. But we must also note that from the first he reprinted at least a little frontier material and that even before the match-ing of expensive thoroughbreds for lush purses declined in the early 1840's, a number of lively amateur writers were trying their hands at humorous and realistic depiction of backwoods life in their epistles to the *Spirit.* "From Maine to Florida, from the St. Lawrence to the Missouri, a thousand gifted pens are employed in imparting novelty and interest to our columns," Porter rhap-sodized in 1837.[28] We may say, however, that the decline of big-time racing coincided with the main burst of local color writing in the *Spirit.*

By March, 1839, when Porter published in the *Spirit* the first of fourteen full-page steel engravings of famous American race

[27] *The Evening Post,* 87–88; *Spirit,* VIII (1839), 412.
[28] *Spirit,* VII (1837), 276. Cf. William T. Porter (ed.), *The Big Bear of Arkansas* (Philadelphia, 1845), vii–xi.

horses, the sport had seen its best days. Professor Carvel Collins says that the years of widespread interest, large stables, and $20,000 stakes were definitely over. Racing will "rise out of the quagmire into which it has sunk," a frequent correspondent, "N. of Arkansas," predicted in 1844. But it did not. The panic of 1837 and the severe five- or six-year depression which followed may have been one reason. Thus as late as 1845 one of Porter's most famous and prolific contributors, T. B. Thorpe, complained of the "derangement of business" in New Orleans.[29]

Thorpe was an itinerant portrait painter and an editor of fly-by-night newspapers, but the southern planter himself was peculiarly exposed to the effects of a business depression by virtue of his frequent improvidence and wastefulness. ("Prudence! prudence is a beggarly virtue, and I hate the very name of it," cries Colonel Dangerfield in James Kirke Paulding's novel *Westward Ho!*) As a result of this lofty contempt for thrift, the average southern country gentleman was often in debt and derived much of his ready cash from speculation in land. The family of Porter's friend Colonel Wade Hampton had been involved in land speculation for many years. A member of the Barrow clan of Louisiana planters (of whom Senator Alexander Barrow, the most famous, was a frequent *Spirit* contributor) made this New Year's resolution for 1840: "I com'ence this year with full determination to attend strictly to my business and to use every economy till I get out of Debt. My cource [sic] will be a Lesson to my children—that is never to loan What is not your own—if you owe any thing pay it first." One cannot forbear to sum up the whole problem by introducing John Randolph's comment on Virginia estates, even though he made it many years earlier—"plenty of serfs, plenty of horses, but not a shilling." [30]

[29] Collins, *The American Sporting Gallery*, 1; *Spirit*, XIV (1844), 343 (N. of Arkansas was Charles F. M. Noland, a planter.) ; T. B. Thorpe to Carey and Hart, New Orleans, March 8, 1845, in Henry Carey Baird Papers, Historical Society of Pennsylvania, Philadelphia. For general comment see Harold U. Faulkner, *American Economic History* (5th ed.; New York, 1943), 168–69.

[30] James Kirke Paulding, *Westward Ho! A Tale* (2 vols.; New York, 1832), I, 19, and see also Francis Pendleton Gaines, *The Southern Plantation* (New York, 1924), 149, and H. S. Fulkerson, *Random Recollections of Early Days in Mississippi* (Vicksburg, Mississippi, 1885), 12; John Donald Wade, *Augustus Baldwin Longstreet* (New York, 1924), 12; Edwin Adams Davis (ed.) *Plantation Life*

Thus when money became scarce and the turnover of land dropped in 1841 to one-twentieth of what it had been in 1837,[31] it is not surprising that racing no longer flourished on its former scale. Therefore Porter quite possibly encouraged humorous and fictional writing in the 1840's to make up for a dearth of turf news and to widen the appeal of his magazine. That is, he began to fish for southern and western readers other than those who followed the turf, although racing always remained Porter's first love (quite literally; he never married).

But one must also ask: Why did not racing and race news in time come back to crowd out in its turn the tall tales and realistic sketches that had made the *Spirit* so much more than a sporting journal? The answers lie outside the province of this study, in the realm of social and economic history, but a few of them may be suggested. First, the land had deteriorated badly in certain once-prosperous areas of the older South, such as middle Georgia and the tidewater zone. Second, many of the big planters from 1830 to 1850 were in the process of scattering westward into the Mississippi Valley and hacking plantations out of the backwoods far from such older centers of racing as Baltimore, Charleston, and Louisville. Third, the price of cotton remained low throughout the forties, whereas the cost of slaves continued to rise steeply between 1840 and 1860. Fourth, another flurry of wild speculation in land culminated in the panic of 1857—and that flurry was at its worst in the Mississippi Valley, whence Porter got most of his local-color sketches.[32] Finally, there was the steady drift toward conflict between the South and the North.

---

in the Florida Parishes of Louisiana, 1836–1846 As Reflected in the Diary of Bennet H. Barrow (New York, 1943), 19–23, 176; Franklin L. Riley (ed.) "Diary of a Mississippi Planter . . . ," *Publications of the Mississippi Historical Society,* X (1909), 305–481, especially pages 311, 332–33, and 336; J. D. B. De Bow, *The Industrial Resources, Etc., of the Southern and Western States* (3 vols.; New Orleans, 1853), I, 161–64; Ulrich Bonnell Phillips, *Life and Labor in the Old South* (Boston, 1929), 238n.

[31] Benjamin Horace Hibbard, *A History of the Public Land Policies* (New York, 1924), 102–103.

[32] Phillips, *Life and Labor in the Old South,* 100–101, and Chapter IV, *passim;* Wade, *Augustus Baldwin Longstreet,* 239–40; Faulkner, *American Economic History,* 351; Ulrich Bonnell Phillips, *American Negro Slavery* (New York and

One effect of all these movements was surely to reduce the amount of ready cash needed for keeping a stable, trading in thoroughbreds, and planking down the huge stakes and side bets that had prevailed in the thirties, when Colonel Hampton had paid $10,000 for a two-thirds interest in Argyle and the famous Wagner–Grey Eagle match at Louisville was run for $20,000 a side.[33]

Moreover, Porter's "infinitesimal division"—meaning, in the South, large slaveholders—was steadily decreasing, although the average number of slaves was on the increase. In 1850, out of 347,-725 slaveholders there were only 1,733 who held 100 or more slaves, and it is quite likely that only a fraction of these were passionately interested in horse racing. When one remembers that Porter claimed a circulation of 40,000 around 1856, it becomes plain that the bulk of his later readers belong to a new and larger economic and social class—a class which may have shared the values and interests but not the economic resources of the old.[34]

To feel Porter's permanent shift of emphasis from the American and English turf to the American farm and frontier, one may go back to the sample issue of March 30, 1833, already mentioned and look at the few nonsporting items in that number. They include a reprinted story about a duel between two midshipmen, a comic Irish yarn, an account of a recent murder trial, and several other police court items. There is also a small department of "Theatrical Chit-Chat," as well as brief reviews of Fanny Kemble's biography of Francis I and of a reissued book of tales by Maria Edgeworth. A few short items cut from "Skinner's Excursions in India," the "Encyclopedia Metropolitana," and various newspapers fill up the

London, 1918), graph facing 370; Hibbard, *A History of the Public Land Policies*, 221–22.

De Bow shows that the population of Arkansas and Mississippi increased 221.1 and 175 per cent respectively between 1830 and 1840. The rise for North Carolina and South Carolina during the same period was only 2.1 and 2.3 per cent. See De Bow, *The Industrial Resources, Etc., of the Southern and Western States*, III, 432.

[33] Collins, *The American Sporting Gallery*, 7.

[34] Bureau of the Census, *A Century of Population Growth* (Washington, 1909), 136; Brinley, *Life of William T. Porter*, 266.

holes and corners. In all, perhaps one-eighth of the space is devoted to original nonsporting articles.

Compare this unrewarding issue with, say, that of August 8, 1846. In the first place Porter had increased the early four-page *Spirit* to eight pages in 1836 and to twelve in 1839. Of the twelve-page issue just cited, Porter is said to have boasted that it contained "nearly SEVEN PAGES OF ORIGINAL MATTER, from the pens of no less than *thirty-three correspondents!*" [35] Moreover, about half of this material consists of realistic or humorous sketches, or tall tales. A great change had indeed taken place in the subject matter of the magazine.

Change or no change, however, Porter had to steer clear of social, economic, and political issues. A de-emphasis of politics was absolutely essential to a sporting paper published in the North which would have to find its chief support among the horse racing and hunting interests of the South and West. At the same time a wise editor would prefer not to rile the very considerable number of sporting gentry who clustered round the Union Course on Long Island and the large number of tracks in New Jersey, upper New York State, and, according to Professor Collins, even in New England. On the day before the bitter presidential election of 1832 the *Spirit* proclaimed, "We have abjured politics . . . but in looking over the columns of our exchange papers, we detect such a railing spirit of party, and see such exhibitions of rancorous hatred, and almost ferocious wrath, rendered more intense as the time of battle draws nigh, that our attempts to pen an article consonant to that genial spirit which becomes our mild and cheerful pages seem entirely out of tune with the Spirit of the Times." In 1843 Porter was still proclaiming, "No Smoking (Nor Politics) Allowed Here!" Moreover, Porter was nonpolitical from preference as well as from expediency. He was temperamentally genial, "his evident mission on earth being, as he contended, to oblige everybody." [36]

In his antipolitical attitude Porter was part of a definite movement of his times. Politics seems to have been an absorbing topic,

[35] Walter Blair, *Native American Humor* (New York, 1937), 83.

[36] *Spirit*, I (November 3, 1832) ; XIII (1843), 37; Brinley, *Life of William T. Porter*, 88.

especially in rural areas where other forms of diversion were few, but a reaction against politics as a subject of discussion was under way in certain circles. Paulding commented acidly that "the devotees of sects and parties are exceedingly prone to imagine that every book, whatever may be its nature or object, is intended to operate in favour of or against their cherished doctrines." Timothy Flint declared that "the most formidable impediment to American literature of all, is the coarse and absorbing appetite of the great mass of the community for politics." [37] And George Wilkins Kendall and his partners resolutely steered the *Picayune* away from political quarrels; in fact, Kendall's biographer thinks this policy is a big reason for the success of the paper, early and late.

Readers of the *Spirit* likewise participated in this antipolitical movement. "Our attention has been called to this matter from several quarters," wrote Porter in regard to staying off of political questions. "A Young Turfman," writing from Natchez, warned, "I am sorry to see a little squinting toward politics in your paper." And there were other warnings to stay away from political subjects, for instance, from "Trebla" of New Orleans.[38]

In general, Porter was highly successful in avoiding the pit of political controversy. The bank and currency questions, Indian policy, the pre-emption acts, the Texas and Oregon annexations, the Mexican War—rarely did the pros and cons of these issues creep into his pages. Only abolition merited his serious attention, and that not too often. When he allowed his contributors to touch on politics at all, the tone was usually one of humor or satire, and the pieces in question had other aspects of interest. Pete Whetstone, an Arkansas rip-roarer, comes out with a typical appeal to backwoods voters: "Pete is no orator; but when it comes to killing a bear, or finding a bee tree, he is *there*. Pete aint good at figures, but he can read big print. If he goes to the Legislature, he will do his best for you . . . . Pete has a couple of gallons over at the doggery;—step over and drink." In another article an unlettered

[37] Paulding, *Westward Ho!*, I, 3; Timothy Flint, "Obstacles to American Literature," *Knickerbocker*, II (September, 1833), 161–70.

[38] *Spirit*, XIII (1843), 37; VIII (1838), 220; "Sayings and Doings in New Orleans," *Spirit*, XIII (1843), 349, by "Trebla." This name, of course, is simply "Albert" spelled backwards. Franklin J. Meine thinks that this writer may have been Albert C. Ainsworth, of New Orleans.

loafer is represented as saying: "Put not your trust in politicianers
. . . . Haven't I served my country for five years . . . going to
meetings and battling my daylights out . . . got licked 50 times
. . . and all for what? . . . . Why for nix . . . what's a trade
when a feller's got a soul? . . . . I loved my country and I
wanted an office . . . . I've a mind to knock off and call it half
a day." [39]

The above passages were all contributed to the *Spirit* several
years before James Russell Lowell, through Birdofredum Sawin,
expressed a similar disillusion regarding service in the Mexican
War. Such bits of illiterate "eloquence" may also be considered
forerunners of the work of Robert Henry Newell (Orpheus C.
Kerr, that is, "office seeker"). The Mexican War did rate a lot of
space because so many of Porter's Whig friends and correspondents
in the Southwest took part in this supposedly Democratic show.
One such participant was "Azul" of Alabama and Mississippi,
who tells Porter's readers that "I kept a Diarrhea of oll the
princepal events." However, Lowell's antiwar "The Recruiting
Sergeant" was reprinted in the *Spirit* along with other extracts
from *The Biglow Papers*, and the war and related issues received
a few light slaps in other contributions. Concerning "Jimmy K.'s"
message on the Oregon question, one loafer asks his fellow derelict
on the levee "wot a 'Merikin President has to do with furrin'
relashuns anyhow. I haint none nor never had. I was born on the
sile, and I was riz on the sile, and I ollers calc'late to stay on the
sile." His friend counters this rural isolationism by explaining
laboriously why Oregon is ours: "Aint it put down so in the map
of the U-nited States, and kolored yaller? . . . O'course Oregon's
ours! . . . So's Texas; and so'll Kelleyforny, and Kennedy
[Canada], and Kuby, be fore long, or else I'll live on stinkin'
mackerel." The author's point is made when a cop finally comes
up and runs in both the spread-eagle imperialist and his isolationist
fellow traveler for vagrancy. [40]

This "a plague on both your houses" attitude is fairly typical

[39] *Spirit*, VII (1837), 121; VI (1836), 65.
[40] *Spirit*, XVII (1847), 203; "Hosea Biglow and His Doings," *Spirit*, XIX
(1849), 73–74; "A Review of the President's Message," *Spirit*, XV (1846), 546.

of the few political pieces which Porter passed on to the printers. Actually he seems not to have liked the war. He printed a dry New England comment submitted by "an odd sort of a fellow" to a contest sponsored by the Massachusetts Peace Society, which had offered five hundred dollars for the best essay "on the origin and result of the Mexican War." The "essay" in its entirety read:

Chapter I.—On the origin of the war.—1. Texas.
Chapter II.—On the result of the war.—2. Taxes.

The editorial comment in the *Spirit* was, "Give Mr. 'Odd Sort of a Fellow' the five hundred dollars, Mr. Peace Society." [41]

But what could Porter do about the war? As an editor he could not brush aside such an undertaking, in which both Whigs and Democrats of the Southwest were keenly interested. He did stress factual reportage from the front rather than controversy behind the lines, and long, often serialized firsthand accounts of the campaigns came from such friends of Porter as Albert Pike, Captain William Seaton Henry, and Thomas Mayne Reid (later a writer of adventure novels for boys). [42] This sort of war copy displaced much of the English and Continental news and features throughout most of 1846, 1847, and 1848. The Mexican War, then, may have been another force which indirectly propelled Porter toward a more thoroughly "American" policy.

But no evidence exists that Porter suffered any psychic trauma from a conflict of his antiwar leanings with an implicitly prowar policy. Generally, he followed the line of least resistance in politics; occasionally, he even showed some heat in opposing that

[41] *Spirit*, XVII (1847), 221.

[42] Two of Pike's many contributions were "Letter from the Central Division of the Army," *Spirit*, XVI (1846), 523, and "Buena Vista, a poem, Written for the *Spirit of the Times*," *Spirit*, XVII (1847), 109. Captain William Seaton Henry, under the pseudonym of "G** de L***," wrote a long series of factual letters to the *Spirit* in 1846 and 1847. These were collected and published in book form as *Campaign Sketches of the War with Mexico* (New York, 1847), reviewed in the *Spirit*, XVII (1847), 230. A typical account by Mayne Reid is "Sketches by a Skirmisher," *Spirit*, XVII (1847), 109–10. T. B. Thorpe, author of "The Big Bear of Arkansas" and other sketches for the *Spirit*, wrote no identified war correspondence for Porter but produced three "quickie" books based on his experiences with Taylor's forces, *Our Army on the Rio Grande* (1846), *Our Army at Monterrey* (1847), and *The Taylor Anecdote Book* (1848).

bête noir of his southern friends, Abolitionism. In a politically minded country this was the one major political and economic issue which was taboo to many editors. Professor Nevins states that when Longfellow's *Poems on Slavery* came out in 1842, the shocked editor of *Graham's Magazine* wrote the author that the word "slavery" was never allowed to appear in a Philadelphia magazine. Until a later date *Harper's* in New York likewise objected to mention of the slavery issue. James Hall, editor of the *Western Monthly Magazine* and writer of romances of the frontier, also buried the question. William Henry Channing, who edited the *Western Messenger* from a transcendental point of view, assisted by James Freeman Clarke, could not always keep his editorial fingers off the national hot potato; nevertheless he touched it with professed reluctance. On one occasion he allowed himself to print a series of pro and con articles on the slavery question but decided twice to drop the matter and finally did bring the series to the end with a curt note in which he said: "We think most sincerely that no good can come from agitating the public mind on this subject. Such agitation only serves to excite passion, instead of leading to conviction." [43] His remarks might have been made by Porter himself.

Thus in the two decades previous to the 1850's slavery was usually kept in the editorial closet—the national skeleton. Ironically, the hotter grew the general controversy, the more Porter succeeded in suppressing his personal feelings and keeping the issue out of his magazine. After 1836 such angry attacks as this definition of "The Abolition-Super-Philanthropic-Monster: Whom bigotry and fanaticism have rendered a knave and who hopes to cheat heaven into a belief of his 'good will to man' by cutting the throats of neighbors, and marrying his daughter to his footman Cuffee," become extremely rare.[44]

On the other hand, Noland of Arkansas raps both the Abolitionists and "Southern fire-eaters who meet them with the cry of

[43] *Western Messenger*, II (November, 1836), 178, 262.
[44] *Spirit*, VI (1836), 1. For some later anecdotes with a proslavery moral see "Negro Ball in Boston," *Spirit*, VIII (1838), 10; "A Practical Joke," *Spirit*, XVII (1847), 90; "A 'Crowner's Quest,'" *Spirit*, XIX (1849), 374; "The Darkies' Ball," *Spirit*, XXI (1851), 219. For some direct attacks on abolition see *Spirit*, VI (1836), 16; VI (1836), 239; XII (1842), 492; XV (1845), 237.

'disunion.' " Noland was a Whig and the Whigs of the South and border states, as Arthur C. Cole has pointed out, stood for national union if not always for unity. Another writer, the agricultural pioneer Solon Robinson, who contributed many factual articles on scientific farming as well as some local-color sketches of unscientific farmer-squatters, declared anxiously that slavery "will split this union." Moreover, all the items cited in which slavery is a main topic are spread over thirty years of a weekly magazine, and such related developments as the Compromise of 1850 and the struggle for Kansas are almost ignored in Porter's pages.[45]

The Tall Son's dislike of controversy and his rare tact can be appreciated even more fully if one examines his method of handling correspondents who waxed warm in long-distance arguments over horses and other nonpolitical matters. Tempers ran high in the ante-bellum South, and the back-country cavalier in particular kept his dueling pistols cleaned and ready. Albert Pike had fought at least one duel. Noland, also of Arkansas, had killed an opponent on the field of honor; a third Arkansas correspondent, Matt Flournoy Ward, had killed a school teacher for punishing his boy. In the *Spirit* a correspondent writing as "O'Kelly" disagreed with Noland over a horse race and summed up caustically, "I think it would not be a very bad plan to bet against his predictions." Porter published the letter but declared in a prefatory note: "Acquainted as we are with 'N.' and 'O'Kelly,' we should regret if any ill feeling was indulged by either towards each other." Porter further promised "to see fair play" if they would only be content to argue the matter out verbally. Another time "Allatoona" tartly accused "Skysail" of mendacity and added, "Should Skysail be inclined for a row, a line to Allatoona from Skysail will receive attention." Porter rose diplomatically to the occasion: *"Note by the Editor.—*'Hold your horses!' What's the use of a row? You had better 'kiss and make up.' Life is short enough anyhow. If you *will* fight, enlist and go to Mexico, which will be equal to securing a pit ticket to 'Kingdom Come!' as pretty much all the *Star* men get killed off there." The allusion is to the

---

[45] " 'N. of Arkansas' on His Way Home," *Spirit*, XX (1850), 168; " 'Col. Pete Whetstone' Again 'About,' " *Spirit*, XX (1850), 168; "Dan Looney's Big Fight in Illinois," *Porter's Spirit*, I (1856), 159; "A Relic of the 'Good Old Times,' " *Spirit*, XIX (1850), 577.

heavy mortality among the officers in the American forces. Was this bit of timely chaff effective? There is no further mention in the *Spirit* of this "row." And if one finds few examples of such verbal tiffs over a third of a century, it is probably because Porter usually tossed such inflammatory letters into the circular file.[46]

IV

But did the *Spirit*, after all, reach the readers for whom it was intended? We need to know, if possible, how many people were exposed to the back-country writing in the *Spirit*, how they reacted to this writing, and whether they themselves lived in log cabins, pillared plantation mansions, gabled New England farmhouses, or narrow flats in Manhattan.

Porter regularly pointed with pride to a world-wide circulation. A typical claim is that the *Spirit* "has a Foreign circulation un-equalled, probably, by any other in the country; it has found its way into all the European capitals, into the East and West Indies, and is read with as much *gout* at Canton, Batavia, Sydney, and the Sandwich Islands, as partial friends would induce us to believe it is at home." He also claimed that there was "not a single military or naval station" in the United States in which the *Spirit* could not be found. But we do not have to rely altogether on the claims of the enthusiastic founder and editor. We know that Porter maintained a regular sales agent in London in 1841 and perhaps for some time thereafter. We also know that the London papers occasionally reprinted material from the *Spirit;* one of the letters of Noland is requoted in the *Spirit* from the London *New Sporting Magazine* after having been reprinted in that journal from Porter's paper.[47]

[46] *Gen. Albert Pike's Poems. With Introductory Biographical Sketch by Mrs. Lilian Pike Roome* . . . (Little Rock, 1900), 23–27; obituary of Noland in the *Spirit*, XXVIII (1858), 291; Josiah H. Shinn, "The Life and Public Services of Charles Fenton Mercer Noland," *Publications of the Arkansas Historical Association*, I (1906), 335–38; William F. Pope, *Early Days in Arkansas* (Little Rock, 1895), 118–23; James Raymond Masterson, *Tall Tales of Arkansaw* (Boston, 1942), 63, 327; "A Kick at 'N.' from 'O'Kelly,' " *Spirit*, VII (1837), 29; "The Wood With the Bark Off!" *Spirit*, XVII (1847), 477.

[47] *Spirit*, XIX (1849), 1; XXI (1851), 1; "Latest from Europe," *Spirit*, XI (1841), *passim;* "A Line from the New Sporting Magazine," by "N. of Arkansas," *Spirit*, XI (1841), 85.

As for the popularity of the *Spirit* at home, the number of Porter's correspondents, particularly those from the South and West, indicates that the magazine was circulating to some extent on the frontier. Let us look at a few examples from among many. In a "Letter from an Officer of the U.S. Dragoons," a regular contributor from Fort Leavenworth who signs his letter "Wisconsin" praises the *Spirit* as a relief from the monotony of garrison life and the general illiteracy of the *Platte Eagle* and the Liberty (Missouri) *Banner*. Several of his brother officers, stationed at or near Fort Gibson, in the Indian Territory, were also frequent correspondents.[48] One of these declared, "I believe that there is not a garrison on this or Red River at which the paper is not taken, and several officers, independently of the several Post Libraries, are subscribers." "Captain," another West Point man, wrote from eastern Florida in 1839, during the last Seminole Indian war, and said that he was the only officer on the post, that his *Spirit* was not reaching him, and that he wanted it badly as he had no companionship and no other reading matter. He added that five volunteers had just been killed.[49]

Further evidence of southern and western circulation appears when Noland promises to get fourteen subscriptions for Porter and attaches a private letter which, according to "Nota Bene by the Editor," "covered $50, and we don't know how many more subscribers, after counting a baker's dozen we stopped." Another gentleman wrote from Milliken's Bend, Louisiana, enclosing ten dollars (the current yearly price of the magazine) from a new subscriber. The Louisiana writer quipped that he got this man by *not* lending him the *Spirit*. Yet another Florida reader sent in six new subscriptions.[50]

The *Spirit* also traveled to California in the wake of the gold

---

[48] *Spirit*, XIV (1844), 78. See also "A Sporting Adventure in Arkansas," by "an Officer of the U.S. Army," *Spirit*, XII (1843), 531. One might balance this with the several letters from a naval officer of the U.S.S. *Vincennes* and from the navy surgeon aboard the U.S.S. *St. Mary's* who signed himself "Grs. X." "Allatoona" and "Skysail" were also naval officers.

[49] "Letter from an Officer in the U.S. Army," dated "Fort Gibson, Cherokee Nation," *Spirit*, XIV (1844), 73; "Letter from 'The Captain,'" *Spirit*, IX (1839), 175. See also "Prairie Dogs of the Far West," *Spirit*, XIV (1844) 55.

[50] *Spirit*, VIII (1838), 69; XI (1841), 414; VIII (1838), 60.

seekers, and the best-known humorist of the West, Captain George Horatio Derby (John Phoenix) drew from it the inspiration for at least one of his sketches. Stephen C. Massett, a strolling actor and humorist whose *nom de plume*, "Jeems Pipes of Pipesville," had been suggested by Porter, saw the *Spirit* on file in the raw boom town of Crescent City. The editor of the Portland *Oregonian* seems to have known Porter personally and to have taken pains to get the *Spirit* mailed to the banks of the Willamette.[51]

From such readers we learn something about the geographical distribution of the 40,000 subscribers claimed, according to Brinley, by the editor for *Porter's Spirit* in 1856. Of course, we must not forget that those were the days of "circulation liars" and that such claims could seldom be checked properly. Moreover, our main interest at the moment is the pervasion by the *Spirit* of the Old Southwest. It is therefore pertinent to note that in 1840, near Holly Springs, Mississippi, the mailman's horse was drowned in a freshet which carried away "large packages of the *Spirit of the Times*" and other magazines.[52]

But aside from circulation in its own form, material from the *Spirit* must have reached many other southwestern readers in the pages of local newspapers. Editors borrowed from each other's periodicals with a right good will, and the *Spirit* was certainly reaching a number of editorial desks in the hill, bayou, and cotton country. Porter made a practice of reprinting plugs for the *Spirit* from other papers, and in its pages we may find literally dozens of testimonials such as that of the *Arkansas Intelligencer*: "We always devote to this popular journal a regular hour," and of the Tennessee *Star-Spangled Banner*: "We assure you, *most puissant* 'Spirit,' that all we said was merited, and more besides. It is one of the documents that we take our coffee over, and take to bed

[51] "Pistol Shooting—A Counter Challenge," *Spirit*, XXV (1856), 568, reprinted from George Horatio Derby, *Phoenixiana; or, Sketches and Burlesques. By John Phoenix* (New York, 1856), 67–70. This item begins, "I copy the following paragraph from the 'Spirit of the Times' for July 15th." That paragraph is a challenge by a self-styled marksman, and Phoenix then burlesques such challenges. See also Massett, *Drifting About*, 248; *id.*, "Col. Pipes in Oregon," *Porter's Spirit*, I (1856), 19–20; " 'One of the Boys' in California," *Spirit*, XXI (1851), 7.

[52] Frank Luther Mott, *American Journalism* (New York, 1941), 237n.; Brinley, *Life of William T. Porter*, 266; *Spirit*, X (1840), 49, credited to the *Marshall County Republican* of Holly Springs, Mississippi.

with us, as we used to take our comfortable old grimalkin, of winter nights, in our childhood days." Occasionally Porter would string some of these plugs together under a single tag-line. In two such clusters of testimonials we find statements from the Alabama *Tribune,* the *Southern Planter* (Richmond, Virginia), the Lexington (Kentucky) *Intelligencer,* the New Orleans *Picayune, Crescent,* and *Bulletin,* the Franklin (Tennessee) *Weekly Review,* the Vicksburg (Mississippi) *Whig,* the Fayette (Missouri) *Democrat,* the Boonville (Missouri) *Observer,* the Columbus (Georgia) *Times,* and other southern sheets, as well as from a number of papers in the northern states.[53]

V

Well then, Porter certainly built up a nationwide circulation for his sporting magazine. Was not the *Spirit* therefore a success financially? Perhaps it was, off and on; at least it survived for thirty years. But it did so literally in spite of Porter, who wrecked commercially what he had built up editorially. Recurrently he endangered the venture by a succession of astounding errors in business judgment—errors that arose directly from his attitude as an editor toward his readers.

First of all, in 1836 the magazine jumped in price from three dollars to five; at the same time it doubled in size, growing from four to eight pages. Five dollars was a lot of money to pay for any periodical in those days. The average subscription price for a weekly or monthly was three dollars per year; at five dollars the *Spirit* cost as much as the big "quality" monthlies. The *Knickerbocker* and the *Southern Literary Messenger* cost five dollars; *Graham's Magazine* only three dollars. Further, we have mentioned that Porter began publishing a costly series of engravings of race horses in 1839, during a depression and when racing was headed downhill. Yet in that same year Porter did an amazing thing; he raised the price of the *Spirit* to ten dollars. He also increased the size of the paper from eight pages to twelve—all this

[53] *Spirit,* XV (1845), 218; XVII (1847), 455; "What People Think of the 'Spirit' and the 'Chronicle,' " *Spirit,* XIII (1843), 61; see also *Spirit,* XIII (1843), 123. Cornelius Mathews of the *Yankee Blade* puffed the *Spirit* several times; e. g. see *Spirit,* XV (1845), 218; XVI (1846), 102, 378; XVIII (1848), 426.

in the face of the hard times following the panic of 1837. Brinley comments on the large, careless generosity of all the Porter brothers with money, and indeed William had raised the price of the advertisements in 1837 simply in order to drive out undesirable advertisers.[54] But mere willingness to spend money and a desire to give good service do not explain Porter's doubling his price at such a time. Nor was it just the result of his belief in the future of the turf. He himself mentions these factors but does not emphasize them in his editorial defending the price raise:

"In answer to solicitations for advice from the most distinguished Breeders and Turfmen throughout the Union, before many of whom, as our oldest and best friends, we frankly laid our whole project, we were told, with assurances of their hearty support, to 'Go Ahead!' . . . They urged that inasmuch as the 'Spirit of the Times' was the accredited organ of an interest embracing only men of liberal views, of taste, and of property, it should be complete in its design, and in all its appointments elegant, and they assured us that we had only to make it worthy of them to command their best wishes, and to ensure their cordial support. Gentlemen connected with the Turf, and admirers of Field and Rural Sports generally, whatever may be their particular passion, are proverbially liberal, and such mainly constitute the subscribers to this paper. The price of a horse, a gun, a dog, or anything which contributes to their enjoyment, is no object with them, provided it fully meets their views, and it is believed that they have too much pride to suffer a paper devoted to them and their amusement to languish for want of that liberality which characterizes them in their ordinary pursuits, or to be second to the organ of any other interest, either in its size, appearance, or character." [55]

Something has already been said about the well-authenticated liberality of southern gentlemen, from Colonel Dangerfield to Colonel Sellars.[56] Even so, it was one thing for such plantation

[54] "To Our Readers," *Spirit*, VII (1837), 4.
[55] "To Old Subscribers," *Spirit*, IX (1839), 1.
[56] But see also Joseph G. Baldwin, "How the Times Served the Virginians," *Flush Times in Alabama and Mississippi* (New York, 1853), 72–105.

princes as Colonel William R. Johnson, of Virginia, the "Napoleon of the Turf," and Colonel Wade Hampton, of South Carolina, with his extensive sugar, rice, and cotton plantations worked by 5,000 slaves to talk to Porter about "going ahead" with doubling the price of his magazine, but it was another to take the losses if such gentlemen failed to support Porter on the scale to which he hoped to become accustomed. When one remembers the earlier quoted figure of 1,733 large slaveholders for the entire country, it is not surprising that in 1841, less than two years after raising his price, Porter admitted that the *Spirit*, like racing in general, had suffered from the hard times. Moreover, in 1839 he had spread his resources even thinner by purchasing a monthly, the *American Turf Register*, and four years later he was editing another—and short-lived—weekly of the turf, the *American Sporting Chronicle*. All in all, it is scarcely surprising that in 1842 Porter lost the ownership of both the *Spirit* and the *Turf Register*. To avoid bankruptcy he sold out to John Richards, the printer of the *Spirit*, a hearty man, fond of bowling and of shrewd business deals, who had come over in his youth from England and built up a large publishing concern. One of Richards' major decisions as proprietor of both the *Spirit* and the *American Turf Register* was to discontinue the latter magazine in 1844. Another was to cut back the price of the *Spirit* to its old figure of five dollars.[57]

Porter continued to sit in the editorial chair and seems to have retained a free hand in all matters of policy not directly connected with the business side of the office. On March 5, 1842, he announced sturdily: "The Editor's attention being now solely directed to his peculiar department, he confidently hopes to render it much more racy, varied, and interesting, while the new Publisher and Proprietor will make every effort to place the paper in the hands of its readers in a style of unusual elegance." Nevertheless he also gave vent to a certain degree of disillusion:

[57] *Porter's Spirit*, IV (1858), 5; *Spirit*, XI (1841), 1 (For a prospectus of the *American Turf Register* see the standing advertisement in the *Spirit*, 1839–1842; concerning the *American Sporting Chronicle*, see also *Spirit*, XIII (1843), 13, 36); *Spirit*, XXIX (1859), 1; XIV (1844), 54; Brinley, *Life of William T. Porter*, 97, 142–43; David W. Judd (ed.), *The Life and Writings of Frank Forester* (2 vols.; New York, 1882), I, 76.

"After having thus devoted ten of the best years of our life, with all the means, the influence, the industry, and the ability we could command, we have realized—what!—Why *on paper*, quite a snug little property, but, in truth, not the first red cent! With nearly Fifty Thousand Dollars due it, this journal passed from ours into other hands, for an amount which would not command a moderate race horse! . . . Had we the past ten years of our life to live over again, and were offered the wages of a journeyman wood-sawyer we should certainly *hesitate* before giving up the 'wages' for the 'popularity,' the *saw* horse for the *race* horse." [58]

Porter's disillusion apparently did not last; he edited the *Spirit* for fourteen more years with no perceptible change in policy. He certainly lacked sound business judgment, but it cannot be said that this lack was the sole cause of his failure. He failed in part because he overestimated the lavishness and resources of the southern gentleman. One thinks again of old Asa Porter, with his immense estate and his love of fine horseflesh, the tradition of open-handedness associated with the family, and young William's revulsion from Puritan morality and schooling.

Moreover, in the autumn of 1838 Porter had made the first of his several tours of the South and West. His purpose was "to make ourselves personally acquainted with the gentlemen, the country, and the various interests involved in the Sports of the Turf." He traveled from Baltimore to Wheeling, down the Ohio through Cincinnati and Louisville, thence to Vicksburg, Natchez, and New Orleans. On his return he cut through the Deep South and then up the Atlantic Coast, thus making a complete circle and visiting every part of the South with the exception of the Florida peninsula. The tour of the sporting editor was evidently something of a triumphal procession: "We can but attempt to acknowledge the unremitted attentions which were showered upon us at Mobile, Montgomery, Columbus, Augusta, Columbia, Charleston, Washington, and other cities . . . . Returning fresh from 'the race horse region,' and laden with the information a personal observa-

---

[58] *Spirit*, XII (1842), 12; "A Profit and Loss Account," *Spirit*, XII (1842), 102–103. Many an editor of course had to sing a sad song about subscribers who failed to pay up. So did Richards. See *Spirit*, XIII (1844), 558.

tion has afforded us, we shall be better enabled than ever to cater for the tastes and wishes of our Southern readers." [59]

Dazzled by this overwhelming show of southern hospitality, Porter evidently interpreted those "tastes and wishes" to mean that he should raise the price of the magazine, with results already indicated. But this tour undoubtedly aided him also in establishing contact with such backwoods writers as Charles F. M. Noland, "Boots," and "Obe Oilstone." The contributions of Obe Oilstone and T. B. Thorpe, two of the liveliest in Porter's string of humorists, began in 1838 and 1839 respectively. Thus the gradual switch in the *Spirit* from emphasis on sporting material to the stressing of local realism and folklore may be traced in part to the panic of 1837 with the resultant decline of big-time racing and perhaps also to the ensuing migration of planters westward and to Porter's own journeys to the South, especially his tour of 1838.

[59] *Spirit*, VIII (1838), 4; Brinley, *Life of William T. Porter*, 43–47, 101–41.

CHAPTER TWO

The Sporting Editor as Critic

I

BY the late 1830's two roads had emerged from the yellow wood of literary uncouthness in America. One was the path of British imitation, a path already well trodden. The other was the less clearly marked trail of exploitation and development of native themes and native styles. A number of American writers had tried to travel both roads. Washington Irving's polite imitations of the *Spectator* occasionally annoyed even the British; of his early writings a reviewer in *Blackwood's* complained in 1824 that they had "a languorous softness that relegates them almost to the realm of feebleness." This unfavorable verdict was later seconded by one of his own countrymen who insisted in the *North American Review* that *A Tour on the Prairies* was "a sort of sentimental journey, a romantic excursion." The Grecianized Indians and the cliffs like Moorish castles in this volume are well known, yet Irving did once note someone's brief delineation of squatter life in a piece which compares favorably with many items in the *Spirit of the Times*. "Polly Holman's Wedding," which, significantly, was not published in Irving's lifetime, includes a practical joke played by the family of a Kentucky squatter on a government express rider, the marriage of the squatter's daughter, and a frolic afterwards. The only element which this sketch lacks to give it an authentic frontier flavor is a bit of dialect. Unfortunately, Irving never let a frontiersman tell a story in his own language, but at least he did attempt to travel the road which led toward the frontier.[1]

[1] Cited by Fred Lewis Pattee, *The Development of the American Short Story* (New York and London, 1923), 24, and *id.*, *The First Century of American*

Cooper too wrote tales of frontier life in a language adapted on the whole to the depiction of life and manners in an eighteenth-century drawing-room. But this inconsistency goes deeper than the mere use of language. Henry Nash Smith has suggested in *Virgin Land* that Cooper's mind was the theater of a conflict between the aristocratic ideals of a squirearchy represented by his own wealthy father and Tory ancestors, and the democratizing influence of the frontier. Cooper's writing, says Professor Smith, came out of that conflict. Smith further points out that dialect in Cooper's novels is definitely a class mark; only low-caste characters like Natty Bumppo use it.[2] One might add that the farther down the social and moral scale Cooper's characters are, the more convincing they are likely to be in speech and action. Ishmael Bush, the squatter of *The Prairie*, is a more concrete and vital creation than Leather-stocking, particularly in the chapter in which he judges, condemns, and executes his wife's brother; and Chingachgook, the old drunken Indian of *The Pioneers*, seems far better actualized than Chingach-gook the romantic warrior of *The Last of the Mohicans*. Let us be grateful that Cooper got as far as he did along the westward path.

As editor of the *Spirit*, William T. Porter likewise spread his long legs in attempting to travel both roads at once. Like Cooper he commands our interest today in proportion to how far he was able to trek westward along the faint early trail of native realism and by how much he was able to broaden that path for his contributors and readers. Yet he showed the same tendency as Cooper to draw back from the democratic wave of the frontier and to look eastward toward the British upper classes. He tried to develop his magazine along the lines of *Bell's Life in London* and in addition he reprinted many of the *Sketches by Boz*, the *Yellowplush Papers* of Thackeray, and various tales and excerpts from the novels of Charles Lever, Charles Surtees, and others. So great, apparently, was the demand for Dickens among readers of the *Spirit* that

---

Literature 1770–1870 (New York, 1935), 295; *North American Review*, XLI (July, 1835), 12, also quoted by John Francis McDermott (ed.), *The Western Journals of Washington Irving* (Norman, Oklahoma, 1944), 41; Stanley T. Williams and Ernest E. Leisy (eds.), "Polly Holman's Wedding: Notes by Washington Irving," *Southwest Review*, XIX (July, 1934), 449–54.

[2] See also Smith's "Introduction" to Cooper's *The Prairie* (New York, 1950), xii–xx.

Porter even perpetrated a forgery entitled " 'Marmaduke Myddle-ton,' a New Work by 'Boz,' " and good-naturedly chaffed rival editors who had fallen for it and had pirated some of the false sketches.[3]

More significant than his reprinting of British works was Porter's habit of encouraging his native correspondents by comparing them favorably to British writers. In 1840 he praised William P. Hawes (Cypress, Jr.) for his tall yarn "A Shark Story" and the then-anonymous writer of "Jones's Fight" and "A Quarter Race in Kentucky" by saying: "And we do not exaggerate when we declare our belief that as such, there are none now contributing to the English Sporting Magazines equal to them." [4]

Porter also hands them some typical praise for their being both humorous and sporting writers, and he praises the author of "A Quarter Race" for his graphic power and the naturalness of his characters. He makes an equally typical attempt to tease these amateurs into further creative effort: "What can be done to incite them to activity?"

In a puff for *The Big Bear of Arkansas*, a volume of sketches from the *Spirit* which he had just finished putting together, Porter declared with his usual enthusiasm that "we have compiled a volume containing twenty-one several sketches, not one of which is unworthy of Hood, Dickens, or Theodore Hook." [5] Yet, is this traveling by a British-made compass so inconsistent after all? Dickens, Thackeray, and others, in their early works at least, were trying to write humorous sketches of local character types drawn with exaggerated traits in bold relief. Does not this parallel the rough exaggeration and bald depiction of regional traits that one finds in American frontier humor?

Fred Lewis Pattee did not seem to think so; in *The Feminine Fifties* he claimed that Dickens' chief influence in America was that of a stimulus to the fiction which appealed to feminine tears and sentiment. How then is one to explain this statement of

[3] Lawrence H. Houtchens, "The *Spirit of the Times* and a 'New Work by Boz,' " *Publications of the Modern Language Association of America*, LXVII (March, 1952), 94–100.

[4] *Spirit*, X (1840), 361.

[5] Porter (ed.), *The Big Bear of Arkansas*, 32.

Porter's editorial policy: "If we confine our originals to notices of *New Books, Reviews,* and *Magazines,* and discussion of current letters, we shall make ample amends by our selections from the *choice Belles-Lettres* of America and Great Britain." And what shall we say of his early notion of organizing *The Big Bear of Arkansas* according to the plan of Frederick Marryat's *A Pacha of Many Tales?* Marryat's work, a crude satire on the romantic orientalism of Byron, Thomas Moore, and possibly of the *Arabian Nights,* concerns a pacha, or pasha, in a generalized Moslem country, who makes his own barber, Mustapha, his vizier. Mustapha and others tell him tales from the Arabian Nights. Various frontier writers, including Porter's contributor Samuel Adams Hammett, were to utilize the framework device by means of the old variant of a group of yarn-spinners in a tavern. Nevertheless one is glad that Porter finally dropped his notion of copying the structure of Marryat's verbose and clumsy volume.[6]

How, too, shall we square Porter's frequent borrowing from the British with his prideful statement of February 2, 1839, that the contents of this week's volume are "almost entirely original"; or his statement of purpose in the preface of *The Big Bear of Arkansas?* Here he says: "A new vein of literature, as original as it is inexhaustible in its source, has been opened in this country, within a very few years, with the most marked success." He states that the pioneers of this continent have moved on even to the Pacific, "but they have left behind them, on all hands, scores of original characters to be encountered nowhere else under the sun." In the Southwest, especially in Mississippi and Arkansas, are "some of the most extraordinary men who ever lived 'to point a moral, or adorn a tale.'" He admits that some of them are hard drinkers and rough customers, but most are merely good story-tellers who also have good sense. "Of adventures and scenes in which these characters stand out in bold relief, this volume is

[6] *Spirit,* VI (1836), 8. Cf. *Spirit,* VII (1837), 4; William T. Porter to Carey and Hart, January 18, 1845, in Henry Carey Baird Papers, Historical Society of Pennsylvania; [Samuel Adams Hammett], *A Stray Yankee in Texas. By Philip Paxton* (New York, 1853).

A number of the tales in Hammett's book appeared in the *Spirit,* usually underwritten "P. P."

"The Big Bear of Arkansas"

mainly composed, relieved occasionally by sketches of men and things in some of the older southern states."

In these statements of intention there seems nothing in any way imitative of the British. Porter's introduction to *A Quarter Race in Kentucky*, his second collection of stories by contributors to the *Spirit*, shows his desire to sample the local color, not only of the South and Southwest, but of "the Universal Yankee Nation." In the prefaces to Porter's two collections he certainly seems a two-hundred-per-cent American, and his proposal to use Marryat as a model becomes even more striking by contrast with his attack on that same English author for his unfavorable review of Nathaniel Parker Willis' *Pencillings by the Way*. Porter struck out thus: "We have never read so disgraceful a criticism—if it be a criticism—as Capt. Marryat's review of Willis's *Pencillings* . . . . It makes our blood boil that any man, however gifted, or however high his rank, should charge it upon an *American* citizen as a matter of shame and disgrace that he is not of noble lineage." Four months later Porter threw another stone at Marryat and in addition scored American critics for their "sullen doggedness" and "meagre commendation" of Willis' book, taking an especial pot shot at "the old aristocracy of Boston and the saplings and suckers thereof." [7]

Of course, one may say that Marryat and the other critics merely attacked one of Porter's friends, and that the loyal, impulsive editor promptly blew up. But this is too simple and too easy an answer. Willis was indeed a friend of Porter and at one time co-edited with George Porter, one of William's brothers, a short-lived literary journal, the *Corsair*. Their intention in this periodical, by the way, was to pirate the best of contemporary English writing.[8] But Willis' connection with George Porter is no reason for thinking William any the less sincere in his attack on British snobbery and on the vested critical interests of the Boston, New York, and Philadelphia press.

Nor did the passage of years bring a clear-cut resolution of Porter's contradictory views. The attack just quoted was made in 1836. In that year Porter puffed his own magazine for its original native material, but in the same volume he announced his intention to use extensive selections from "the choicest English Belles-Lettres." In 1839 he boosted the price of the *Spirit* partly in order

---

[7] *Spirit*, VI (1836), 52, 172, 204. Eventually a duel between Willis and Marryat was narrowly averted; see Henry A. Beers, *Nathaniel Parker Willis* (Boston, 1885), 197–206.

[8] Brinley, *Life of William T. Porter*, 73, 75–78; Mott, *A History of American Magazines*, 356–58; Beers, *Nathaniel Parker Willis*, 239–43.

to give more space to the British turf. The following year he praised Cypress, Jr., and the author of "A Quarter Race in Kentucky" for outdoing the sporting writers of England. In 1845 he brought out *The Big Bear*, a book of original sketches of the West and South, intended at first to be strung on a frame suggested by an English author whom Porter had once lashed for derogating American society and an American writer. He followed this with another volume of indigenous matter. His activity on behalf of American writers was at its height in the middle forties, and from then to the end of his career he continued to print copious tales and sketches of the backwoods. Even so, a "fave notice" of *Vanity Fair* appeared in 1851, the same year in which he was praising both Dickens and Melville for breaking with the tradition of writers who continually rely on "overdone incidents" and who imitate "defunct Scotts and Radcliffs [sic]." (This praise occurs in a long, shrewd, and highly favorable review of *Moby Dick*.) Perhaps Porter realized that certain established writers were, like himself, pioneers of realism.[9]

Right up to his last days at the desk this Yankee editor continued to fill many column inches of the *Spirit* with chunks and snippets from the works of Dickens, Thackeray, and the lesser writers of *Punch*, and in the forties and fifties one finds no more such anti-British explosions as the attack on Marryat in 1836. The more Porter mellowed toward the British in theory, the more he seemed to favor the Americans in practice.

True, Porter was never much of a theorizer; his theory was a rationalization after the fact of his editorial performance. However, that performance was hampered by his inconsistent devotion at the same time to polite British literature and to impolite, rough-shod American humor and realism. This inconsistency is but an

---

[9] *Spirit*, XXI (1851), 494. The next year Porter printed the only known review which was favorable to *Pierre*, in "New Publications," *Spirit*, XXII (1852), 336. Melville scholars have stated that *Pierre* received no favorable attention, but I give the brief in full:

"Pierre; or the Ambiguities. By Herman Melville. —Every work written by this author possesses more than common interest, and abounds in strange and wild imaginings, but this book outstrips all his former productions, and is quite equal to Moby Dick, or the Whale. It is certainly one of the most exciting and interesting ever published, and it must be read to be clearly appreciated, but none will regret the time spent in its perusal."

aspect of his self-identification with the ideals and mores of the southern gentleman (who always felt akin to the English squire), and his consequent attempt to put the *Spirit* entirely at the service of that very small class of large planters as they followed the sport of kings. This attempt nearly wrecked his paper economically, and in the realm of literary taste it caused him to accept a tremendous amount of slush in the way of moralizing essays, floridly romantic tales by both men and women, and unutterably trashy occasional verse, much of which appeared cheek by jowl with the realistic and folkloristic humor for which we now study the *Spirit*. In short, Porter broke a lot of ground for American realism, but had he not had an English thoroughbred—imported by a gentleman slaveowner—hitched to his editorial plow, he would have broken much more.

One must not forget that Cooper was a Jacksonian Democrat with a nasty temper and Porter was a Whig with an even temper. Yet Porter, like Cooper and also like Irving and Poe, admired the English for their gentlemanly ways and, like them, looked with favor on the ideal of an oligarchy of wealth, intelligence, and culture.[10] But all four men took a serious interest in the frontier as possible literary material. To see how thoroughly within the main stream of American thinking were Porter and his most important contributors, one need only compare Poe's comments on Longstreet's *Georgia Scenes* (1835) with a note by William Tappan Thompson, the Georgia author of *Major Jones's Courtship* (1843). Poe says of Longstreet's work: "Seriously—if this book were printed in England it would make the fortune of its author." He also hits at "the long indulged literary supineness of the South" and hints that the book may not sell because of this inertness.[11] Thompson, speaking in the character of Major Jones, makes this sardonic comment:

"I didn't know what upon yearth to make of seein my letters gwine the rounds in the papers, till I saw that 'Spirit of the Times'

[10] James Fenimore Cooper, *The American Democrat* (Cooperstown, 1838), 104–15, 184–86.

[11] *Southern Literary Messenger*, II (March, 1836), 287–92. See also Poe's somewhat more critical review of *The Big Bear of Arkansas* in the *Broadway Journal*, I (May 24, 1845), 331.

what you sent me. Our people's monstrous loud about Southern
genus and Southern institutions, and Southern feelin, and Southern literature, and all that, but they never find out they've got
anything good at home, until the Northern people tell 'em of it.
That's the secret—and sense the New York and Boston papers has
begun to publish my ritins, I can find 'em in lots of papers all over
the South." [12]

One doubts whether an uneducated Georgia farmer would
normally have much to say about southern literature. However, as
Porter's slap at Boston critics in connection with Marryat and
Willis shows, he was also at one with Thompson and Poe in that
their interest in frontier writing was bound up with a distrust of
certain genteel northern circles.

Incidentally, Poe at least was wrong. According to Longstreet
himself, the first edition of *Georgia Scenes,* published in Augusta
and amounting to nearly 4,000 copies, was sold out entirely except for 250 which were lost, "and all this without sending a single
volume north of the Potomac." [13] The southern public was ready.
It only needed a means of supply. Porter and the *Spirit* furnished
that means.

II

Porter, unlike Irving, Cooper, Poe, and Paulding, was in
close and constant touch with the backwoods through his many
written and personal contacts and through his interest in racing,
hunting, and fishing. As a result he was far more active on behalf
of backwoods writing than any of the other figures named. Even
outside of the *Spirit* he accomplished a good deal; specifically, he
edited two popular collections of backwoods humor and acted as a
sort of literary agent for two of the most popular southern writers,
Thomas Bangs Thorpe and Johnson Jones Hooper. He may well

[12] *Spirit,* XIII (1844), 590–91.
[13] Augustus B. Longstreet to James B. Longacre, September 1, 1842. A copy
of this letter is owned by Professor William Charvat of the Ohio State University,
to whom I am indebted for a transcript. Further data on the growth of southern
interest in southern writing is furnished by Shields McIlwaine, *The Southern
Poor-White from Lubberland to Tobacco Road* (Norman, Oklahoma, 1939),
40–74.

have made some contacts also for William Tappan Thompson and others, even as he acted as go-between for "Country Gentlemen" who wanted horses, guns, fishing tackle, and a variety of other goods bought for them in New York.[14]

The Big Bear of Arkansas (1845) and *A Quarter Race in Kentucky* (1846) are the third and fourth volumes respectively of southern and western humor to come off the press in America. Longstreet's *Georgia Scenes* had appeared in 1835; Thompson's *Major Jones's Courtship* in 1843. On January 18, 1845, Porter wrote to Carey and Hart, Philadelphia publishers of humor and miscellaneous works. This is the earliest letter of their correspondence which has been preserved:

"Gentn

Your favor of the 14th is before me and I lose no time in acknowledging it and how much satisfied I am with the compliment paid the 'Spirit of the Times.'

You allude to a few of the *recent* 'crack' stories—not the *richest*, however, that have appeared in its columns, allow me to assure you. 'Jones's Fight,' though a capital thing, is not comparable with another story, earlier given in the 'Spirit' by the same writer . . . . There is material for half a dozen volumes of the size of 'Maj. Jones's Courtship,' and I make no doubt the volume you propose will be immediately succeeded by others of a similar character. I have no idea of the trouble of compiling such a volume, but should imagine that each story should be introduced with some appropriate remarks. Marryatt's [*sic*] 'Pacha of Many *Tales*' might be a good model. In the course of the day I will hunt up something of the kind, and also look over my files." [15]

Thus it looks as if the initial proposal for a volume of sketches from the *Spirit* came from someone in the firm of Carey and Hart —whether from Abraham Hart (then the leading member of the firm) or a subordinate does not matter. What does matter is that all Porter needed was a suggestion, and the firm's proposal oper-

[14] "To Country Gentlemen," *Spirit*, XV (1845), 1. This advertisement ran for years.
[15] Porter to Carey and Hart, January 18, 1845, in Henry Carey Baird Papers.

ated on him like the touch of a button on a high-voltage motor. With truly electric zeal he must have started to work as he promised, because less than one month later he writes as though he had already finished compiling the volume. He says, "I am gratified you entertain so favorable an opinion of the Southwestern Sketches, and am confident I can make a still more interesting compilation for a second volume, as I intend taking a wider range. I shall commence upon it forthwith." [16]

By the middle of February work on the engravings was going forward, but on March 3 Porter was still sending over some of the sketches needed to fill the first volume. In his letter of that date we learn of still another project on the fire:

"Am much obliged for your offer of sheets of Hooper's sketches in advance. Who knows but I may have been, or be, the means of making his 'fortune?' 'Tall oaks from little acorns,' etc. I congratulate you upon making an arrangement with him . . . . 'Talking of guns!' I enclose you a note from T. B. Thorpe, Esq., the author of the 'Big Bear of Arkansas.' Thorpe is a man of decided genius. The 'Big Bear' hardly gives one an idea of what he has done or is capable of. He is postmaster of Vidalia, Louisiana, (a little village opposite Natchez, Miss.)—editor of the 'Concordia Intelligencer,' and by profession, a portrait painter. So see what you can do for him. He is as nervous as our friend Henry Inman, but like him is a capital good fellow. He is well known to 'the press gang' on both sides of the Atlantic and every man who ever saw him will 'go his death' on him. Some of his sketches in the Great Valley of the Mississippi and of the 'characters' encountered there are equal to anything in the language, in my humble opinion. You will see that, like many other young writers, he looks to 'this child' as a sort of 'literary godfather.' " [17]

Porter had already helped to make Thorpe popular by the publication of "Tom Owen, the Bee-Hunter" in the *Spirit*.[18] We see Porter now bringing forward two authors, Thorpe and Hooper,

[16] William T. Porter to Carey and Hart, February, 14, 1845, in Porter Papers, New-York Historical Society Library.
[17] William T. Porter to Carey and Hart, March 3, 1845, in Porter Papers.
[18] *Spirit*, IX (1839), 247 and XXIX (1859), 1.

who had not previously achieved book publication. In a letter dated March 15 Porter says:

"I have written a long letter to Thorpe, to New Orleans (care of the Eds. of the 'Picayune') . . . ascertaining your suggestions in relation to his forthcoming sketches . . . . I have received a letter from Hooper, of the 'East Alabamian,' enclosing 'Daddy Bigg's Scrape at Cockerell's Bend.' This last he intends revising for you, at his leisure, and asks your permission to do so! God bless him, he can have anything connected with the 'Spirit,' the editor included, if he wishes.

"I have 'got out' a portion of the 'copy' of the 2 vol. of sketches, but it is not in a fit state to send you. Rather than Darley should be idle, however, I will send you two or three articles for him to read and in a day or two will send more. I can furnish the introduction at my leisure.

"That Maj. Douglas's story is indeed 'some!' But if you will read 'A Quarter Race in Kentucky' and 'A Shark Story' I think you will agree with me that *they can't be beat!*' Before placing it in the printers' hands I must ask you to erase the several introductions (the portions enclosed in brackets) as original ones will be written to supply their places.

"Pray let me have any duplicate illustrations of 'The Big Bear' . . . and . . . a proof of the Editor's Preface. Would it not be gratifying our different writers to re-publish it, or a portion of it, in the 'Spirit?' As a dozen different members of 'the press gang' are spoken of, it might not 'set you back any' in the sale of the work." [19]

Here we see the editor and agent hard at work. Apparently at least two and possibly three projects in which Porter was involved were now underway at Carey and Hart—*The Big Bear* and *A Quarter Race* (which may be thought of as a single venture), a book of sketches by Hooper, and one by Thorpe. This letter also suggests that Porter has taken the initiative away from Carey and Hart in publicizing *The Big Bear*, since this is his second request

[19] William T. Porter to Carey and Hart, March 15, 1845, in Porter Papers. The parentheses are Porter's.

A QUARTER RACE IN KENTUCKY,

AND OTHER TALES.

EDITED BY W. T. PORTER, ESQ., OF THE N. Y. SPIRIT OF THE TIMES.

PHILADELPHIA:

T. B. PETERSON, No. 102 CHESTNUT STREET.

"A Quarter Race in Kentucky"

for permission to publish illustrations from that volume in advance. Since the publication of the book was apparently postponed from April 1, 1845, to May 16, 1845, the date on which it actually appeared, Porter was indeed able to publish a couple of engravings in advance, plus brief excerpts from two of the stories.[20]

By June 7 Porter was working hard on the second volume of sketches culled from the *Spirit* (*A Quarter Race in Kentucky*). A letter of that date reflects his scrupulous attention to the wishes of his contributors and reveals how both Porter and the author were striving for an accurate representation of backwoods traits. Editor and contributor had the same goal—realism in the sense of fidelity to life:

"Gentm
[First word undecipherable] my return from your city I have rec'd a note from the author of 'A Quarter Race in Kentucky,' in which he calls my attention to an error in the text, which I will thank you to correct in the proof.

The expression
'he could look his own head,'
has always been printed
'look (*at*) his own head'
The word 'at' is superfluous. To make the expression plain he suggests the following note
* 'A backwoods invention to super cede [*sic*]
the use of a fine tooth comb.'
* 'The original mode of *hunting* small *varmints.*' " [21]

This letter suggests that Porter was sending proofs of each story to its writer and trying to make sure that any emendations or corrections made by the author were carried out by the publisher. Such changes of text to please the various authors may have been no light task. *The Big Bear* contained twenty-one sketches and tales; *A Quarter Race*, thirty-three; and the number of contributors to each was nearly equal to the number of tales. As far as we can tell, only Thorpe, Thomas Kirkman, "The Turkey Runner"

[20] *Spirit*, XV (1845), 33. See also *Spirit*, XV (1845), 117, 126.
[21] William T. Porter to Carey and Hart, June 7, 1845, in Porter Papers, Manuscript Room, New York Public Library.

(Alexander McNutt), and William P. Hawes are represented more than once.[22]

However, the process of preparation slowed down during the ensuing year and a half, partly owing to the shortage and slowness of engravers, and partly, no doubt, owing to the publishers' unwillingness to bring out a second group of backwoods sketches before the first had had a good run. Meanwhile, Porter, in addition to editing these two volumes and helping Thorpe and Hooper to place theirs, was putting in a word for yet another of his contributors, Captain William Seaton Henry. Thanks in part to Porter's correspondence with Harper and Brothers on behalf of Henry's *Campaign Sketches of the War with Mexico,* that volume, which originated as a series of dispatches to the *Spirit of the Times,* was published in 1847.[23]

A Quarter Race in Kentucky was probably issued in the last days of 1846,[24] but it obviously grew in Porter's mind and in the external world almost simultaneously with *The Big Bear of Arkansas,* being slowed down only in the final stages. The two books may well be treated as two volumes of a single set, the first being, as its subtitle indicates, "Illustrative of Characters and Incidents in the South and Southwest," and the second being "Illustrative of Scenes, Characters, and Incidents, Throughout 'The Universal Yankee Nation.'" Both are set up in the same manner, which is *not* that of *A Pacha of Many Tales.* Instead of being linked in a framework, the tales are almost entirely disparate, but each is "introduced with some appropriate remarks," as Porter had wished. These introductory paragraphs are on the whole brief, mellow, and in keeping with the humorous atmosphere of the volumes as a whole. Subtitles are furnished which in themselves contribute a tinge of mild humor. For instance, "Jones's Fight" is subtitled

22 The two stories of Hawes (Cypress, Jr.), "A Shark Story," and "A Bear Story," are reprinted from Henry William Herbert (ed.), *Sporting Scenes and Sundry Sketches . . . of J. Cypress, Jr.* (2 vols.; New York, 1842), I, 37–46, 47–53.

23 William T. Porter to Abraham Hart, November 20, 1845, in Porter Papers, New York Public Library; Porter to Carey and Hart, October 18, 1846, in Porter Papers, New York Historical Society Library; *Spirit,* XVII (1847), 230.

24 *Spirit,* XVI (1847), 540.

"A Story of Kentucky—by an Alabamian"; "Swallowing an Oyster Alive" is called "A Story of Illinois—By a Missourian"; and "A Quarter Race in Kentucky" is listed as "By a North Alabamian." One or two samples of Porter's brand of commentary may also be given. Here is how he introduces "That Big Dog Fight at Myers's/ A Story of Mississippi—By a Mississippian":

"The writer of the following story is one of the most entertaining companions we ever met. Like the elder Placide, or Gabriel Ravel, he has the keenest perception of the ludicrous imaginable; in him this is combined with an inexhaustible flow of spirits, and a rare fund of wit and humour peculiarly calculated to 'set the table in a roar.' For several years he has been a most acceptable correspondent of the New York 'Spirit of the Times,' and while his stories have 'ranged from amazin to onkimmon,' there is not an indifferent one among them all. His extraordinary merit as a storyteller is only equalled by his modesty; 'not for the world' would he permit us to name him. We are free to say, however, that he is a country gentleman of Mississippi, 'of about our size,' and that he resides on a river-plantation nearly equidistant from the regions of 'the cotton trade and sugar line.' " [25]

Over another story, "Going to Bed Before a Young Lady./ By Judge Douglass, of Illinois," Porter writes in typical fashion, "Judge Douglass, of Illinois, is decidedly the most original and amusing member of the western bar—or we are no judge." [26] In like manner a number of the other prefaces either give some information about the writer or make some quip or comment calculated to encourage him to write more, or both. Although sometimes inaccurate, they are a valuable and as yet partially unexploited source of information about the identity of several of the anonymous authors.

In spite of the disparateness of the tales, both volumes, taken as a set, possess a decided unity of tone and manner. In *The Big Bear* this unity may be chiefly owing to the unity of subject matter.

[25] Porter (ed.), *The Big Bear of Arkansas*, 54. For identification of this author as P. B. January see Meine (ed.), *Tall Tales of the Southwest* 383.
[26] Porter (ed.), *A Quarter Race in Kentucky*, 52.

But unlike its predecessor, *A Quarter Race* does not confine itself to the Southwest. Of the thirty-three sketches no less than eight are from areas other than that part of the frontier. The locale of the two by Hawes is Fire Island, New York, and Hawes himself was a New Yorker, but the stories are nonetheless tall, especially "A Bear Story." [27] Three stories and a poem come from authors living in or near Boston, hub of literary respectability and target of Irving, Poe, and Porter. One of these stories, "The Fastest Funeral on Record," by Francis A. Durivage ("The Old 'Un") is a rough little piece about the driver of a funeral carriage who simply couldn't resist a race with a rival hack—even though he had a body in his vehicle. Two stories from Pennsylvania complete the eastern score. One of these, "Somebody in My Bed," by U. J. Jones of Harrisburg, is set in a ramshackle, isolated tavern in the northern part of the state and is somewhat on the spicy side.

Thus the temptation urged upon his readers by Porter to try their hands at humorous sketches, particularly those involving racing, hunting, fishing, or related subjects, was not confined in its appeal to the South and Southwest. More important, the flavor, technique, and subject matter of frontier writing—back-country sport, the rough practical joke, the use of dialect—were at the command of some eastern as well as western writers. In *A Quarter Race* the spread is nationwide. And was the circulation of both these volumes also nationwide? Porter testified to the popularity of *The Big Bear,* which soon sold out an edition of 4,000 copies printed at a cost of only $610. New editions were issued in 1846, 1850, 1851, and 1855. [28] As for *A Quarter Race,* the firm of T. B. Peterson and Brothers added this volume to their "Library of Humorous American Works"—encouraged, no doubt, by the brisk sale of this work and of *The Big Bear.* [29] The first edition of *A*

---

[27] *Ibid.,* 188–96.

[28] *Ibid.,* 5; entry of March 26, 1845, "Carey & Hart Record Books," unpublished mss., Historical Society of Pennsylvania; Nelle Smither, "Library of Humorous American Works," unpublished Master's thesis (Columbia, 1936), 51–56.

[29] The snarled bibliographical history of this series is largely unraveled by Miss Smither. Abraham Hart, successor to Carey and Hart, began the "Library" in 1849; T. B. Peterson continued the series in 1851. The first three numbers of the series were: [Solomon Franklin Smith], *Theatrical Apprenticeship and Anecdotal Recollections of Sol. Smith, Esq.;* [Denis Corcoran], *Pickings from*

Quarter Race, also numbering 4,000 copies (cost, $708.16), was followed by editions in 1850, 1852, and 1854.[30] Moreover, several of the authors represented in one or both of the Porter volumes published collections of their own sketches (including those preprinted in the *Spirit*) within the next two years. Thorpe, Hooper, Joseph M. Field, Sol Smith, John S. Robb, Francis A. Durivage, George P. Burnham, and Henry Clay Lewis ("Madison Tensas") brought out volumes before or during 1848. Porter had helped to start quite a snowball.

III

Among these writers at least two, Thorpe and Hooper, relied directly on Porter for assistance in achieving book publication. The Porter-Thorpe relationship is given a full and careful treatment by Dr. Milton Henry Rickels, but we might notice that Thorpe knocked around the Mississippi Valley for eighteen years (1835–1853), editing or writing for various Louisiana newspapers and painting portraits of such notables as Zachary Taylor and Senator Joseph Walker of Louisiana, and of such well-to-do delta planters as Bennet H. Barrow. Once he fell in with a local squatter whose great passion in life was bee hunting. Thorpe went out hunting with this man and afterwards wrote a sketch based on the bee hunter for a village paper. The drowsy editor let it lie in his drawer for three months and finally returned it as not interesting enough for publication. Thorpe too let it gather dust for awhile but finally fished it out and sent it to the *Spirit,* where it was received without fanfare and published in the issue of July 27, 1839. "Mr. T., living in the 'backwoods,' was not aware of its great popularity, until he went to New York some three years afterwards, where he found himself quite a lion, as that single article had rendered him 'famous.' " This tale of "Tom Owen, the Bee Hunter" marked Thorpe's first publication of narrative material in a national magazine. In it the emphasis is on dialect humor and

the *Portfolio of the Reporter of the New Orleans Picayune,* and Frank Forester [Henry William Herbert], *My Shooting Box.* Selections from all three had previously been printed in the *Spirit of the Times.*

[30] Entry of December 15, 1846, "Carey & Hart Record Books"; Smither, "Library of Humorous American Works," 28–30, 42, 52, 57.

vivid description, in contrast to Irving in *A Tour on the Prairies*
and Cooper in *The Prairie* and *The Oak Openings*. Both treated
bee hunters in their usual patronizing, sentimental manner, as did
Richard Penn Smith in *Col. Crockett's Exploits and Adventures
in Texas.*[31]

Less than a year later Thorpe went to New York, where he
undoubtedly met Porter. The Tall Son of York encouraged the
chunky son of Massachusetts to write more about the southern
backwoods, and Thorpe did two more sketches before leaving the
city. Rather ungratefully, Thorpe later claimed that the popularity
of "Tom Owen" was the direct and sole cause of his writing
further material about the back country. Be that as it may, his
reputation now rests, not on that sketch but on his second truly
humorous tale, "The Big Bear of Arkansas," which appeared in
the *Spirit* of March 27, 1841. In the next four or five years a long
string of pieces on life and manners in the delta backwoods flowed
from Thorpe's pen, and most of them appeared in the *Spirit*
either at first or eventually. With two or three exceptions, the
bulk of these pieces are not very interesting, being written
"straight," that is, in polite language, with the emphasis on mere
description of natural phenomena or sporting excursions.[32]

"The Big Bear of Arkansas," of course, gave its name to Porter's
first collection of tales from his magazine. Before the book appeared in the stalls Thorpe had sent 100 pages of a collection of
his own to a London publisher, but the house failed and the material was returned to the Louisiana artist, whereupon he began
negotiating with New York publishers, through Porter and other
friends.[33] Thus, only the shuttle of chance (to borrow a metaphor

[31] Milton Henry Rickels, "Thomas Bangs Thorpe: His Life and Works," un-
published Ph.D. dissertation (Louisiana State, 1953), 37–179, *passim;* Davis (ed.),
Plantation Life in the Florida Parishes, 228, 257, 415; "Men and Things of
Louisiana," *Spirit,* XX (1850), 270; "New Publications," *Spirit,* XXIII (1853),
457–58; *Spirit,* XXIX (1859), 30; T. B. Thorpe, *Mysteries of the Backwoods*
(Philadelphia, 1846), 7–8.
[32] *Spirit,* X (1840), 421; "Wild Turkey Shooting," *Spirit,* X (1840), 253;
"Primitive Forests of the Mississippi," *Spirit,* X (1840), 361; "A Piano in Arkan-
sas," *Spirit,* XI (1841), 409–10; "The Devil's Summer Retreat, in Arkansaw,"
Spirit, XII (1842), 295–96, given as "Bob Herring, the Arkansas Bear Hunter" in
Porter (ed.) *A Quarter Race in Kentucky,* 130–45.
[33] T. B. Thorpe to Carey and Hart, March 8, 1845, in Henry Carey Baird
Papers.

"How Simon Suggs 'Raised Jack' "

from Melville) operating within the general historical fabric
enabled Porter to call himself "a sort of 'literary godfather' " to
this budding author. Thorpe's first collection, *The Mysteries of
the Backwoods*, eventually came out in 1846 under the Philadelphia imprint of Carey and Hart.

Porter was also sitting up with the young reputation of Johnson J. Hooper, creator of the one and only Simon Suggs. How
Hooper's "Taking the Census" proved "an open sesame to fame

and immortality," how publication of this piece in the *Spirit* was
followed by warm notes of encouragement by Porter, how selections from *Some Adventures of Captain Simon Suggs* appeared
shortly thereafter in the magazine, how Porter held up the printing of *The Big Bear* to include one of the stories about "the shifty
man," and how he labored as hard to put *Simon Suggs* through the
press of Carey and Hart as he did on his own volumes at about the
same time—all this is told with zest and scholarship by W. Stanley
Hoole in *Alias Simon Suggs,* his biography of the Alabama humorist and newspaperman. A single omission in Hoole's admirable
study may be rectified in this place. William Tappan Thompson's
Major Jones's Sketches of Travel reveals that Hooper met the
genial Georgia major in New York and that the two made that
city their base of operations for about seven weeks in June and
July, 1845.[34] Since *Simon Suggs* was released on or just before
September 20, according to Hoole, there is every reason to believe
that Hooper and Thompson met Porter and that they "touched
knees under mahogany" at Monteverde's while they talked fun,
fishing, and frolics—and about the publication of Hooper's forthcoming volume. Thompson, we know definitely, made the *Spirit*
office his headquarters whenever he was in the city.[35] Anyhow,
shortly after this trip *Some Adventures of Captain Simon Suggs*
came rolling off the press with this dedication, which well sums up
the attitude of many regional humorists toward York's Tall Son:

[34] William T. Thompson, *Major Jones's Sketches of Travel . . . in His Tour
from Georgia to Canada* (Philadelphia, 1848), Letters XIII–XX, 107–89. The
first of these eight letters from the North was dated June 2, 1845, the last July 22,
1845. During this time the two made side trips to Boston and Lowell in "Yankee-
doodledom" and to Niagara. Thompson may also have spoken to Porter and to
Carey and Hart in Philadelphia about the publication of his *Chronicles of Pineville*
(1845).
[35] *Spirit,* XVI (1846), 228; Brinley, *Life of William T. Porter,* 83.
    Porter and Hooper shared an interest in sport as well as humor. In 1846 Porter,
despite his multiple work load, re-edited an English work, *Instructions to Young
Sportsmen . . . By Lieut. Col. P. Hawker . . . to Which Is Added the Hunting
and Shooting of North America, with Descriptions of the Animals and Birds. Carefully Collated from Authentic Sources* (Philadelphia, 1846). Porter did more than
collate; he added a number of sketches of hunting and fishing in the New World,
some of which had previously appeared in the *Spirit.* Hooper's sporting activity
eventually crystalized in *Dog and Gun; a Few Loose Chapters on Shooting* (New
York, 1856).

To William T. Porter, Esq.
Editor of the New York Spirit of the Times,
The Following Pages are Respectfully inscribed,
As Well in Token of the Writer's Regard
As Because
If There Be Humour in Them,
They Could Have No More Appropriate Dedication.

CHAPTER THREE

The Spirit and Its Writers

I

WALTER BLAIR, among others, has done what he could to ruin his eyes by peering at the small print and dull paper of the *Spirit* or at microfilm reproductions thereof. In his condensed essay on "Humor of the Old Southwest (1830–1867)" he shows how a yarn which he has traced to a New England almanac was sent to the *Spirit* from Buffalo, New York, in a much altered version. Then a correspondent from East Baton Rouge Parish, Louisiana, tried to top it with another version which used some details from the New England version that were not in the Buffalo story.[1] Thus did the writers in Porter's crew spin a web of mutual influence, a fabric in which waves of stimulation and borrowing started at many points and traveled, crisscrossing and interweaving, in all directions to all corners of the country. And upon this homespun tapestry let us superimpose a moving picture, that of the realistic short story evolving, sometimes intermittently, sometimes steadily, from the factual letters in which Porter's early correspondents reported merely the where, when, how, what, and why of turf meetings and hunting excursions.

One must never forget that nearly all of these writers were amateurs. They began to send in letters and articles because they thought they had something to say within the magazine's main area of interest—sports, especially racing, hunting, and fishing. These occasional wielders of the pen fell roughly into two categories: gentlemen planters and sports-minded journalists. A number of officers and a few country lawyers and doctors were also included, but in most cases the officers, lawyers, doctors, and

[1] Walter Blair, *Native American Humor* (New York, 1937), 84–85.

members of the "press gang" were also planters or at least num-
bered members of the planter class among their close friends. That
is, the interests of the well-to-do planters who wrote for the *Spirit*
and of the persons not engaged in agriculture who did likewise
may be considered identical. We have already dealt with Thorpe
and Hooper, but we may backtrack long enough to note that
Thorpe was a guest at a planter's home at the very time he encountered the original of "Tom Owen, the Bee-Hunter," [2] and
that he once made this frank comment: "Finally, if I should come
north I should wish by industry to acquire a competency, a position
in society, and whatever else pertains to a gentleman." [3] Hooper,
moreover, was a stanch Whig and had for fellow travelers Thompson and Porter himself at a time when the southern Whigs were
definitely the party of property and privilege in the South.[4]

In the first part of his preface to *The Big Bear of Arkansas*
Porter in effect describes how the sporting interest among his
gentleman correspondents bloomed into a widespread, zestful depiction of frontier life and manners. Although it glows with his
usual enthusiasm, Porter's preface is fairly accurate: "A new vein
of literature, as original as it is inexhaustible in its source, has been
opened in this country within a very few years, with most marked
success," he declared. He cites the *American Turf Register and
Sporting Magazine*, which he had edited for awhile, and the New
York *Constellation*, which he had edited briefly in the early 1830's,
as the first American journals catering to writers of the kind that
contributed to the *Spirit*. Of the *Spirit* itself he wrote:

". . . ere long it became the nucleus of a new order of literary
talent. In addition to correspondents who described with equal
felicity and power the stirring incidents of the chase and the turf,
it enlisted another and still more numerous class, who furnished
most valuable and interesting reminiscences of the far West—
sketches of thrilling scenes and adventures in that then compara-

---

[2] *Spirit*, XX (1850), 270.
[3] T. B. Thorpe to Carey and Hart, December 5, 1845, in Thorpe Papers, New
York Historical Society Library.
[4] Thompson, *Major Jones's Sketches of Travel*, 143ff; Hoole, *Alias Simon
Suggs*, 60–65, 68–80.

tively unknown region, and the extraordinary characters occasionally met with—their strange language and habitudes, and the
peculiar and sometimes fearful characteristics of the 'squatters'
and early settlers. Many of these descriptions were wrought up
in a masterly style; and in the course of a few years a generous
feeling of emulation sprung up in the south and south-west,
prompted by the same impulses, until at length the correspondents of the 'Spirit of the Times' comprised a large majority of those
who have subsequently distinguished themselves in this novel and
original walk of literature."

Porter praises the writing of Cooper and Paulding, but he says
that the flatboatmen and backwoodsmen of these two authors belong
to an earlier, presteamboat era. Later pioneers than those of
Cooper and Paulding have moved on even to the Pacific. "But
they have left behind them scores of original characters to be
encountered nowhere else under the sun." Porter goes on to list
some of the correspondents who have written about these frontier
characters. He mentions C. F. M. Noland, T. B. Thorpe, "Col.
Mason, 'Captain Martin Scott,' of 'coon' remembrance, Gen. Gibson, Maj. Moore, Gen. Brooke, and a troop of other gallant officers
of the U.S. Army whom we are not permitted to name." He also
names Audubon, Timothy Flint, Albert Pike, Charles Fenno Hoffman, George Catlin, " 'Mary Clavers' (Mrs. Kirkland)," Captains
Carleton, Henry, and Johnston, "ex-Gov. Butler and Mr. Sibley,
the Indian agents," M. C. Field, and George Wilkins Kendall.
He says that these writers and "several others whose identity we
are not at liberty to disclose, have all vastly magnified, by their
writings, the eager curiosity to know more of the distinguishing
traits of character of the denizens of the many comparatively un-
peopled regions of the West and Southwest."

A cross-sectional analysis of Porter's crew of writers generally
bears out these prefatory comments. True, Audubon, Flint, Hoffman, Catlin, and Mrs. Kirkland contributed no original material
to the *Spirit;* their appearance in its pages was entirely by way
of reprinted selections. Further, the *Spirit* was first in its field only
as a national outlet and must be distinguished from such purely
local and regional outlets as the St. Louis *Reveille* and the New

Orleans *Picayune*.)For that matter, a few literary men had been collecting frontier yarns long before the *Spirit* existed. Fifteen years before the publication of *Westward Ho!* Paulding, to name one, had collected tall talk and tales in *Letters from the South* (1817), which originated far from the flatboat trade of the Ohio Valley and are closely related to much of the piquant local color material in the *Spirit*. Thus Porter had his forerunners; part of his significance lies in the extent rather than the priority of his material. Let us further keep in mind that the action of the *Spirit* in promoting frontier writing was essentially twofold; it published much original writing by frontier correspondents, and it republished much of the same kind of subliterature from journals of strictly local or sectional circulation.

II

By recalling occasionally this twofold role of the *Spirit*, one may concentrate for awhile on Porter's service to his original correspondents without losing perspective. In the beginning Porter's intent was merely to found a sporting journal. Paid correspondents were practically unknown in those days and we have noted that in order to obtain proper news coverage in his field a sporting editor had to secure the services of obliging sportsmen or fans who would send him, for nothing, newsworthy accounts of various turf and field events. In one of the sparse files of the *Spirit* for 1832 we find a plea for secretaries of racing clubs to report on the results of their respective fall meetings. In these few issues, however, only one writer, "D. W." of Franklin, Missouri, can be labeled with certainty as a regular contributor.[5]

"D. W." is mainly interesting because two of his three surviving articles indicate a pattern which was to be paralleled later in the writings of many contributors. Both of these two letters are informal sporting epistles; one records a deer hunt in which the author took part and the other a fishing expedition of which he was likewise a member.[6] The fishing epistle, however, includes a bit

[5] *Spirit*, I (October 20, 1832); "Washington Irving," *Spirit*, II (October 13, 1832).

[6] "Angling in Missouri," *Spirit*, II (February 16, 1833); "A Day's Hunting in Missouri," *Spirit*, II (March 9, 1833).

of conversation in dialect between two of his fellow anglers. Thus "D. W." has moved one step away from mere sporting narrative toward lifelike representation of character. The twist he gives to the reportorial epistle of sport is thoroughly typical of Porter's livelier correspondents.

Indeed the entire evolution described in Porter's prefatory remarks to *The Big Bear* was in a sense a struggle between two literary forms—the informal essay of the *Spectator* type (applied to sport primarily) with its restricted compass and polite diction, and a looser, more flexible type of writing, the oral tale of the backwoods transmuted into print with its earth-drawn material and its rougher, freer style. Even readers and writers of the *Spirit* were somewhat conscious of their literary molder; a Louisville correspondent signed an epistle "Spectator," and T. B. Thorpe himself declared that Hooper's *Simon Suggs* reminded him of the essays in that magazine.[7] Later we shall try to determine whether this conflict of literary forms is but the refracted image, brought to a focus, of a wider conflict between social groups.

"Delta," another early correspondent who is typical of many later contributors, sent in two tall tales, one of a monstrous snake and one of "Colonel Wanderwell," an infinitely digressive sportsman who can never finish a yarn. "Delta" was a rare spirit, and if he contributed more stories it is a pity that they have not survived. In a sense he by-passed the step-by-step development from purely sporting epistles to dramatic tales of frontier character in action; even so, both of "Delta's" tall tales have to do with sporting.

In 1836, after the reorganization and enlargement of the *Spirit*, the stream of sporting correspondents began to trickle steadily and finally to flow into the busy office of the editor. On March 26 of that year appeared a letter by the man who was to become the most frequent correspondent Porter ever had. Headed "A Glance at the Southern Racing Stables, etc.," this epistle was just what its title implies—a brief survey of horses, breeders, trainers, and recent importations of thoroughbred stock in the

---

[7] *Spirit*, XII (1842), 164; "The Spectator and Simon Suggs," *Spirit*, XV (1845), 471. See also Louis J. Budd, "Gentlemanly Humorists of the Old South," *Southern Folklore Quarterly*, XVII (December, 1953), 232–40.

cotton belt, particularly in Alabama.[8] It was underwritten "N. of Arkansas." In the next twenty-two years it was to be followed by over two hundred sporting epistles, tall yarns, and dialect sketches by the same person. "N. of Arkansas" was Charles Fenton Mercer Noland, a planter and newspaperman who lived most of his life in or near Batesville, in the Ozark foothills of northern Arkansas.

Noland was rather a colorful personality. Born in Virginia and enrolled at West Point at the age of fourteen, he soon dropped out and migrated to Arkansas. He served in the Black Hawk war as lieutenant in the company of mounted rangers, came home, killed the nephew of the governor of the state in a duel, and left again. He seems to have come back to Batesville some time in 1835.[9] During the balance of his life he ran an upland cotton plantation, edited a Whig newspaper, and served in the state legislature. He was a strong racing fan and kept a small stable, but he was more famous as a wit and teller of tales both in conversation and in print. Legends grew up around him even in his lifetime; one early writer says, "Observe him in a circle of Desperadoes—listen to the roars of laughter aroused by his wild anecdotes—hear him sing his favorite, 'Such a gittin up stairs,' or 'The Hudson was a Bully Boat;' look at the hilt of the long knife in his bosom, or the half dozen pistols that swing around his beaded Indian belt; or see him practicing at ten paces, driving out the centre every shot, or bringing down the sparrow on the wing . . . ." The writer goes on to describe Noland as a man of ordinary height, blue eyes, fair hair, slender build, and of a melancholy cast of countenance, "as if afflicted with some deep-sealed sorrow of the soul." [10]

This overdrawn portrait does suggest that Noland was the

[8] *Spirit*, VI (1836), 45. Masterson thinks he may have begun his contributions earlier.

[9] "Death of Charles Fenton Mercer Noland," *Spirit*, XXVIII (1858), 291; William F. Pope, *Early Days in Arkansas*, 20; Josiah H. Shinn, "The Life and Public Services of Charles Fenton Mercer Noland," *Publications of the Arkansas Historical Association*, I (1906), 330–43. For a convenient discussion of his life and work see Masterson, *Tall Tales of Arkansaw*, 29–54, from which I have borrowed many ideas and facts about Noland.

[10] Alfred Arrington, *The Lives and Adventures of the Desperadoes of the South-West* (New York, 1849), 73–74, quoted by Masterson, *Tall Tales of Arkansaw*, 32–33.

sort of man about whom tales could grow. Actually he seems to have performed no deeds of desperation beyond his one affair of honor, and after that episode he was opposed to dueling the rest of his life. But as a physical outline this description seems fairly authentic and it also shows the Byronic tradition of the gloomy hero operating on the sensibility of Noland's contemporary biographer. We know that he did suffer from consumption, and it killed him at forty-six. For the rest, Noland, in his wit and humor, his interest in racing, his more or less colorful background, his love of a good story, and as we shall see, the slant of his social views, was typical of Porter's writers. He will make a good test case.

Within a few months of his first venture as a correspondent of the *Spirit* Noland wrote five more letters, all concerned with hunting and racing.[11] But in the last of these dull, gossipy epistles he mentions a man who killed five buck deer on his way from one salt lick to another. This exploit he presents as fact; then he refers to another hunter who "used up three in one shot." This incident is obviously tall. He gives a short account of a desperate fight between two Negroes and a panther; this episode too seems offered as factual. Then he switches to a certain Farmer Smith, of whom he gives a terse but telling sketch. Farmer Smith is small, pugnacious, and hard of hearing, and when a "man's mouth went as if it said liar, he hit him on suspicion." After some more tattle of the turf, Noland signs off with "Lazily and warm, I subscribe myself, truly yours."

Up to this time (August, 1836) Noland may be seen to have passed through three distinct stages as a writer, though these stages are not necessarily chronological. First, he has departed from matters of interest only to sportsmen and given a couple of sporting episodes which are unusual or picturesque enough to have a wider interest. Second, he has left the purely factual long enough to slip in a bit of fantasy. Third, he has given a brief character sketch of the kind discussed by Porter in *The Big Bear of Arkansas.* (I deliberately use the terms "steps" and "stages" with a progres-

[11] "Deer Hunting in Alabama," *Spirit*, VI (1836), 129; "From a Virginia Correspondent," *Spirit*, VI (1836), 129, 147; "John Bascombe, Bertrand, Sen., Pacolet, &c," *Spirit*, VI (1836), 186; "Wild Sports of the West," *Spirit*, VI (1836), 221.

sive connotation since it seems to me that when a backwoods correspondent had mastered one of the elements enumerated above, he had then progressed a certain distance toward becoming a fully rounded writer of frontier tales and articles. For example, Thorpe's tale "The Big Bear of Arkansas" is deservedly the most famous specimen of its genus, and it may be so because it involves all four of the aspects mentioned—sporting narrative, vivid realism, piquant dialect, and fantasy made convincing through realistic detail.)

Noland's next letter was likewise an intermixture of racing news and nonsporting material. "Will you have a snake story? A true one by the way," he says in introducing a famous tall tale. Then he tells of a volunteer soldier who felt the bite of a snake while he was squatting on his heels. Ill and terror-stricken, the luckless victim was abandoned to die. He recovered enough to rejoin his company and squatted again in their midst, but promptly jumped up again in pain. Someone finally discovered his trouble— "You d——d fool, your spurs have stuck into you." [12]

A long string of letters follows, most of them consisting, like the above, of turf news interspersed with lively factual hunting stories and genuinely tall yarns, with now and then a bit of dialogue. But the next important milestones for "N." were his sustained use of dialect and his complete elimination from the yarn proper of the person of the educated narrator. Both steps were achieved in the letters which he sent under the name of "Pete Whetstone." This rough and rude backwoods character lives on the Devil's Fork of the Little Red River and writes in a semiliterate dialect which is "heavy" enough to be distinctive but not so pronounced as to afford awkward reading. He introduces himself in this manner: "Dear Mr. Editor,—Excuse my familiarity for you must know us chaps on the Devil's Fort [*sic*] don't stand on ceremony; well, week before last, daddy sent me down to the Land Office at Batesville, with a cool hundred shiners, to enter a piece of land—I tell you it took all sorts of raking and scraping to raise the hundred.

[12] "Bulletin from Arkansas," *Spirit*, VI (1836), 229. Cf. [George Washington Harris], "A Snake-Bit Irishman," *Spirit*, XV (1846), 549, reprinted in George W. Harris, *Sut Lovingood* (New York, 1867), 108–113; also "Philip Paxton" [Samuel Adams Hammett] in *Spirit*, XIX (1849), 51–52, and *A Stray Yankee in Texas*, 229–31.

'Squire Smith let me have forty, but he wouldn't have done it, but for a monstrous hankering he has, after sister Sal." Pete then complains of the government's refusal to accept paper money— this was written shortly after Jackson's Specie Circular—and praises the *Spirit of the Times*. He goes on, addressing the editor in a brag with echoes of Paulding's Nimrod Wildfire: "I just wish you could come to the Devil's Fork. The way I would show you fun, for I have got the best pack of bear dogs, the closest shooting rifle, the fastest swimming horse, and perhaps, the prettiest sister you ever did see." [13]

Pete then describes a tavern gang, and Dan Looney, the bully of Raccoon Fork, yells, "I say it publicly and above board, the Warping Bars can beat any nag from the Gulf of Mexico to the Rocky Mountains, that is now living and above ground, that drinks the waters of the Devil's Fork, one quarter of a mile, with any weight, from a gutted snow bird to a stack of fodder." This bit of boasting seems much more genuine and less a literary borrowing than the previous brag. Then comes a match horse race and finally a brawl between the Devil's Fork and Raccoon Fork gangs: "I tell you there was no time to swap knives—I pitched into Dan— 'twas just like two studs kicking—we had it so good and so good for a long time—at last Dan was using me up, when Squire Woods (who had got through whipping his man) slipped and legged for me, and I rather think gave Dan a slight kick—Dan sung out and the Devil's Fork triumphed." [14]

It should be clear that Noland in 1837 had created the first sustained character of the southwestern frontier to tell a story entirely in his own person. He was thus the first southwestern author to eliminate his own cultivated personality entirely from the story as far as direct presentation of character and atmosphere was concerned. Seba Smith had written the *Life and Adventures of Major Jack Downing* (1833) in dialect, but in the South no au-

---

[13] Colonel Nimrod Wildfire describes himself as having "the fastest horse, the prettiest sister, the quickest rifle, and the ugliest dog in the states." Quoted from newspaper accounts of this play by Nelson F. Adkins, "James K. Paulding's *Lion of the West*," *American Literature*, III (November, 1931), 249–58. Cf. the brags in B. A. Botkin (ed.), *A Treasury of American Folklore* (New York, 1944), 12–15, 27–28, 50–66.

[14] *Spirit*, VII (1837), 36.

thor had attempted such usage in any work which reached a national public. Even Longstreet in *Georgia Scenes* told the stories in his own person, using dialect only when his characters spoke to one another. Despite their often lusty, gusty humor, one rarely forgets that the cultivated gentleman is telling these tales with the moral intent of refining and smoothing the rough society thus depicted.

Altogether Noland wrote forty-five Pete Whetstone letters, generally dashed off without any special plan or program whenever the *Spirit* moved him. On the positive side Noland's letters are sharply realistic, unblurred by sentiment, and show an unusual ability to write from two points of view, that of the satirical, detached onlooker, "N.," and that of the wholehearted participant in backwoods affairs, Pete Whetstone. On the negative side Noland is often repetitious; his themes are few—racing, drinking, gambling, and fighting—and his style is rambling, episodic, careless, and inconsistent—the work, in short, of a rural sportsman who wrote at first to discuss his hobby and later simply to amuse himself and perhaps a few others. His view of the lower class of whites is implicit but clear enough in his presentation of Pete and his friends as merely a bunch of tavern roisterers who have no family life, do no work, and do not even do well the things they brag about—matching horses, hunting, and fighting. That there undoubtedly were such characters in the southwestern backlands does not alter the fact that Noland's view is narrow and distorted and that both its authenticity and its narrowness were surely responsible for part of his popularity with other readers of Porter's magazine.

As a writer Noland may be fairly termed a frontier dilettante, even as Nathaniel Parker Willis and Fitz-Greene Halleck were New York dilettantes, with all the aristocratic tastes that the word connotes (Porter, be it remembered, moved in the same Knickerbocker circle). Part of his equipment consisted in a certain degree of education and training in letters which, in the South, was a monopoly of the agrarian aristocracy to which he belonged. Without that education and training neither Noland nor any of Porter's other contributors could have written much for publication. The point is that, effective though he often was and pioneer though he certainly was, Noland could surely have done much better had not writing been strictly a sideline in the mores of the cultivated southerner. As it was, Noland's favorable social and economic position enabled him to transmute some of the oral tales and crude life of the backwoods lower classes into printed sketches and yarns, but at the same time this favorable position imposed rather severe limits on his accomplishments in this field.

The typical nature of Noland's pattern of development and his achievement as a taleteller is sharply underscored by his immediate popularity and the host of imitators, good and bad, that shortly crowded the columns of the *Spirit*. One correspondent was sure that Pete was real and that he had actually seen him at a race meeting held in Washington, D.C. Another wanted (and got) a daguerreotype of Noland.[15] "Trebla" (Albert C. Ainsworth?), a frequent and gossipy correspondent from New Orleans, avowed that "People in this fever-land 'think a heap' of 'N.' " "N. Junior," "M. of Florida," and others frankly imitated either "N. of Arkansas" or Pete Whetstone or both.[16] "M. of Florida" illustrates two of the stages of development found in Noland's work; he was a sporting correspondent and he deviated into dialect.

III

But four men who were admittedly influenced by the Arkansas yarn-spinner deserve special attention because of their activity and their illustration of all phases in the growth of frontier writing. A boisterous Virginian calling himself "Boots" saluted Porter in his first letter: "Well, Mr. Porter, seeing as how Mr. Pete Whetstone has not rubbed agin the steel lately, so as to put forth some of those bright scintillations from 'the Devil's Fork of the Little Red,' that used to illuminate your pages, I takes occasion when the big lights ain't a-shining to let my little taper glow some, and to tell you that I have just rid out from town on a short-tail animal,

[15] *Spirit*, VIII (1838), 93; XI (1841), 325.
[16] *Spirit*, XVI (1846), 378; VII (1837), 260, 348. For further evidence of Noland's popularity see *Spirit*, VIII (1838), 169; also page 333 (in which one learns that a certain race horse has been named Pete Whetstone) ; *Spirit*, IX (1839), 379; XI (1841), 246; XVIII (1848), 99.

which one of the 'fair sex' laughed at 'by the light of the moon,' and axed me if his tail were cut off, jam'd up, or 'driv' in?' " [17] A string of letters followed in the next three years, on horses, dogs, guns, women, and a little—a very little—politics. Boots favored two national banks, one in Philadelphia and one in Charleston, saying, "When I was trimming my little canoe one day in the mill-pond, I noticed that pullin' all the weight on one side sorter turned her over; so now I either sets right in the middle or puts one leg one side and t'other t'other." Though not common in the *Spirit,* use of such a concrete, homely analogy or anecdote to make a political point was extremely widespread elsewhere. Boots also gave a vivid and sprightly description of "a crowd of Legislators who are a fixin' for a party!" In the same letter Boots further trod on the edge of forbidden territory by mentioning a slave auction. His real purpose, however, was to characterize "the Mayor of the Slashes," a local personage, and Porter appended no editorial warning.

Even those letters devoted mainly to turf news were done partially in dialect, and Boots worked in a couple of tall tales. After meeting Porter in New York he wrote about a friend named Chapman, who "has a most remarkable grandfather and grandmother. He told us all one night his grandmother washed up so many clothes she had no where to dry 'em so his grandfather, 'a most wonderful man!' took two poles (the North and South Poles) and made propping sticks of 'em and hung grandmother's clothes on the Equinoctial Line." The epic sweep of this tale reminds one of a Davy Crockett yarn in which Davy greased the frozen axes of the earth with bear oil to start the globe turning again.[18] In another letter Boots tells of a yarn-spinner at the Norfolk races who informed him that there is "a big sink in the Floridas that lay right in the heart of a level country, and was suddenly so deep that the 'bottom had drapt clean out by ——!' "

It may be seen that Boots represents all three of the levels or stages undergone by Noland and that, like the Arkansas gentle-

---

[17] *Spirit,* VII (1837), 333. Other pieces by Boots which are cited or discussed in the text are in *Spirit,* VII (1837), 365; IX (1840), 560; X (1840), 366.

[18] Richard M. Dorson (ed.), *Davy Crockett, American Comic Legend* (New York, 1939), 16–17.

man, Boots was a sportsman who occasionally tried to draw pictures with a little local color. Like Noland too, he is careless, diffuse, and gossipy, and it is a pity that Porter or someone else did not seriously urge this sportsman and legislator to pay more real attention to that one talent for which he is here remembered.

At least one friend of Boots was inspired by him to write a sporting epistle in dialect to the *Spirit*. Thus we see Noland influencing a correspondent who in turn influenced at least one other correspondent to depart from mere sports reporting—a typical chain reaction.[19]

Another contributor who began to write humorous articles directly through Noland's example was "Obe Oilstone" (Phillip B. January), who said he was kin to Pete Whetstone and Jake Grindstone.[20] Obe launches out into sustained dialect narrative in several letters—he has gone the whole way and is really writing sketches and stories, not epistolary reports. "Chase of the Spectral Fox" is in form a dialect sporting epistle, in substance an exciting short story. A hunter tells how a certain wily Reynard always eluded the dogs and men in about the same place, a little briar patch near the grave of an old miser who had been murdered many years before. Despite the protests of a deputation of slaves, a hunting party goes out for a fifth and final try at this mysterious animal. Apparently cornered, the fox eludes them as he has before, although "They had run the thing right in the ground and not 100 yards from the grave!" Hunters and reader alike are getting a creepy feeling when the dogs finally do catch and tear the prey, which is only a fox after all,[21] though it may be akin to Thorpe's Big Bear of Arkansas, not then celebrated, who "was an unhuntable bar, and died when his time come."

Other letters of Obe, or January, include an epistle of the turf (in dialect), a faked duel between two loafers,[22] and a tale about a man who bit a dog. "That Big Dog Fight at Myers's" has been

---

[19] "Letter from a Friend of 'Boots,'" *Spirit*, IX (1839), 294.
[20] "Quarter Racing in Mississippi," *Spirit*, VIII (1838), 310.
[21] *Spirit*, X (1840), 223. Cf. "A Fox Chase," *Spirit*, IX (1839), 487.
[22] *Spirit*, VIII (1838), 310; "The Last Duel in Loaferville," *Spirit*, XIV (1844), 33.

"That Big Dog Fight at Myers's"

reprinted in our time and ranks with "The Chase of the Spectral Fox" as an example of Obe Oilstone's narrative prowess and his power to capture the piney-woods atmosphere. As so often happens, the events of the tale are less important than the life and spirit breathed into the yarn by the narrator, a "character" of the first water. Uncle Johnny is perversely and slyly digressive, and his language, like that of Hooper's Daddy Biggs, is colorful and pungent:

" 'Youth, H——! yes, like the *youth* of some of my old friends' sons—upwards of thirty, an' they're expectin' to make *men* out'n 'em yet! I tell you what, young men in my time'd just get in a spree, sorter open thar shirt collars, and shuck tharselves with a growl, and come out reddy-made men; and most on 'em has staid reddy for fifty-one year! I ain't failed now yet, and—'

" 'Uncle Johnny, for God's sake stick to the dog story: we'll hear all this after—'

" 'Ah, you boy, you never will let me tell a story *my* way, but here goes:' "

Then the old man rambles artfully into the story of old Irontooth, who amuses a tavern crowd by getting down on all fours and fighting a vicious dog with teeth and hands. This core incident may have a historical origin.[23]

Obe made Uncle Johnny tell two more good stories in the next three years, though the old man's literate creator lapsed, in the main, into "familiar epistles" written in conventional and therefore uninteresting (for our purposes) English, with the exception of that in which he reveals that he based his portrayal of old Irontooth on a living person. In the same letter he testifies to the influence of Porter's magazine by saying that he, Obe, is now known around Natchez as the author of the dogfight story, "All, too, 'Owen' to your 'Spirit.' "[24]

Obe didn't write much after 1848, but Porter's correspondents did not easily forget the rollicking Mississippian. A contributor from Virginia related a story much like "That Big Dog Fight at Myers's," although he implied that the events in his tale too had actually happened.[25] Having once, through Obe's influence, got started writing for the *Spirit*, this man introduced a narrator who

[23] *Spirit*, XIV (1844), 391, reprinted in Porter (ed.), *The Big Bear of Arkansas*, 54–61. Cf. Everett Dick, *The Dixie Frontier* (New York, 1948), 140.

[24] "Uncle Johnny's Tooth Pulling Story," *Spirit*, XV (1845), 51, reprinted in Porter (ed.), *The Big Bear of Arkansas*, 167–74; see also "Another Story Uncle Johnny," *Spirit*, XVIII (1848), 43.

[25] "The Dog Fight at Morris's," *Spirit*, XIX (1849), 330. "A Louisiana Sell," *Spirit*, XX (1850), 410, is underwritten "O. O."

spun a much better yarn later about a loaded revolver laid too near a hot coal: "directly the infernal thing went to ˉhopping and a-shooting, and a-hopping and a-hitting; and the more *I* jumped, the more it hit, until it hit me four times, and t'other feller once." [26]

Two other readers sent in anecdotes about Obe himself.[27] Once again one sees how Noland stimulated a contributor who in turn started other pens a-scratching. Noland and Pete Whetstone also seem to have given the necessary push to the "Man in the Swamp," a Mississippian, who told about "A Rollicking Dragoon Officer." This tale concerns a tall, dashing, quarrelsome captain who throws a match into a powder barrel in order to get a seat in a crowded store. His action empties the store in a twinkling—but the keg of "explosive" contains only madder, and he had known this all along. Like a number of the realistic yarns used by Porter, this one, set in Rushville, Illinois, is based on an actual incident involving a real person. Captain Jesse B. Browne (or Brown) of the First Dragoons, U.S.A. was the man, and he seems to have been quite a local "character." [28]

Hateful Parkins is obviously an easterner and writes from Maine and New York, but his dialect is not much different from Pete's—he is an example of the dangers of stylization, although his creator is lively enough:

"Says I 'how d'ye do?' 'Well enough for Pete, anyhow,' says he, 'and if you want a small bet I'll shock you.' 'Good,' says I, and I flap'd my quarter down right on the grass. 'There,' says I, 'go on the top of that just another sich!' He larfed, and slipping a *thousand* under my nose, sang out, 'hollo, stranger! what culler are

[26] *Spirit*, XXIII (1853), 302.
[27] *Spirit*, XVII (1847), 85; XX (1850), 377.
[28] "Anecdote of a Dragoon Officer," *Spirit*, XV (1845), 159, reprinted under the title mentioned in the text in Porter (ed.), *A Quarter Race in Kentucky*, 103–106. Cf. Rourke, *American Humor*, 116; Hawkins Taylor, "General Jesse B. Brown," *Annals of Iowa*, Series 1, X (July, 1872), 198–99. See also Anon., "Fort Des Moines (No. 1), Iowa," *Annals of Iowa*, Series 3, III (April–July, 1898), 351–63; Mary R. Whitcomb, "Reminiscences of Gen. James C. Parrott," *Annals of Iowa*, Series 3, III (April–July, 1898), 364–83; Jacob Van Der Zee, "Fort Des Moines (No. 1)," *Iowa Journal of History and Politics*, XII (April, 1914), 178–82.

you?' 'White,' says I. 'Green,' says he . . . . '*Not quite so green,*' says I. He larfed, and the way I liked that Kurnel warn't lazy." [29]

This Pete is neither the first nor the last Yankeeized ring-tailed roarer to be found in the *Spirit* or out of it. The famous Sam Slick himself is a hybrid of the Yankee peddler and the western screamer.[30] Major Job Whetstone, like Parkins, wrote only one letter that need delay us; he has Black Harris, well-known mountain man, retell his and Jim Bridger's yarn about the "putrified" forest. Harris adds a couple of fish tales.[31]

Thus did an obscure Arkansas planter gain a reputation and provide the push that started a number of other *Spirit* correspondents along the trail leading to vigorous, racy depiction of backwoods life and characters. Noland's influence radiated outward from Batesville in ever-widening circles like concentric ripples from a stone dropped into a pond. Sometimes this influence is direct and observable; often we can only infer it. One need not suppose that Noland or any other one person influenced a majority of Porter's correspondents to try their hand at writing. A number made rather self-conscious declarations of intent without reference to any other writer. One new contributor says bluntly: "Mr. Porter, if you think the following account of a Fox Chase, in the olden time, worthy of a place in your columns, insert it; if not, throw it under your table. Here it is." The article turns out to be a lively account of a Frenchman who, ignorant of the ways of sporting gentlemen, commits the heinous crime of shooting the fox instead of letting the dogs run him to earth. An army officer in Baton Rouge declares that since Porter has printed his first letter he was trying another one: "I am no writer . . . I give you the Hunt; if you think it worth publishing, do so—if not, burn it." Porter did not burn it, but he should have. And a Philadelphia man said he was no sportsman but that "It is not necessary that every line in

[29] *Spirit*, IX (1839), 174–75.

[30] "An Original Character," *Spirit*, XIII (1843), 506, reprinted in Richard M. Dorson, *Jonathan Draws the Long Bow* (Cambridge, Massachusetts, 1946), 95–96; Thomas Chandler Haliburton, *The Attache or Sam Slick in England* (Paris, 1843), 59–62; V. L. O. Chittick, *Thomas Chandler Haliburton* (New York, 1924), 337–42.

[31] "Buffalo Hunting in Missouri," *Spirit*, XIII (1843), 365. Cf. George Frederick Ruxton, *Life in the Far West* (Edinburgh, 1849), 5–8.

the paper should smell of buffalo hump or decayed cattle. There is enough folly in the world, if properly touched up, to please even the 'Sporting' readers of the 'Spirit.' " [32]

In such phrases did various readers coyly or not so coyly reveal an urge to see themselves in print—an urge that surely played no small part in bringing manuscripts into Porter's office literally by the dozen.[33]

IV

But there were other clusters or cycles of contributors besides the "Noland cycle" (a cycle may be defined as a group of contributors associated in any way, whether by proximity, acquaintance, or influence). One such cluster might be called the Fort Gibson, or "military" cycle. Fort Gibson was an important frontier post and the capital of the Indian territory. Several officers from there, from Fort Leavenworth, from Fort Scott, and from other posts farther away wrote and told fellow readers of the *Spirit* how they hunted foxes, wolves, buffalo, Indians, and Mexicans, and some of them salted their letters with dashes of anecdote and folklore. Captain Henry (G** de L**), author of *Campaign Sketches of the War with Mexico,* has already been mentioned. Henry contributed with varying frequency for about ten years, but only a few anecdotes spring into life from his generally factual pages. A certain colonel retells how the fox and the gopher agreed to run a race through the pine barrens of eastern Florida. There were many gophers about, and the gopher agreed to wear a sprig of holly so the fox could recognize him as they ran. The gopher was apparently to run underground through the network of burrows in the warren. As the fox dashed along among the gopher hills a gopher kept popping up ahead of him from a different hill each time and always wearing a sprig of holly. Of course the gopher had made an arrangement with his friends, and the fox finally ran himself to death.[34]

[32] "Fox Hunting," *Spirit*, IX (1840), 559; "Western Hunting Adventures," *Spirit*, XII (1842), 216; "Introduction of a New Correspondent," *Spirit*, XVI (1846), 302.

[33] *Spirit*, XX (1850), 294.

[34] *Spirit*, XIV (1844), 457–58.

Long ere this the reader will have recognized the ancient story of the tortoise and the hare, readapted to a new country with different fauna. Other bits worth salvaging from the flood of Henry's prose are a tale of how the fox caused the 'gator to be thoroughly charred in a prairie fire in revenge for the 'gator's eating his little ones, and a story about how an old farmer cheated the devil.[35]

Noland did have a connection with the Fort Gibson cycle in that he at least once attended a race meeting and visited a friend there. On the very day that Noland left the post one of its officers mentioned his departure and "the feast of reason and the flow of wit which I have enjoyed in his society." This captain adds that the Fort boasts color and sport worthy of Pete's pen and cites a tall individual in a fox-skin cap who offers a bet to an officer in these terms: "Well, Capting, though you are a blooded nag, and I am but a scrub, I'll bet you $10 on the race." Another rough customer brags, "I'm a clever man at home, a great man on a race course, a mighty man to improve a small town in a new country, and I'm good company anywhere." [36] This letter illustrates how the humorous writing of these army correspondents grew largely out of their interest in sporting matters.

War and gambling, too, bred their share of yarns. "Wisconsin" writes about a Broadway dandy on a Mississippi steamboat who is baffled and dismayed by such riverboat gamblers' slang as "Oh, come along, we'll put 'er through straight from the mark, and pile on the chips until we bust you, or get bust ourselves; so don't try to play possum on this child." The dandy is sure the gamblers are aiming to blow up the boat.[37]

Paradoxically, when the U.S. Army set out to chide, chase, or chastise the Pawnees or Sioux, or when, in 1846, they were bound for the Rio Grande, its officers waxed dull and prosaic. They seem to have mistaken the *Spirit* for a military journal or a lady's magazine like *Godey's,* and in their accounts of camp and field, racy humor and color give place to what may be termed "report

[35] *Spirit,* XV (1845), 261; XIV (1844), 109.
[36] "Fort Gibson (Arks.) Races," *Spirit,* VIII (1839), 428, by Noland; "Letter from 'Captain' on Breeding," *Spirit,* IX (1839), 19.
[37] "Anecdotes of Western Travel," *Spirit,* XV (1845), 189–90. Another good story from the same pen is contained in "Indian Reminiscences," *Spirit,* XIV (1844), 85.

realism" or lurid sentimentalism. Their developing urge to write vividly but without gloss was not equal to the strain of war and wartime subject matter. Historical data one finds in abundance, but little that makes literary history.[38]

V

At least two more cycles deserve to be mentioned. One is connected primarily by a similarity of pseudonyms. Two Massachusetts journalists began to write sketches for the *Spirit* and for other papers from which Porter promptly borrowed their work. "The Old 'Un" was Francis A. Durivage of Boston and "The Young 'Un" was George P. Burnham of Roxbury. Many of their sketches were collected in a book entitled *Stray Subjects Arrested and Bound Over* (1846), with their proper names attached.[39] In the middle forties and early fifties racing epistles and descriptive sketches appeared under the names of "The Very Young 'Un" of Alabama, "The Middle Aged 'Un" of Bayou Sara, Louisiana, and "The Little 'Un," also of Louisiana. "The Little 'Un" is stated in his obituary notice in the *Spirit* to have been Coddington C. Jackson, a planter and horse fancier of Louisiana.[40]

Another cycle revolves around the literary development of George Washington Harris, author of the *Sut Lovingood* yarns and in some ways the most talented of the southwestern realists. Like Noland, Harris took up the pen at first to contribute sporting epistles to the *Spirit*. Soon he began to brighten them with bits of atmospheric detail and character portrayal. Finally he wrote sketches and tales which were entirely concerned with depicting customs, characters, and incidents of the backwoods.[41]

[38] For example see [Lieutenant J. Henry Carleton], "Dragoon Expedition to the Rocky Mountains," *Spirit*, XV (1845), 183; *id.*, "Return of the Dragoons from the Rocky Mountains," *Spirit*, XV (1845), 386; [Thomas Mayne Reid], "Sketches by a Skirmisher," *Spirit*, XVII (1847), 109–111.

[39] Burnham collected other sketches of his own in *Gleanings from the Portfolio of the Young 'Un* (Philadelphia, 1848). For comment on Durivage and Burnham see Porter (ed.), *A Quarter Race in Kentucky*, 47, 125.

[40] See, for example, "The Night Old Armistead Brought the News," by "the Very Young 'Un," *Spirit*, XV (1845), 495; "Sayings and Doings in New Orleans," by "Little 'Un," *Spirit*, XIX (1849), 218; also "Death of 'The Little 'Un,'" *Spirit*, XXV (1856), 534.

[41] Most of the above material is drawn from Donald Day, "The Life of George Washington Harris," *Tennessee Historical Quarterly*, VI (March, 1947), 3–38; *id.*, "The Life and Works of George Washington Harris," unpublished Ph.D. disserta-

This metalsmith, steamboat captain, farmer, and journalist wrote all four of his sporting epistles in 1843, using the pen name of "Mr. Free" and seasoning his letters with local color.[42] He was then silent for a year. In the summer of 1845 the "Man in the Swamp" wrote from Vicksburg, Mississippi, challenging a phrase used by Harris and remarking sadly that East Tennessee isn't what it used to be; religion and politics have replaced the old-time frolic as sources of entertainment. This letter prompted Harris to reply with his first full-length story, "A Knob Dance—a Tennessee Frolic." [43] In an introductory note he good-naturedly raps the "Man in the Swamp" for mislocating Knoxville on the map and says "Wonder if he was at 'ar-a-frolick' while he was in East Tennessee? I reckon not or you would have hearn of it before now in the 'Spirit of the Times.' " Harris used the *nom de plume* of "Sugartail," which, Dr. Donald Day tells us, is a term applied in the mountains to the donkey because his tail resembles a stalk of sugar cane. A subsequent letter signed "Roderick" but possibly written by the "Man in the Swamp" refers to this story and asks the question: "Have you heard anything of the 'Smokey Mountain Panther?' a book to be published by 'Sugartail' and 'the Man in the Swamp?' It is now in the womb of the future, but I trust they will bring it forth 'ere long. It is to be illustrative of the manners and customs of East Tennessee—containing an account of Bear and Panther fights, Quarter Racing, Card playing, anecdotes of the Rev. Mr. Anley, etc., etc., with illustrations." [44] Harris made a trip to New York about this time and may have discussed this proposed book with Porter, but the volume seems to have died a-borning.

"Sugartail" had another yarn in the *Spirit* in January, 1846,[45]

---

tion (Chicago, 1942), 11–23. See also Day's "The Humorous Works of George Washington Harris," *American Literature*, XIV (January, 1943), 391–406, and "The Political Satires of George Washington Harris," *Tennessee Historical Quarterly*, IV (December, 1945), 320–38.

[42] Of interest are "Quarter Racing in Tennessee," *Spirit*, XIII (1843), 79, and "Sporting Epistle from East Tennessee," *Spirit*, XIII (1843), 313. Dr. Day identifies "Mr. Free" by a notice in the Knoxville *Press and Herald*, December 14, 1869.

[43] *Spirit*, XV (1845), 267, reprinted in Porter (ed.), *A Quarter Race in Kentucky*, 82–90, as "Dick Harlan's Tennessee Frolic."

[44] "Sayings and Doings in East Tennessee," *Spirit*, XV (1845), 446.

[45] See note 12 above.

but then he lapsed into a long silence. Two fun-loving friends who wrote for the *Spirit* as "Charlie" and "Dresback" tried repeatedly to stir him into literary activity but failed, although one of them personally handed a sketch by Harris to Porter in New York. Porter rejected it, as he did many tales, because he deemed it too highly spiced even for the *Spirit*.[46] The Tennessee cronies of Harris went on writing for Porter's periodical,[47] but nothing more by Harris appeared until 1854. In that year he contributed "Sut Lovingood's Daddy Acting Horse." Dr. Day, a keen student of Harris, points out that this tale was "Harris's first story under the pseudonym that was to bring him his greatest fame, and the last story that he wrote for the *Spirit*." [48]

Other cycles of correspondents exist or could be constructed around various nuclei. The three parishes of northeastern Louisiana, Concordia, Madison, and Tensas contributed more than their share of correspondents, some of whom were mutually acquainted. T. B. Thorpe, Robert Patterson, and Henry Clay Lewis (Madison Tensas) could have just as well formed the basis of a "Concordia cycle." [49] There were also clusters of correspondents who owed their stimulation to Hooper's writings; others were associated by having written for the New Orleans *Picayune* or the St. Louis *Reveille* as well as for the *Spirit*.

VI

A survey of the writers in Porter's crew would not be complete if one did not look at a few of those gentlemen who, though showing an Elizabethan reluctance to publish works under their own names, have been balked by chance and research in their attempts

[46] "Letter from a Tennessee Joker," *Spirit*, XVIII (1848), 517–18. Cf. "A Mississippi Correspondent 'Down on His Luck!'" *Spirit*, XX (1850), 294.

[47] For instance, see "A Musical Tennessee Landlord," *Spirit*, XVI (1847), 603, by "Dresback"; and "Stirring Up an Old Correspondent," *Spirit*, XVIII (1848), 73; "A Practical Joker in a Soft Spot," *Spirit*, XVIII (1848), 325; "Familiar Epistle from Tennessee," *Spirit*, XIX (1849), 157, all by "Charlie."

[48] Day, "The Life of George Washington Harris," *Tennessee Historical Quarterly*, VI (March, 1947), 23.

[49] Originally all three parishes were part of Concordia Parish. Madison Parish was carved out in 1838 and Tensas Parish in 1843. A Concordia cycle could have been augmented by such writers as "F. H. D." of Vidalia and H. J. Peck of Sicily Island.

at anonymity. Some of these gentry (using the word in a double sense) would not even trust the convivial editor with the secret of their identity. Over "A Quarter Race in Kentucky" in 1843 appeared the editorial comment that this sketch, first published in the *Spirit* nine years ago, was by an author who for over two years had guarded his anonymity by having his communications copied by someone else and sent five hundred miles from his home for mailing to the *Spirit*. Porter said he had discovered the man's name only through "the merest accident, in New Orleans, in conversation with one of his intimate friends," and that this gentleman had only written two articles, "one of which, *'Jones' Fight'*—is, like the 'Quarter Race,' equal to any sketch of the kind in the language." [50]

Luckily for the cause of knowledge and bibliography, Porter made his publishing house a confidant when he was collecting material for his two humorous anthologies. In a long letter, already quoted in part, Porter said to Carey and Hart:

" 'Jones's Fight,' although a capital thing, is not comparable with another story, earlier given in the 'Spirit' by the same writer, who is none other than Thomas Kirkman, Esq of Alabama, the owner of the famous Peytona and a gentleman of immense fortune. He would not have his name divulged, however, for any amount, and I mention it to you confidentially. Gov. McNutt of Mississippi, and Gov. Butler of S. Carolina have written some of the most side splitting stories ever published in this country. This *entre nous.*" [51]

In a day and age when most folks are proud of their authorship of even a scrap of verse in the Eddie Guest style, this diffidence about putting one's own name to one's work is striking and perhaps seems a little affected. The gentleman doth protest too much? But remember that this humorous stuff was not considered literature; it was the masculine humor of the barroom and race track, cleaned up a bit for printing. Thomas Kirkman, no doubt one of the pillars of society in his home area of Florence, Alabama, probably felt the way Longstreet did when he called his own

[50] *Spirit*, XIII (1843), 265.
[51] Porter to Carey and Hart, January 18, 1845, in Henry Carey Baird Papers.

sketches "mere bagatelles" but thoroughly enjoyed retelling them.[52]

The "Gov. McNutt" mentioned in the letter is Alexander Gallatin McNutt, governor of Mississippi from 1838 to 1842. McNutt, a self-made lawyer and planter with a checkered political and personal past, has aroused violently contradictory feelings in the breasts of local historians.[53] One thing is certain, he was just the kind of man to write for the *Spirit*. "McNutt was a master of broad humor and smutty anecdote, which he freely retailed," wrote J. F. H. Claiborne, and Horace Fulkerson, who heard him frequently, referred later to his power of manufacturing a side-splitting story out of his fancy with a little foundation on fact.[54] Perhaps Porter felt that such a man didn't really care whether he was known as a humorous writer or not; anyway, in his prefatory note to one of McNutt's tales Porter almost let the cat out of the bag: "He is nearly connected with a late governor of one of the principal cotton-growing states; and under the signature of 'The Turkey Runner,' his original sketches of life and manners in the south-west have made him a formidable rival of 'Tom Owen, the Bee Hunter.' His two favourite characters, who figure in almost all his hunting stories, are 'Jim' and 'Chunkey.' . . . . They were both employed by Governor McNutt on a remote plantation of his on the Sunflower river, in a perfect wilderness." [55]

McNutt wrote at least nine sketches under the name of "The Turkey Runner." [56] The series is remarkable for being just that—a series, connected by more than a mere name. Although some of the various episodes are dissociated and complete in themselves,

[52] Wade, *Augustus Baldwin Longstreet*, 213–14.

[53] Cf. Reuben Davis, *Recollections of Mississippi and Mississippians* (Boston, 1889), 83–85; Robert Lowry and William H. McCardle, *A History of Mississippi* . . . (Jackson, 1891), 298; Henry S. Foote, *Casket of Reminiscences* (Washington, 1874), 198–215; Dunbar Rowland, *History of Mississippi, the Heart of the South* (Chicago and Jackson, 1925), I, 595.

[54] J. F. H. Claiborne, *Life and Correspondence of John A. Quitman* (2 vols.; New York, 1860), I, 219; Fulkerson, *Random Recollections of Early Days in Mississippi*, 14.

[55] Porter (ed.), *The Big Bear of Arkansas*, 118.

[56] "A Swim for a Deer," *Spirit*, XIV (1844), 15; "Scenes on Deer Creek and the Sunflower," *Spirit*, XIV (1844), 91; "Chunkey's Fight with the Panthers," *Spirit*, XIV (1844), 137; "Hunting in the Swamps and Bayous of Mississippi and Louisiana," *Spirit*, XIV (1844), 163; "'Falling Off a Log' in a Game of 'Seven-Up,'" *Spirit*, XIV (1844), 343; "Catching Buffalo with a Gig," *Spirit*, XIV

the characters of the two hard-drinking, hard-fighting, fun-loving, sharp-dealing backwoodsmen Jim and Chunkey are sustained to a degree matched among Porter's contributors only by Hooper with his Simon Suggs yarns. Chunkey is a real ringtailed roarer of the Davy Crockett variety. He kills a panther in a hand-to-hand fight, hates specie, but likes credit, liquor, and bear meat. When Jim is having a desperate fight in the river with a swimming buck, Chunkey goes calmly off and leaves him, because, as Jim says, "If his own daddy was drounin' and he wanted a drink, he'd go to the liquor gourd afore he'd go to his daddy." To pay him off, Jim gets Chunkey into a card game, but Chunkey outwits Jim, drinks up their jointly owned bottle of whisky, and throws dirt in Jim's eyes when the latter tries to pitch into him. Yet the relationship of these tales to the purely sporting epistle is still clearly discernible in their subject matter and occasionally their style.

The other governor mentioned by Porter in his letter was undoubtedly Pierce Mason Butler of South Carolina, author of at least two sketches in the *Spirit*. He should not be confused with the planter of the same name who led such an unhappy married life with Fanny Kemble; the two families of Butlers were not even related.[57] Some time after resigning his governorship in 1838, he was appointed Federal Indian agent to the Cherokee Nation. The Cherokee Agency was at Fort Gibson, and during his tenure at that post, 1841–1845,[58] Butler did what humorous writing has been identified as his.[59] One of these sketches is an earthily realistic picture of a backwoods wedding at which an unwilling girl is married to a loutish squatter. The other concerns a big mountaineer who

(1844), 349; "The Chase in the South West," *Spirit*, XV (1845), 225–26; "Another Story of Jem and Chunkey," *Spirit*, XV (1845), 399; "A Frightful Adventure on the Mississippi," *Spirit*, XVII (1847), 67. Tales by McNutt were reprinted in Porter (ed.), *The Big Bear of Arkansas*, 118–39, and *A Quarter Race in Kentucky*, 91–95.

[57] Theodore D. Jervey, "The Butlers of South Carolina," *The South Carolina Historical and Genealogical Magazine*, IV (October, 1903), 296.

[58] Royal V. Hart, Interior Section, National Archives, Washington, D.C., to the author, January 2, 1953.

[59] "Western Life and Manners," by "a New Arkansas Correspondent of the 'Spirit of the Times,'" *Spirit*, XIV (1844), 25–26, reprinted in Porter (ed.), *The Big Bear of Arkansas*, 154–58; "The Tin Trumpet," *Spirit*, XIV (1844), 493, reprinted in Porter (ed.), *A Quarter Race in Kentucky*, 197–203. Butler may also have written the tale of a shooting in the Cherokee Nation, entitled "Death of Tom Merritt," *Spirit*, XIII (1843), 20–21, as well as other sketches.

discovers that he is being taken in a poker game, beats up one of the sharpers, and gets his money back. Two sketches farther from the parlor romances of the time could hardly be imagined.

Although no governors of North Carolina contributed to the *Spirit*—as far as is known; one cannot be too sure—John Winslow, of Fayetteville, a circuit court lawyer and member of a distinguished family of the Old North State, has been identified as the author of a trio of connected dialect letters having to do with the courtship and wedding of Billy Warrick and Barbry Bass, a serial memorable chiefly for the depiction of old Mrs. Bass, who scoffs at such frills as lace nightcaps, "britches opening before," and "injun rubber things blowed up that the gals in town ties around their wastes and makes 'em look bigger behind than before—for all the world like an 'oman was sorter in a curious way behind." Thus does the old lady denounce the latest trend in bustles. In another scene the gossip flies thick and fast as old Mrs. Bass and old Mrs. Collins swap views on "prechin and mumps, and the measly ointment, and Tyler gripes" in a chimney-corner scene that suggests the old women chattering about the escape of the Negro runaway Jim in *Huckleberry Finn*.[60]

Porter reprinted all three of the Billy Warrick letters in *The Big Bear of Arkansas*. The authorship of one of the other tales chosen by Porter for republication has perhaps been concealed from some readers because of a misprint. The story "Somebody in My Bed" is listed in *A Quarter Race in Kentucky* as by "W. J. Jones, Esq., of Harrisburg, Pa." In the *Spirit* this tale had appeared under the designation "U. J. Jones." W. J. Jones eludes identification, but Uriah James Jones was a well-known journalist, novelist, and local historian who wrote a number of other pieces for the *Spirit*.[61]

[60] See "Mr. Warrick in Distress," *Spirit*, XIII (1844), 577; "Mr. Warrick in Luck," *Spirit*, XIV (1844), 49; "Marriage of Bill Warrick and Barbry Bass," *Spirit*, XIV (1844), 373, all reprinted together in Porter (ed.), *The Big Bear of Arkansas*, 90–105. Less interesting sketches by Winslow are "A Trip to County Court," *Spirit*, XIV (1844), 379; "Reflections of the Piney-Woods Boy," *Spirit*, XV (1846), 591–92. "To Correspondents," *Spirit*, XIV (1844), 373, reveals Winslow to have been an avid fisherman.

[61] Cf. *Spirit*, XV (1845), 489, and Porter (ed.), *A Quarter Race in Kentucky*, 168. Jones also wrote "An Irish Bird," *Spirit*, XVI (1846), 152; "Jack Muggins's Ghost," *Spirit*, XVI (1847), 607–608; "Two Good 'Uns from U. J. Jones," *Spirit*, XIX (1849), 494; "Nine Cheers for Old Zim," *Spirit*, XIX (1849),

"Somebody in My Bed" is worth further attention because it contains the only important editorial revision made of any of the sketches in *The Big Bear* and *A Quarter Race*. Of the first volume Porter had written to Carey and Hart: "There may be, in the course of it, an occasional indelicate expression or allusion that it would be, perhaps, desirable to expunge. In such an event will you direct your proof reader to do me the favor to expunge, alter or amend in such manner as may seem unto him right and proper?" [62] One must remember that this was a time when legs were coyly designated as limbs and when an irate southwestern writer could refer contemptuously to "the exalted tastes of the Miss Nannyites, who dress the legs of their tables in frilled pantelettes, and faint over a nude cherub." [63] Nonetheless Porter barred Mrs. Grundy from his office when he was editing his two collections of humor, except when he was going over Jones's story. Like so many other tales of the backwoods this one was purportedly heard in a tavern from the lips of a good yarn-spinner. The Doctor recounts how he came home from an unlovely dissection and found an attractive girl asleep in his bed. He took hold of the coverlet and pulled it down to her waist:

" 'She had on a night dress, buttoned up before, but softly I opened the first two buttons—'
" 'Well!!!' said the Captain, wrought to the highest pitch of excitement.
" 'And then, ye Gods—what a sight to gaze upon—a Hebe—pshaw, words fail. Just then—'
" 'WELL!!!!' said the captain, hitching his chair right and

499; "An English Traveller's Adventure in a Western Menagerie," *Spirit*, XXI (1852), 602–603. Data on Jones's life are in U. J. Jones, *Simon Girty the Outlaw*, ed. by A. Monroe Aurand, Jr. (Harrisburg, 1931), ix; William H. Egle, "Appendix" to U. J. Jones, *History of the Early Settlement of the Juniata Valley*, ed. by Floyd G. Hoenstine (Harrisburg, 1940), 353–56; *Notes and Queries Historical and Genealogical Chiefly Relating to Interior Pennsylvania*, Series 1, II (1895), 215; Anonymous introduction, J[onathan] F[alconbridge] Kelly, *The Humors of Falconbridge* (Philadelphia, 1856), 23–24.

[62] Porter to Carey and Hart, February 14, 1845, in the New York Historical Society Library.

[63] "Fire in the Rear," *Spirit*, XXI (1851), 136, credited to the New Orleans *Delta*. Captain Marryat, in *A Diary in America*, II, 246–47, claimed to have actually seen a piano thus decorated, at Niagara.

"Billy Warrick's Courtship and Wedding"

left, and squirting his tobacco juice against the stove that it fairly fizzed again.

"'I thought that I was taking a mean advantage of her, so I covered her up, seized my coat and boots, and went and slept in another room!'

"'*It's a lie!*' shouted the excited captain, jumping up and kicking over his chair. '*It's a lie!* I'll bet you fifty dollars that you *got into the bed!*'"

In the *Quarter Race* version of this mildly naughty yarn the last sentence was left out entirely and the story ends with the second exclamation, "It's a lie!" For this reader the abbreviated ending is thus weakened in diction and rhythm with no special loss of suggestiveness.

Other contributors well known in their times included Thomas Dunn English, author of the song "Ben Bolt" and enemy of Edgar Allan Poe. English wrote dialect sketches as "Thomas the Rhymer." There were also Henry P. Leland, brother of Charles Godfrey Leland, among whose tall yarns was an early analogue to Mark Twain's story of the jumping frog, and Alexander Porter, United States Senator from Louisiana.[64] Judge Porter was surely one of those who entertained the sporting editor during his tour of 1837, and one can hardly avoid the conclusion that he was among the advisers who turned the Tall Son of York's face permanently toward the South and West. Perhaps he was also one of the lavish, optimistic gentlemen who dazzled the editor into expanding the services and raising the price of the *Spirit* in the face of a national panic, with consequent peril to his paper.

VII

Certain tentative conclusions may be drawn from this brief survey of the background of Porter's correspondents. First, the *Spirit* acted as a collector of, a forum for, and an influence upon a far-flung body of readers and writers. Second, the informal sporting epistle seems to have been the basic form of a great many contributions to Porter's pages. Third, the humorous and realistic short story of backwoods life tended to grow organically, step by step, out of this type of factual sporting narrative. Fourth, the writers of these tales were so interested in accurately depicting regional life and characters that they frequently proclaimed their use of models from life.

[64] "New Publications," *Spirit*, XIX (1849), 372; "Another 'Spirit' Correspondent 'Around!' " *Spirit*, XXIV (1854), 530 (Poe attacked English as "Thomas Dunn Browne"); "Frogs Shot Without Powder," *Spirit*, XXV (1855), 170, reprinted in Bernard DeVoto, *Mark Twain's America* (Boston, 1932), 340–42; "Death of Judge Porter," *Spirit*, XIII (1844), 588; Charles Daubeny, *Journal of a Tour Through the United States, and in Canada* (Oxford, 1843), 136, 141–46.

Lastly, these writers as a group were predominantly followers of the turf or chase. As such they tended to be men of means, property, and affairs. They were members of the upper class economically and the ruling class socially, but they were of a back-country and frontier ruling class and could not isolate themselves completely from the white lower classes among whom they dwelt in the pine woods and canebrakes. Hence the ability of these gentlemen to look at their social inferiors closely and describe them vividly.

These writers were also men of some education, which set them apart as a class even more surely than did the possession of land, slaves, or specie. Even if we assume Thorpe and Patterson to have worried along on a shoestring in their capacity as editors of the *Concordia Intelligencer,* they had far more in common with wealthy planters like Alexander McNutt or Alexander Porter than with Chunkey or Tom Owen, the bee hunter. Consequently these contributors were bound to infuse their writings with the outlook and prejudices of their class. Walter Blair has made this point briefly in *Horse Sense in American Humor,* where he affirms that southern humorists liked their homespun characters for tall tales, strange doings, color, and the techniques of oral yarn-spinning. "But often the writer was likely to take pains to show that, when matters of importance—like politics—were concerned, he took no stock in the insight into such matters of a poor man." Harris' figure of Sut Lovingood, as Blair says, is, like Simon Suggs, an example of the no-account poor white. Blair points out that when Harris wanted to express his political views he used the general formula for Civil War humor—"to set up a numb-headed and rather vicious character, show how he traitorously sympathized with the wrong side, have him, in an irritating fashion, give his rascally aid to the enemy, and then have him tell his story." Examples are Bill Arp for the southern side and Petroleum V. Nasby for the northerners. Blair's thesis is well demonstrated by Alexander McNutt in his depiction of Chunkey as a man who liked credit and hard liquor and hated specie. McNutt himself seems to have been a hard-money and temperance man during his gubernatorial administration.

Even when the authors seem kindly disposed toward their characters, as is true of Winslow and frequently of Noland, much of the humor of their pieces stems from the foibles of the ignorant —comic dialect, misspelling, bewilderment in the big city, absurd antics when courting, and ignorance of the law and its procedures. Another large slice of this humor derives from the poor whites' allegedly excessive devotion to the arts of swindling, lying, cheating at cards, racing "ticky-tail hosses," drinking "byled corn," and biting off fingers and gouging eyes when they fought, which was quite often. The views of these gentlemen writers and their friends on comedy, then, were like those of Queen Bess's gallants—implicitly neo-Aristotelian; that is, for them comedy resulted from the foibles and follies of the lower classes. That the well-to-do and the educated had their faults few would have denied, but these faults were not considered proper subject matter for comic writing.

And yet this is not the whole picture. We cannot say that the gentlemen who wrote for the *Spirit* were not more in sympathy with their material than they perhaps would have cared to admit even to themselves. Even when they openly condemn, there is a good deal of ambiguity in their condemnation. Who can say that Chunkey, as he walks cockily off after having swindled his pal, can be wholly despised? Are we not made to feel rather that Jim got what he deserved for his inordinate fear of snakes? Jim Doggett, the hunter of "The Big Bear of Arkansas," is carefully dissociated from the narrator; he is a liar, a braggart, a superstition-monger, and a heavy drinker. Yet he is a powerful and commanding personality who dominates all others on the boat, and wins our affection too. Moreover, some of these writers did present other aspects of squatter life than the tavern, the race track, and the game trail, as shall be seen presently.

Finally, an important over-all effect of local-color humor in the South was that it helped to increase the self-consciousness of the entire region. After an evening with the *Spirit* a southern reader could hardly help but feel that his was a way of life distinct, for better or for worse.

CHAPTER FOUR

Planters and Poor Whites

I

A FRONTIER author, lawyer, editor, banker, and politician, James Hall, wrote in the preface to his *Legends of the West* (1832) that "The sole intention of the tales comprised in the following pages is to convey accurate descriptions of the scenery and population of the country in which the author resides . . . . they are founded upon incidents which have been witnessed by the author during a long residence in the western states, or upon traditions preserved by the people, and have received but little artificial embellishment." [1] In the 1853 edition Hall added, "The descriptions are obviously such as could not have been gathered from books; they are valuable only in proportion to their fidelity; and they are accurate."

Brave words! But one will search vainly in Hall's works for writing uncluttered by sentimental, euphemistic diction, orotund Johnsonian periods, and the polite avoidance of anything like indecorum in relation to sex or the rougher aspects of backwoods life. In fact an anonymous writer in the *North American Review* found Hall sadly lacking in realism and asserted that "His mind is shut up in his own ways of thinking and feeling, and his writings, in consequence, give no true reflection of Western character." [2]

Were other writers and editors as perceptive as this reviewer in recognizing the inhibitive influence of the East upon westerners?

[1] James Hall, *Legends of the West* (Philadelphia, 1832), i. Cf. Longstreet's preface to *Georgia Scenes.*

[2] Anonymous review of Hall's *Legends of the West* in the *North American Review*, XII (July, 1836), 2, also cited by Pattee, *The Development of the American Short Story*, 58.

All too often the answer is no. An editor of the *Texas Mercury* raved grandiloquently: "In no country are the elements of poetry found more abundant than in America. Here nature is on the grandest scale. A Niagara, with its majesty, is calculated to excite the imagination, and inspire with grandeur the conceptions of the most unimaginative mind." Professor Boatright quotes this passage in *Folk Laughter on the American Frontier* and he suggests that this editor's own diction offers one explanation of why so many American writers failed to live up to the promise of the country. Boatright says, "Literary men of the frontier from Timothy Flint and James Hall to Hamlin Garland were as emphatic as the country editors in their insistence that the frontier abounded in materials suitable for great art . . . . Yet when they ceased to theorize and began to practice, they proved themselves hardly less slaves to the traditions of another culture than did the editor quoted above."

A large proportion of Porter's correspondents did break away in part from the apron strings of the sentimental, genteel school of fiction. Yet it is true that throughout his editorial tenure Porter reprinted a good deal of western fiction written with the conventionally sugared ink. Selections from Hall, Flint, Irving, Cooper, Charles Fenno Hoffman, and other writers of that stamp appear frequently in the pages of the *Spirit*. With these writers we are not concerned. We are bound to notice, however, the partial allegiance to the older tradition which is evident in even the amateur writers who contributed most of the realistic material in Porter's magazine. For instance, a certain D. L. Brown, who claimed to have fought alongside Kit Carson himself, calls the great scout "The Rob Roy of the Rocky Mountains." [3] As far as is known, neither Porter nor his readers saw anything incongruous in this blending of Walter Scott, historical romancer and aristocrat, with Kit Carson, an active trapper and guide who personified the western freedom from class, law, and custom.

Sentimentalism of a slightly different hue is shown by one of the few women to try her hand at writing for Porter. Her theme offers possibilities for a starkly powerful and tragic narrative. A

[3] *Spirit,* XVI (1847), 573.

woman and her child are attacked by a panther near their lonely frontier cabin. The woman, armed only with a pair of shears, kills the beast after a heroic struggle. Her left arm, however, is so badly mangled that amputation is finally necessary. Here is how the author renders the thoughts of the woman when she sees the panther about to spring on her child: "The golden hair would be dabbled in red blood; the lips which had so often been pressed to hers in the rich kiss of holy affection, would be torn and crushed between the ravenous jaws of the monster! That little body, now so warm and beautiful with life, in a moment would be a shapeless mass, gorging the fierce appetite of a wild beast." [4] This thoroughly morbid sentimentalism is as unhealthy in its way as is *Charlotte Temple* with its sensationalistic content of seduction, violence, and ruin.

It is in the treatment of the better known heroes of the early southwestern frontier—specifically Davy Crockett, Mike Fink, and Jim Bowie—that elements of the polite school of fiction may be seen in the clearest contrast to the roughness of the frontier writers. The school of Scott, Irving, and Hawthorne's "d——d mob of scribbling women" demanded that its heroes in fiction be absolutely ideal in character—brave in combat, defenders of the right, and worshippers of women. The members of the fair sex were supposed to be as weak-kneed physically and intellectually as they were stout morally. Except in the Crockett almanacs women actually figured little in the frontier hero legends and then usually as mere motivation for male deeds of derring-do. The hero-cycles were masculine in content, but their protagonists were romanticized and sentimentalized to a degree not found in the frontier yarns attached to the less heroic figures of the poor-white hunter or the squatter on public lands.

Significantly, the contributions to the hero-cycles of Crockett, Fink, and Bowie which appeared in the *Spirit* are neither many nor striking. Porter preferred more realistic fare. Moreover, Fink in the time of the *Spirit* was already a historical rather than a contemporary figure, having flourished roughly from 1815 to 1830,

[4] *Porter's Spirit*, II (1857), 71. Cf. [George Philip Burnham], "Starving Mad," *Spirit*, XV (1845), 10.

and the national vogue for Crockett and Bowie as heroes had about run its course by 1837, the approximate date at which Porter began publishing frontier material in large quantity. Too, many of the hero yarns which he did use were reprinted from magazines and almanacs which have received considerable scholarly treatment in recent times. Walter Blair and Franklin J. Meine, who have unraveled and rewoven many threads of the Mike Fink legend, have this prefatory remark to make about the Fink stories: "Thus, though we timid people of the twentieth century find them romantic and glamorous, for their contemporaries, these frontiersmen were daringly real." This comment may be applied in general to the hero-cycles of this period. But in the case of Jim Bowie, one student of frontier lore has found material in the Spanish archives of Louisiana which shows that whatever else Bowie had done, he and members of his family also perpetrated land frauds on a vast scale.[5] Here the chasm between myth and fact yawns particularly wide.

Nonetheless, a few items in the *Spirit* deserve a pause before one flips the pages. In most of these items the heroes are invested with the chivalry and flawless morals required by eastern taste in fiction, but they also reflect something of the crudeness and breeziness of the frontier. For example, during Crockett's first winter in Washington as a representative from Congress, the erstwhile backwoodsman goes to the zoo. He kills a wildcat just by looking at him and offers to whip the lion in a fair fight. Someone asks him if the monkey favors Jackson in looks; Crockett replies that he favors "Mr. ———" of Ohio. The gentleman from Ohio happens to be present and takes exception to the remark. Crockett relates that his rejoinder was, "I had either slandered the monkey or Mr. ——— of Ohio, and if they would tell me which, I would beg pardon." Mr. ——— threatens to challenge him to a duel, whereupon Crockett agrees to fight him if he wishes —with bows and arrows. There is no combat. Clearly the mythic killer and braggart of the first part of the story is not the urbane

---

[5] Edward S. Sears, "The Low Down on Jim Bowie," in Mody C. Boatright and Donald Day (eds.), *From Hell to Breakfast* ("Texas Folklore Society Publications," [Vol. XIX] Austin and Dallas, 1944), 175–99. More sympathetic are J. Frank Dobie, "Bowie and the Bowie Knife," *Southwest Review*, XVI (Spring, 1931), 351–68; C. L. Douglas, *James Bowie, the Life of a Bravo* (Dallas, 1945).

fencer of the second part. A version of the same story in a later issue presents Crockett in a less polished role. He starts to apologize and then breaks off with, "Hang me if I can tell whether I ought to apologize to you or to the monkey." Crockett likewise appears as something less than a gentleman in an alleged speech of his which was submitted to Porter by George D. Prentice, editor of the Louisville *Journal*. Crockett informs the cheering Texans at Nacogdoches that, "I was for some time a Member of Congress. In my last canvass, I told the people of my District, that, if they saw fit to re-elect me, I would serve them as faithfully as I had done; but if not, they might go to h——l and I would go to Texas. I was beaten, gentlemen, and here I am." [6] A somewhat different version appearing in the *Spirit* seven years later is credited to Haliburton's *Sam Slick*.[7] In both versions the speech is not exactly in tea-table taste, although the speaker may have had good grounds for resenting the fickleness of the electorate.

Another aspect of the sentimental, eastern view may be seen sharply contrasted with the frontier attitude in the following item. The diction is that of the East; the characters are of the West with certain "refining" eastern characteristics: "Col. Bowie, who invented the wonderful knife which bears his name, has, it is said, two beautiful and highly accomplished daughters, who can bring down the deer in his swiftest flight, and hit the boss of the target at every shot—possessing that combination of Spartan energy and courage, with the excellence of modern refinements, which forms the perfect woman."

Rezin Bowie, the brother of Jim, is the member of the family referred to. It is said that Rezin got his dander up at the frequent mention of his attractive, robust daughters in the papers. He hinted strongly that he was ready to hold personally responsible any editor who continued to give his family such publicity. The name of Bowie promptly vanished from the newspapers.[8]

[6] *Spirit*, II (1833), 129; "Anecdote of David Crockett," *Spirit*, XXII (1852), 177.
[7] "Crockett's Last Speech," *Spirit*, XIII (1843), 409.
[8] "Col. Bowie's Daughters," *Spirit*, VIII (1838), 163, credited to the Boston *Post*; and given also in Marryat, *A Diary in America*, I, 290–94; Edward S. Ellis, *The Life of Colonel David Crockett . . . to Which Are Added Sketches of General Sam Houston, General Santa Anna, Rezin P. and Colonel James Bowie* (Philadelphia, 1884), 225–26.

Mike Fink, in print, seems to have more of the bark left on him than either Crockett or the Bowie family. Fink and Crockett are compared implicitly in a story in the Crockett almanacs. The two test their skill in a shooting match; Mike knocks half a comb out of his wife's hair with a rifle ball and dares Davy to knock out the other half. But Crockett refuses: "Davy Crockett's hand would be sure to shake if his iron war pointed within a hundred mile of a shemale, and I give up beat, Mike." Crockett thus conforms to the chivalrous, worshipful attitude toward women which was expected of the hero in the sentimental novel. Mike does not so conform; in fact he usually treats his women roughly (once he seared a girl in a bonfire of leaves). Nor does he conform in an even taller tale. An inquisitive Yankee on a steamboat wants to meet Lige Shattuck, an old pilot who had known Mike in the heyday of the latter's career. The Yankee is sent up to the pilot house, where he begs Lige to tell him a story about Mike. Lige winks at his fellow pilot and says that Mike once ate a whole buffalo robe. The astounded Yankee asks the reason for such an action. "Why, the fact is," said Lige, "the doctors told him he had lost the coating of his stomach, as he drank nothing but New England rum, he thought he'd dress his insides up in suthin' that 'ud stand the cussed pizen stuff, so he tried buffalo with the hair on, and it helped him mightily." [9]

Mike is entirely the ring-tailed roarer here. Moreover, in this story we are granted an opportunity to see one aspect of the process by which he became a roarer in legend, whatever he may have been in fact. The greenhorn has asked for a story; the westerner obliges with a tall one. Lige Shattuck, the taleteller, may himself have been an authentic character; at least he is so represented in another story which appeared in the *Spirit* three years before the one just quoted. [10]

In another item Mike is said to have been the friend of the tough leader of a counterfeit gang, and in such oft-cited stories as

[9] Dorson (ed.), *Davy Crockett, American Comic Legend*, 32–34; "Lige Shattuck's Reminiscence of Mike Fink," *Spirit*, XVIII (1848), 89, reprinted from the St. Louis *Reveille*.

[10] "The Way 'Lige' Shaddock 'Scared Up a Jack!'" *Spirit*, XV (1845), 4, reprinted in Porter (ed.), *The Big Bear of Arkansas*, 175–77.

"Trimming a Darky's Heel," by John S. Robb, and "The Disgraced Scalp Lock," by T. B. Thorpe, he commits actions which seem brutal to moderns, like shooting the heel off a negro to prove his marksmanship, or shooting away an Indian's scalp lock —his badge of honor—for essentially the same reason. Further, in "The Death of Mike Fink," by Morgan Neville, he accidentally kills his best friend—something the hero of the sentimental novel was rarely permitted to do. Yet Mike does feel in some degree the soft, heavy hand of sentimentality. The tales by Robb, Thorpe, and Neville are told in thoroughly polite, conventional language, have tight, melodramatic plots, and abound in sentimental cliches. Mike dies with the words on his lips, "I didn't mean to kill my boy." For that matter, Blair and Meine point out that "The Death of Mike Fink," the first literary treatment of the Fink legend, appeared originally in an annual, the *Western Souvenir,* edited by James Hall. The annuals, or gift books, were traditional repositories of polite and sentimental verse, essays, and fiction, and the *Western Souvenir* seems to have been no exception, despite the fact that Hall or an associate preceded Vernon Louis Parrington by many years in clearly recognizing the spurious, unwestern nature of some of the Crockett humor.[11]

Lest the reader tend to overestimate the elegance and cultivation of the hero tales in the *Spirit,* here is one more yarn of Crockett the uncouth. On Crockett's return to his constituents after his first session in Congress, a group of them began to ask him questions about Washington:

" 'What time do they dine at Washington, Colonel?' asked one. —'Why,' said he, 'the common people, such as you, here, get their dinner at one o'clock, but the gentry and big bugs dine at three. As for us Representatives, we dine at four, and the aristocracy and the Senate, they don't get their victuals till five.' 'Well, when

11 "The Old Bear of Tironga Bayou, Arkansas, . . ." by "De Grachia" [Matt Flournoy Ward], *Spirit,* XVI (1847), 603; *Spirit,* XVI (1847), 605; *Spirit,* XII (1842), 229–30, reprinted in Blair and Meine, *Mike Fink,* 139–52; *Spirit,* XIV (1844), 437; "Mike Fink's Death," *Spirit,* XII (1842), 217; Ralph Thompson, *American Literary Annuals & Gift Books 1825–1865* (New York, 1936), 32, 95–96; anonymous review of *A Narrative of the Life of David Crockett, Western Monthly Magazine,* II (May, 1834), 277–78.

does the President fodder?' asked another,—'Old Hickory?' exclaimed the Colonel, (attempting to appoint a time in countenance with the dignity of the station,) 'Old Hickory! well if he dines before the next day I wish I may be tetotally———.' " [12]

II

Of the stories about Crockett, Bowie, and Fink, it may be said in general that they reveal the cultivated influence of eastern literary circles in their idealized characters and formal diction. Additional eastern influence may be seen in the way dialect is used in a large number of contributions. A discussion of dialect as used in these sketches, however, should reveal more than merely the influence of sentimentalism on Porter's writers. It has been shown that Cooper followed Scott in putting dialect into the mouths of lower-class characters exclusively.[13] Thus, Leatherstocking and other characters of lowly life speak in local idiom, whereas the Effinghams and other characters of aristocratic birth and station use the conventional rhetoric of the sentimental novel. The upper-class background and prejudices of Porter's correspondents are also manifested, among other ways, in their use of dialect.

Ordinarily it is not possible to separate the eastern influence (which is primarily an upper-class influence) from that of the upper-class background of these southern and western writers. All one may say is that dialect is frequently employed as a mark of social identification by Porter's contributors and that they, like Cooper, tend to put uncouth, local idiom into the mouths of their no-account, poor-white characters as well as to let characters of birth and station speak cultivated or at least grammatically correct English—the King's English, as it were. There are exceptions of course, the best known of which is Thompson's Major Jones, a substantial farmer with a few Negroes. But in the main the racy, highly flavored idiom which for us constitutes a leading attraction in these sketches is spoken only by the illiterate and lowly, while the men of property and prestige nearly always speak a language

[12] "Whim Whams and Oddities," *Spirit*, VI (1836), 1.
[13] Louise Pound, "The Dialect of Cooper's Leatherstocking," *American Speech*, II (September, 1927), 481.

the correctness of which can most conveniently be accounted for by social prejudice, alongside the fact that education was the privilege of the upper classes only. True, nearly all educated men of the South and Southwest were of the upper social strata, but by no means all members of those strata were educated.

One of the most interesting specimens of dialect usage is "The Negroe's [*sic*] Leap," which is signed "Hunt" and is reprinted from the St. Louis *Reveille.* This story is really a place-legend of an Illinois precipice which got its name when an escaped slave, chased by a bandit gang bent on kidnapping him and selling him South again, leaped from the top. Before he jumped he addressed the gang thus: "Hounds of hell! you shall never have my sinews to sell for gold!" But a tree providentially broke his fall, and he landed safe and unhurt. Several months later he ran across his old master and accosted him with, "God bless you, massa—! don't you know me? Take Simon home—he's tired of being a free nigger!" [14] The formal bombast of the first speech is that of the tin-type hero in the sentimental novel; the crude idiom of the second, that of the stage darky. In the same story the author presents his man in two different roles and naïvely assigns him two different dialects. The dialect in each case is a function of a different literary stereotype.

In thus presenting stereotypes of the idealized hero and the comic Negro, this piece is an exception to the general run of backwoods tales. Many more contributions to the *Spirit* are concerned with the speech of the illiterate white hunter or backwoods farmer, and in a number of cases the form of presentation is the letter in misspelled dialect supposedly composed by the character in question. The dialect letter in verse or prose was quite common in the three decades preceding the Civil War. Lowell's *Biglow Papers* were dialect epistles in verse; Seba Smith's Jack Downing letters and Noland's Pete Whetstone letters were dialect epistles in prose. In prose likewise were the letters which comprised *Major Jones's Courtship, Major Jones's Sketches of Travel,* and John Winslow's contributions about Billy Warrick. We shall pass on to certain other pieces in the dialect letter form. For instance Porter re-

[14] *Spirit,* XVIII (1848), 197.

printed from the Concordia (Louisiana) *Intelligencer* three letters
from "Stoke Stout," who Porter thought was one of the two
editors, Robert Patterson, but who Dr. Milton Rickels believes
to have been T. B. Thorpe, the other editor.[15] In the second letter,
which has the strongest narrative thread of the three, Stoke tells
how he was cornered by a bull in a pasture but mesmerized him
long enough to get away. For a moment, though, the issue was
doubtful:

"In this fix I stared the bull in the fase, ans 'twixt the horns, . . .
an' felt I war a fool fur not killin' him 2 yer afore; an I lookt
sharp, and stared, and grind mi teeth, an' winct, an maid mowths
at him, but he only lookt fearser and fearser. An' then I wisht
him sich gude grasse, an' sitch gude wawter, and sitch gude every
ting, az I node he would find in a field, I thot ov a half ov a mile
offe; an' I wished this hard awl the tyme, an' I buggun to swett
powerfullye, an it drapt offe ov me."

In the third epistle Stoke tells a doleful tale about how he has
been flooded out of his lowland cabin and is now

Out ove kabin	out of kash
Out ove kredit	Out of Kumfort [16]
Out ove korn	

From these samples the reader may see that a part of the humor
of Stoke's letters depends merely on the comic errors and misspell-
ings rather than on any peculiar local flavor in the writing. There
are other examples of this rather barren form of humor, such as
the epistle of Timothy Hawkins to "My dear Mister Head-eater
of the Sperrits," and that of the usually lively "Azul of Mississippi," who went to the Mexican War and kept "a Diarrhea of oll
the princepal events." [17]

Such mere playing with words has been found highly unrewarding by more than one student of American humor, and Bernard

[15] Porter (ed.), *The Big Bear of Arkansas*, 147; Rickels, "Thomas Bangs
Thorpe: His Life and Works," 154–55.

[16] *Spirit*, XIII (1844), 589; XV (1845), 38. See also *Spirit*, XIII (1843), 253.

[17] "Timothy Hawkins in a Bad Fix," *Spirit*, XXII (1852), 2; "A Breach of
Promise Case," *Spirit*, XVII (1847), 203.

DeVoto, in *Mark Twain's America*, has tried to make a sharp distinction between the humor of the oral tale based on atmosphere, character, and situation, and the purely verbal high-jinks of Artemus Ward and other such misspellers and punsters. In view, however, of the examples given above and of many more in the *Spirit*, this distinction must be called into question. The humor in the Stoke Stout letters derives not only from Stoke's manhandling of his mother tongue but also from the fact that he emerges as a poor white who is too stupid to know that he should build his cabin on the knoll rather than in the hollow, and too shiftless to lay up cash and provisions against a literal and figurative rainy day.

Another down-at-heel and disreputable letter-writer is "Ruff Sam," purportedly a Mississippi backwoodsman who served for awhile as a volunteer in the Mexican War. After his return, dialect letters based in part on his supposed war experiences appeared in New Orleans newspapers and subsequently in the *Spirit of the Times*. Sam brags of his part in the battle of "Bony Vista" and admits having slaughtered a Mexican prisoner after the man had surrendered to him: "I'll tell you that I did sorter *feel* one of 'em with my bowie knife when he said *amigos* to me; for you see I ain't wantin' sich friends, and I tho't maybe he mout fool me." Another letter is primarily a hunting yarn. In a third Sam tells two neighbor boys that he has killed a huge rattler and that they should go and bring it in. The boys follow his directions and find something that looks vaguely like a snake dead and stiff with rigor mortis; they are dubious about toting such a grisly object, but they pick it up gingerly and start for home. After awhile they become even more dubious. " 'Corderoys and trousers! Did you hear that' sez Zeek. 'Ef he didn't rattle *then*, I ain't got no snake on my shoulder, that's all!'

" 'I've been a watchin' him poke his tung outen this end all 'long,' sez Abe, a rollin his eyes round."

The boys reassure each other that all is well, and on they go, counting the snake's rattles by way of beguiling their fears. Eventually they reach home, throw down their burden, and discover that it is a poplar log. Thus in Ruff Sam's three letters we find a characterization of a low-class hunter, a straight hunting narrative, and a tall tale—three of the principal ingredients in the vast body of material published by Porter and Richards.[18]

Another rough and ready volunteer in the Mexican War is "Pardon Jones" (identified by Copeland as C. M. Haile, a staff member of the *Picayune*), whose letters to the *Picayune* were frequently reprinted in the *Spirit*. Ruff Sam and Pardon Jones resemble Lowell's Birdofredum Sawin only in that all three are presented as uncouth and unscrupulous members of the lowest social class in their respective regions. Birdofredum, however, is a moral vehicle; in his disgust with life in the Army he presents the antiwar views of his creator. There is no antiwar sentiment in the presentation of Ruff Sam or Pardon Jones; both rapscallions enjoyed themselves at the front and behind the lines. The main interest of Pardon Jones is in reporting humorous incidents and situations in the army of occupation—situations which were quite incidental to the fighting and unrelated to the issues being fought over. One example is "Pardon Jones in Mexico," in which we learn how a lieutenant saluted the general's orderly by mistake and how the regiment got up a cacophonous amateur band.[19]

In the case of both Ruff Sam and Billy Warrick, well-read folks are expected to laugh at the way these rednecks lacerate the English language as well as at their ignorance and crudity of morals and manners. The same is true of the two letters from "Kurnell Shingle Splitter," also of Mississippi.[20] The humor of the Colonel—whose title is wholly self-awarded—arises not only from his misuse of English but also from his general ignorance of the great world outside "Hushpuckany Bayou." In the first letter Shingle Splitter and Sal go to the opera in New Orleans, where they behold "a leetle the slickest pair of britches I ever seed stretched over woman flesh." Sister Sal arises and departs in righteous indignation, and one wonders whether the author intended to make his principal theme a moral slap at the licentious customs of the big city. But in the Colonel's next letter Sister Sal

---

[18] *Spirit*, XVII (1847), 437, credited to the New Orleans *Delta*; *Spirit*, XVIII (1848), 14, credited to the New Orleans *Picayune*; *Spirit*, XVIII (1848), 217-18.
[19] *Spirit*, XVI (1846), 362.
[20] *Spirit*, XII (1842), 233, 333.

attempts, with success, to imitate the opera ballet at a frolic back home:

" 'I'll let you know when I was to the opera I larnt the hop, jump and riggle step an if you cant cum them licks, you can just sit down an skin a tater, while I shows them fokes how they does things at Orleans.'

"So wid that Poll, she took on considerable and swore as how she could shake as nasty a leg as any oman in them swamps, and them as wod'ent believe it was'ent no account no how—so to stop a fuss I an unkle Jack bet a jug a licker on the dance. Well wid that sister Sal she struck up a midlin lick and arter a spell she began to go it upon the riggle step and the fokes gin to hollerin an that put the devil in Sal, so that she fetched one of them big wobbles like the gal in Orleans, and nothing was'ent the matter with her that she had not them little tight breaches on—if she had the breaches on I think in my soul she would jist have taken the shine offen all creation. So then Poll took a horn and started in, and arter she lumbered a cupel a times she found out it was no go, and she gin in and told unkle Jack as how he could take the licker."

In both these yarns the humor of situation rises above and through the mere verbal humor of dialect.

Even so, one may find contributions in which oral rather than written dialect—oral as carefully recorded by the writer—forms the chief element of interest. Such contributions fall roughly into three somewhat overlapping types, the electioneering speech, the tale told by a narrator with some special peculiarity of style, and what one might call the "thrust and parry" form of dialogue, in which a suspicious backwoodsman adroitly fends off the questions of an inquisitive outsider.

Cited earlier were examples of the frontier stump speech, in which an ignorant coonskin politician pours forth a stream of cliches, big words, and inflated phraseology, all frightfully mangled and absurdly misused. Sometimes the educated writer emphasizes this two-penny Jackson's ignorance of the political issues at stake; more often he merely stresses the butchery of formal English. In any case the literate reader is expected to smile, along with literate writer, at the backwardness of the speaker. An example of both types may be found in a single issue of 1844. One southern writer, disturbed over the agitation of the Oregon question, declares that he would gladly sacrifice Oregon to the British rather than risk war, but he adds, "Hear what a 'howling tiger' from the 'great west' has to say upon the subject of Oregon and a war with Great Britain." There follows a ranting, spread-eagle oration of which a sample may suffice: "Others say that she [Britain] is the *mistress* of the ocean. Supposin' she is—aint we the *masters* of it? Can't we cut a canal from the Mississippi to the Mammoth Cave of K–ntucky, turn all the water into it, and dry up the d——d ocean in three weeks? Whar, then, would be the navy? It would be *no whar.*"

Subjoined is a letter that supposedly gives an eyewitness account of an election at "Wolf's Mouth" in Arkansas at which the following was heard: "Feller citizens—I'm going to end my speech with a quotation from Se zem the celibrated Latin cricket, when addressed the Carthagenions and Rocky Mountain Cods at the battle of the Cow Pons. Look out! I'm comin'—cock your rifles and be ready! Eat your burute E.' as the immaculate feller said when he got stabbed in the back in the House of Representatives!" This candidate won the election.[21]

Porter was a Whig, and those speeches which have any political slant at all usually reflect a Whig bias in their satire of ignorant Democrats. Thus one "democrat of the Jeffersonian school" swears he is against the "Dandy Arristicraties." But the relative scarcity of political satire in the *Spirit* reflects Porter's desire to keep his paper out of politics. Burlesque of frontier oratory simply as oratory is the rule in this type of selection. A slight variation is the kind of oration in which fun is poked at the backwoodsman's lack of literary culture. In "A Wisconsin Debating Society" the topic is, "Which conferred the greatest benefit on mankind, Mr. Christopher Columbus, or Gen. George Washington?" One zealous defender of Washington affirms that the father of his country fought and won, among other battles, those of Waterloo and New Orleans. He is challenged by a huge frontiersman who shouts,

[21] *Spirit*, XIV (1844), 81.

"Sir, any school boy knows that the battle of New Orleans was fit before General Washington was born. Let the gentleman read Plutarch's lives, the lives of the Signers of the Declaration of Independence, or let him read Arkwright's History of the Black Hawk War, and he'll find that *General Henry Dodge fit the battle of New Orleans!*" [22] As one chuckles he is reminded that Longstreet too wrote a burlesque sketch titled "A Debating Society" and that Huck Finn similarly tangles historical figures and facts in Chapter XXIII of Mark Twain's novel.

Even in the nonpolitical selections the pervading implication is that the ignorant back-country politician is unfit for public office —an old theme by 1840; Brackenridge had developed it much earlier in *Modern Chivalry* (1791). Thus one may explore an implication of Blair's comment that the southern writers regarded the poor white as a source of humor and local color but did not take any stock in his opinions on matters of importance. One may go a step further and see in those sketches in which the peculiar style of the narrator is stressed that Porter and his contributors regarded the poor white primarily as an entertainer—his position was analogous to that of a court jester or clown. His status in these tales (and many others) is dissimilar from that of the comic or stage Negro only in degree, not in kind. By treating the lowclass white as a clown or entertainer Porter and his group in a sense resolved the two contradictory aspects of their outlook as sporting writers and southern gentlemen—their belief in the natural superiority of their kind and their interest in the rude, irreverent stories and customs of the dwellers in log cabins. Let us also note that the picturesqueness and local flavor of the back-country style arises mainly from that very ignorance which, in the eyes of the gentry, was a sign of the inferior status of the narrators. Thus in striving to recapture on paper the distinctive savor of these oral tales, their transcribers were recognizing and to a degree exploiting the ignorance of the lowly backwoodsman even when they admired—no doubt quite honestly—his independence.

In several first-person narratives the tale-teller achieves a pe-

[22] *Spirit*, VI (1836), 207; XXI (1851), 327, by "Homarrache." Cf. "Manners in Missouri," *Spirit*, VIII (1838), 155; "Sam Jonsing on Banking," *Spirit*, X (1840), 298.

culiarly rhythmic style which was recaptured with some success by
the respective contributors of these yarns. In the anonymous "A
Backwoods Sheriff and His Dog" the sheriff tells a simple story
of how his hardy and intelligent hound used to help him hunt
bear. Here is a sample of the style:

" 'Yes I seen 'em squeeze her until she wan't any larger than my
arm and at least nine or ten feet long; you might have wound her
up into a ball as you would have done a hank of yarn. Well, when
she was stretched out on a string, or even tangled up in a knot, I
would shoot the bear, draw her off to one side, throw a little cold
water over her, leave her, and go to butchering. In an hour and
sometimes it would take longer, she would begin to come together
like a jointed snake, and presently she would fetch a yelp, and
come streaking to me, shaped as she ought to be, showing her
teeth, and looking as fresh as if she was a new made dog.' "

This yarn is decidedly tall, in contrast to another example of
piquant rhythm which is reproduced in a "Sporting Epistle from
Florida" devoted mainly to news of the turf. The old hunter is
talking about the climax of a bear hunt:

"Me and the nigger was goin' up, when the old bear she saw us,
and down she came, and the old dog he run her about forty yards
furder, and up a big white rock *he put her;* the old bear she was
comin' down, when the nigger he fired at her and missed her, and
she fell out, and the old dog, who didn't have no tooth in his head,
he covered her; and sich a scraping in the leaves I never seed.
Thinks I, you are a dead dog now, but the old bear she got away
from him, and the old dog he run her through the hammock about
sixty yards furder, and up a white pine *he put her.*"

Although one of these stories is tall and one is not, both are
equally realistic in detail and rhythmic of style.[23] They bring to
mind Simon Wheeler's monotonous yet vivid and subtly accentuated delivery in "The Celebrated Jumping Frog." Mark
Twain may not have known either of these two stories, but at least

[23] *Spirit,* VIII (1838), 175; VII (1837), 348, credited to "M. of Florida."
In all selections quoted from the *Spirit,* italics are those of the editor or original
author unless otherwise stated.

the comparison shows that he was merely the most distinguished of a company of writers who saw possibilities for written entertainment in the yarns spun over the cracker barrel or around the campfire.

Other stylistic peculiarities of various narrators include a tendency to malapropisms and to the accent of the Creole, Irish, or some other minority group which a narrator exhibits in addition to frontier speech mannerisms. Such burlesques of minority groups are by no means confined to back-country writers.[24] Another stylistic peculiarity, which seems richer in interest to the student of backwoods humor, is the continual digression of the narrator. (Dialect epistles such as the Pete Whetstone letters, in which the main interest lies in the character rather than the speech of the narrator, are discussed elsewhere.) In this kind of sketch the narrator perversely rambles from point to point until he loses the entire thread of his story, if he ever had one to start with. The repeated digressions themselves are the main element of the piece.

Such a tale is "Cousin Sally Dilliard," by Hamilton C. Jones, which went the rounds of the newspapers in the 1830's and was republished in the *Spirit* at least three times. Franklin J. Meine has called it "one of the earliest and most widely-read of all the humorous stories." [25] In a North Carolina law court a garrulous old man is called as a witness. He drives the judge and the interrogating lawyer frantic with his stupid—or extremely clever—manner of beginning his story with exactly the same irrelevant phrases each time a question is put to him. Finally he is allowed to tell his story his own way; the result is a discursive tale about his wife and his Cousin Sally Dilliard—a tale which has nothing whatever to do with the case in hand. One is left with the im-

[24] E.g., " 'Running a Saw' on a 'French Gentleman,' " *Spirit*, XV (1845), 333, reprinted in Porter (ed.), *A Quarter Race in Kentucky*, 68–73.

[25] The first republication which I have found is in the *Spirit*, VI (1836), 102, with this headnote: "It is time to give Cousin Sally Dilliard a gentle jog, and let her go the rounds once more. Lend us a lift, brother editors, and let us see what we can do for her—*Ed. Wash. Mirror.*—We give her another and a fifth chance for immortality—*Ed. Spirit of the Times.*" Later reprintings of the tale are in the *Spirit*, VII (1838), 133–34; XIV (1844), 132; XXVII (1857), 483; Porter (ed.), *The Big Bear of Arkansas*, 178–81. See also Meine (ed.), *Tall Tales of the Southwest*, 39. Mr. Meine states that the story was originally contributed to a North Carolina newspaper "somewhere in the thirties." Cf. "A Good Witness," *Spirit*, XV (1845), 93, credited to the *Louisiana Chronicle*.

pression that the witness was only feigning stupidity and had been suborned; this impression is strengthened by the fact that he gave the lawyer "a knowing wink" before he began his first attempt at answering the questions. In a similar story the bribery of the witness is made explicit. The stupidity or venality of the ignorant white and the inability of a country law court to function properly when anything unusual occurs are clearly objects of satire in both of these pungent little tales.

Social satire, however, is not necessarily present in sketches of this type. An example which contains none is the piece about "Colonel Wanderwell," who starts out to tell a hunting yarn and drags it out to an interminable length with digressions on boasters, yellow fever, the technique of training dogs, and other irrelevant topics. He is finally interrupted by his bored listener.[26]

The third general type of dialect yarn is that in which a wary backwoodsman parries the questioning of a too inquisitive stranger. This type of exchange occurs frequently outside the pages of the *Spirit,* and there is no reason to suppose that it may not be older than that magazine. I have called it the "thrust and parry" form, but it might also be referred to as the "Arkansas Traveller" motif, since that famous dialogue is the best known example of this kind of give and take. Professor Masterson considers the "Arkansas Traveller" a synthesis of a number of previous scraps of its kind and thinks it may have originated on the New Orleans vaudeville stage.[27]

The 1836 file of the *Spirit* includes these examples of the "thrust and parry" dialogue:

"*Dull of Appearance*—The *N. Y. Spirit,* has, amongst other excellent things the following: 'Stop that cow,'—'I have got no

---

[26] *Spirit,* II (November 30, 1833).

[27] See the dialect yarns in *Narrative of the Life of David Crockett* (Philadelphia, 1834), 41; Longstreet, *Georgia Scenes,* 215–17; T. B. Thorpe, "Remembrances of the Mississippi," *Harper's New Monthly Magazine,* XII (December, 1855), 39–40. Hooper's "Taking the Census," *Spirit,* XIII (1843), 326, reprinted in *Some Adventures of Captain Simon Suggs,* 149–65, may be considered a cross between the digressive narrative and the thrust-and-parry dialogue. See also Catherine Marshall Vineyard, "The Arkansas Traveler," in Mody C. Boatright and Donald Day (eds.), *Backwoods to Border* ("Texas Folklore Society Publications," [Vol. XVIII] Austin and Dallas, 1943), 11–60.

stopper,'—'*Head* her'—'her *yead* is on the right end,'—'*Turn her*'—'Her *skin* is on the right side,'—'D——n it! *Speak* to her,'— '*Good morning Mrs. Cow!*' The cuteness of this fellow reminds us of the Georgia wagoner, who didn't like much to let out a secret.

" 'What's cotton?' asked a wagoner with a load of one returning empty.

" 'Why, it's cotton' was the reply.

" 'But does it *fetch* anything?'

" 'No,—my team *fetch'd it.*'

" 'I mean—what does it come to?'

" 'Why, to the loom, to be sure.'

" 'Zounds!—how high is it?'

" 'Three tiers at Hamburgh.'

" 'I say stranger—you're a little too cute for me.'

" 'The same to you and all your family.' " [28]

This suspicious Georgia wagoner is close kin to a man paddling a canoe in a Mississippi flood who is likewise hailed for information but neatly parries a series of questions about the flooded area. This sketch is lively, but one yet livelier is "A Musical Tennessee Landlord," by "Dresback," one of the friends of George Washington Harris. This particular dialogue, which takes place between a country fiddler and a stranger who completes the tune for him, is obviously related to the "Arkansas Traveller." [29]

The influence of the gold rush is reflected in another give-and-take between landlord and traveler, a piece which has most of the elements of the "Arkansas Traveller" except for the fiddle. The time of this dialogue is given as 1851 and the setting has been shifted to a tavern near the Bear River in California. The traveler wishes to stay the night at the inn; the landlord informs him that he has no food, no bed, and no fodder for his horse. The traveler finally asks in exasperation, "Well, great heavens, Mister, how do you do?" The landlord replies with a bland bow, "I am very well, I thank you Sir, how do you do yourself?" [30]

[28] *Spirit*, VI (1836), 102.
[29] "Things and Sights in Missouri," *Spirit*, VII (1837), 52; *Spirit*, XVI (1847), 603. See Walter Blair, "Inquisitive Yankee Descendants in Arkansas," *American Speech*, XIV (February, 1939), 11–22.
[30] *Spirit*, XXIV (1854), 61, credited to the *Weekly Brunswicker*.

In "Toby Small's Panther Hunt" another form of parry is used. The man questioned simply echoes part of the question:

" 'Was you much skeered over here?'

" 'Well, want we? Mammy nearly went into fits they say, when she first hearn it, and I thought I should a ———.' " [31]

The point of the exchange is that the questioner thinks he has heard a panther scream and the answerer, knowing that the noise was merely a steamboat whistle, is gulling him by leading him on. This type of thrust-and-parry foreshadows Mark Twain's use of the same device in "The Celebrated Jumping Frog," where Jim Smiley and the stranger fence verbally before the wager and the jump.

Yet another form of give-and-take emphasizes the poverty and stupidity of the poor white dweller in the pine barrens. In sketches with this motif a stranger asks a member of a family in a ramshackle wagon or makeshift dwelling about the health and welfare of the family. The answerer replies sullenly but the stranger, a lawyer, continues his questioning:

" 'Fine situation you have here,' resumed my brother attorney.

" 'Fine, h——l,' responded the host, 'what is it fine for?'

" 'Why, I should suppose you would have sport here in hunting.

" 'Then you suppose a d——d lie! You can't hunt, 'ceptin' you got suthin' to hunt at kin you?' "

We learn that this man's cattle had drowned in the swamp and that the "ager" was shaking his bones into jelly. Yet he refuses to move to a better spot because, "Oh, . . . the lightwood knots are amazin' handy." [32]

[31] *Spirit*, XV (1845), 458, reprinted in *Spirit*, XXVI (1856), 161.

[32] "Animal Men and Vegetable Men," *Spirit*, IX (1840), 557, reprinted in part from *The Knickerbocker*, XIV (August, 1839), 140–43, where it appeared as "My Own Peculiar . . . No. 3." In the unreprinted portion we find that this sullen squatter is also a fiddler who keeps playing a single tune over and over again. Thus the sketch is another cousin of the "Arkansas Traveller." Cf. "Sister Nance and the Ager," *Spirit*, IX (1840), 561, credited to the St. Louis *Pennant*; "Electioneering Eloquence," *Spirit*, XVII (1847), 467; "Light-Wood," by "Uncle Solon" [Solon Robinson], *Spirit*, XXI (1851), 50.

In all cases the sullenness and stupidity of the down-and-out squatter are stressed rather than his stoicism, and no special pity colors the merciless light turned on by the literate contributors. In fact the treatment is more apt to be comic:

" 'Yes, a few on us are goin' to have the shakes this arternoon.'
" 'How many?'
" 'Why, all on us except Sister Nance, and she's such a darnation cross critter the ager won't take on her; and if it did, she is so cussed contrary she wouldn't shake, no how you could fix her!' "

A fourth device of these southern and western correspondents was the tale within a tale, or the oral dialect tale told within a framework of conventional English in which the author introduces the teller and sets the stage—usually a tavern or a campfire. In *Native American Humor* Walter Blair has discussed the role of Porter and the *Spirit* in promoting and developing this form. He also comments on the "box-like structure" of those stories in which a dialect tale-teller introduces another yarn-spinner who proceeds to tell a dialect story within the first tale.

The quality and authenticity of the dialect used in the *Spirit* vary widely. Professor Thomas D. Clark in *The Rampaging Frontier* declared that "Many of the articles appearing in the *Spirit* are in the very best dialect." Some of them, however, are in the very worst, for example, "The Negroe's Leap." We have tried to show that in these dialect epistles and tales the writers of the South and West have stressed and utilized the picturesqueness and unique local color of the lower-class, uneducated white even while they poked fun at his poverty, ignorance, and unfitness for political office. Anyone who thumbs through the files of the *Spirit* will notice exceptions to this rule. He will find dialect philosophers of the Hosea Biglow type who were genuine mouthpieces for the opinions of their authors. He will no doubt enjoy the sensible proverbs of "Major Bunkum," who reminds one of Major Jones and who is really Samuel Adams Hammett. He may also be diverted by the shrewd political satire on the Maine boundary dispute with Britain presented by Hateful Parkins, who may be imitating Jack Downing (Seba Smith). He may relish the observations of " 'Peleg White' Among the Corn Dodgers Out West," and "Yankee Doodle, Esq." in Arkansas and elsewhere. But eventually the reader will find that nearly all of these pieces are by New Englanders except for those by Hammett, and Hammet was a New Yorker who lived in the metropolis both before and after his Texas interlude. Few southern or western writers of dialect yarns in the *Spirit* presented the uneducated backwoods white in any other light than has been here reflected.[33]

I might add that many northern contributors also tended to adopt the upper-class point of view. "H. M.," a sporting man who was apparently an easterner making a long stay in Illinois, gave vent to his feelings in these words: "But what especially stirs up my bile is to hear some animal whose soul can conceive of no higher exploit than to circumvent an opponent in a county election express his surprise at any one's attachment to so futile a pursuit as field sports." [34] One feels that this squib was intended as a blast at the entire coonskin fraternity.

[33] Major Bunkum pieces with proverbial comments in them include "Goin' Off Half-Cocked," *Spirit*, XIX (1849), 25, 51–52; "Bein' Too Smart," *Spirit*, XVIII (1848), 421; "Shootin' Yer Granny," *Spirit*, XIX (1849), 410. A reworked version of the first was included in [Samuel Adams Hammett], *A Stray Yankee in Texas*, 222–31; of the second in *id.*, *Piney Woods Tavern*, 30–38. See also "Letter from the Seat of War," by "Hateful Parkins," *Spirit*, IX (1839), 50. Peleg White's contributions may be sampled in *Spirit*, X (1840), 187, 229; XI (1841), 58; and those of "Yankee Doodle, Esq." in *Spirit*, XIV (1844), 37, 279. See also Hoole, *Sam Slick in Texas*, 1–15, 40–54.

[34] *Spirit*, XI (1841), 67.

CHAPTER FIVE

Jugs, Jokers, Fights, and Frolics

I

A LARGE body of writing in the *Spirit* concerns itself, as stated earlier, with the one-gallus white, who was often a squatter and as such was both disliked and feared by the more substantial farmers and merchants along the frontier. A squatter was a man who settled on state or government land without bothering to buy it or even to file a claim and pay the filing fee at the land office. Naturally he was regarded as a land thief and an evader of his responsibilities by those who had paid for their land in good hard cash. He was likewise regarded as a threat by the order of speculators who formed wildcat banks, bribed the government surveyors and land agents, hired dummies to file claims for land they never intended to develop, promoted worthless land through newspapers and pamphlets, and combined by prearranged agreement to keep bids on good land low at the government land auctions. By such tactics they acquired huge allotments of land at low rates and sold them at exorbitant prices.[1] The bona fide settler was not wanted unless he paid the high price asked.

Moreover illegal settlers on the land created the problem of removal; they often resisted individually and collectively. Sometimes they formed claim associations, under which bond they marched to the auctions and bought the land on which they had already settled at low prices prearranged among themselves. Competitive bidders who would raise the price were warned off by the leveled rifles of the association. Such groups operated all over the South and West, although they were much more prevalent in

[1] Hibbard, *A History of the Public Land Policies*, 108, 214.

Wisconsin, Iowa, and Kansas than in the lower South. The squatters also fought the speculators and men of property by political means. The modified Pre-emption Act which was finally pushed through Congress in 1841 was essentially a bill designed to benefit those settlers who were already farming western land but had not yet paid for it.

In addition to being disliked as an evader of his just payments and a threat to speculation, the squatter was held in some disrepute as a waster of the land. James Flint, an Englishman traveling in the West, differentiated the frontier population according to three levels, the backwoodsman, the subsistence farmer, and the merchant-capitalist. He added that these three classes tended to merge and that one man might rise from backwoodsman to subsistence farmer and finally to merchant status; in other words, the soil-robber might become a sound, progressive cultivator and soil-conserver. Professor Joseph Schafer, however, has affirmed the existence of the distinct social type of the "professional squatter." The farming methods of the professional squatter were likely to be makeshift and inefficient, based on the probability that when the area surrounding his illegal claim became more settled and his title was likely to be contested he would pick up and move farther West, to squat on another plot of unclaimed land. Such a restless, shiftless individual often lived by hunting, fishing, trapping, and, in the Mississippi Delta, selling wood to steamboat captains, as much as by farming.

It is this professional squatter and backwoods farmer-hunters like him who cavort and stalk through so many of the tales in the *Spirit.*[2] Bob Herring, the Arkansas bear hunter portrayed by Thorpe, is a clear-cut example of the professional squatter. Sam Adams Hammett expressed his dislike of the poor white and at the same time granted him a place, of a sort, in society thus: "There was one feller among 'em whose name was Joe White; he was one of a breed you niver meet with in the white settlements, they'd be

[2] James Flint, *Letters from America*, cited by Joseph Schafer, *The Social History of American Agriculture*, 108–109; John James Audubon, *Delineations of American Scenery and Character* (New York, 1926), 137–42; [J. H. Ingraham], *The South-West. By a Yankee* (2 vols.; New York, 1835), I, 253.

vagabonds there, but the Backwoodsmen can't get along without 'em." [3]

The educated gentlemen and their journalistic friends who wrote for Porter's sporting magazine tended especially to stress the poor white's hunting, his sports, and his alleged love of a jug, a fight, and a frolic. Most of the contributions on these themes are products of the previously discussed evolution of factual sporting epistles into wholly fictional sketches and tall tales. For example, "A Panther Hunt on the Blue Ridge" and "Death of the Panther," by "Seebright," a Virginia gentleman, are factual hunt yarns in which the main interest for us lies in the humorous character sketches of Hank the Dutchman and Bob Jones the hunter, both of whom fall essentially into the poor-white category. We are now analyzing the content rather than discussing the evolutionary origins of the selected material; therefore in looking at such a contribution as "Joe Harris and the Panther" we are more interested in the fact that a poor-white hunter's desperate fight with a panther is treated humorously than that the piece is partly a sporting epistle and partly a story with characterization and dialogue. [4]

Another selection in which the genuine dangers of hunting become material for comedy when a lower-class hunter is concerned is "A Bear Hunt in the Diggings." Although the setting of the tale is in California, the main character is clearly a preacher of the southern poor-white class. Charged at close range by a bear, he prays, "Oh, Lord, you know I don't trouble you often with my prayers, like the d——d Methodists, who are always at you for *something*—but for this once listen to me. This 'bar' is a *screamer*, and I haint got my knife; so help me if you can, but if you *can't* help me, *don't* help the 'bar,'—but just you keep dark, and lay low, and you shall see one of the d——est 'bar' fights you ever did

---

[3] "Old Charley Birkham," *Spirit*, XVIII (1848), 402–403. Cf. Hammett, *A Stray Yankee in Texas*, 123. See also T. B. Thorpe, "The Devil's Summer Retreat in Arkansaw," *Spirit*, XII (1842), 295–96, republished in Porter (ed.), *A Quarter Race in Kentucky*, 130–45, as "Bob Herring, the Arkansas Bear Hunter."

[4] *Spirit*, VII (1837), 364–65; VII (1838), 389–90. See also "Wolf Shooting on the Turkisag," *Spirit*, VIII (1838), 81–83, 197–98, likewise by "Seebright." Reprinted in Thomas Chandler Haliburton (ed.), *The Americans at Home* (3 vols.; London, 1854), I, 43–51; also see *Spirit*, XIX (1849), 366.

see." [5] The present author recalls having heard a song on this theme entitled "The Preacher and the Bear."

When humor arises from the fact that the danger turns out to be fictitious, the protagonist may sometimes be identified with the more genteel classes. One of the "Scraps from the Note-Book of a Missouri Lawyer" concerns an attorney who was frightened by the heavy tread of an animal near a bear cave until he discovered that it was only a neighbor's horse. A poor white who is scared needlessly in a parallel situation is Jim, one of the creations of Governor Alexander McNutt of Mississippi. Jim is flicked on the leg by a handkerchief; having been earlier alarmed by an alligator, he decides now that a 'gator has attacked him, and he becomes so frightened that he falls into the river—a mishap which, naturally does not decrease his terror. [6]

But the prowess of the hardy backwoodsman in the chase—a trait with no particular social implications—is generally admired. We have already mentioned Thorpe's "The Big Bear of Arkansas." In a not wholly dissimilar story Billy Scott, a woodsman of Concordia Parish, Louisiana, kills two deer, a he-bear, and a she-bear with cubs, before he runs out of percussion caps. "Never mind," said Billy Scott. "I'll go home and get my breakfast: but am fully persuaded, if my caps had not given out, I should soon have had something to brag about." In another yarn an Irish trapper tells a "man bites dog" story of how he outwrestled a grizzly until the bear finally tore himself loose and fled. Some hunters who finally shot the bear discovered that five of his ribs had been snapped by the hug of this he-man trapper. And an allegedly factual excerpt from the St. Louis *Reveille* tells of an elk-running contest in which a Kentuckian and a Creole half-breed ran down sixteen elk on foot and slew them with their knives. Each man was said to have run over seventy-five miles that day. [7]

[5] "California Sport," by "T—— C——, Esq.," *Spirit*, XX (1850), 184.
[6] *Spirit*, XVI (1846), 277–78; XVII (1847), 67.
[7] "Billy Scott's Bear Hunt," by "M. P. S., Esq., of St. Joseph's, La.," *Spirit*, XII (1842), 202; "Sparring With a Grizzly Bear," by "Will B.," *Spirit*, XVII (1847), 124. Cf. "The Indefatigable Bear Hunter," *Spirit*, XIV (1845), 25, reprinted in *Spirit*, XX (1850), 100–101 and in *Odd Leaves from the Life of a Louisiana "Swamp Doctor." By Madison Tensas, M.D.* . . . [Henry Clay Lewis], (Philadelphia, 1846), 164–75. See also "The Elk Runners," *Spirit*, XIV (1844),

We might—and hereupon do—mention additional yarns of back-country hunting and hunters, such as "Mike Hooter's Fight With the Panther"[8] and other tales by McNutt about Jim and Chunkey. Some of the Pete Whetstone letters are also relevant here, since Pete is usually presented as a disreputable character who is, however, "death on a bar." Let us pass now to other aspects of squatter life. The sports of the backwoods must not be neglected, and as might be expected in a journal of the turf, the sport most stressed in the realistic tales and sketches printed in the *Spirit* was horse racing.

"I am under the impression that There is Something done in the way of Swindling out there at times." Thus wrote William Johnson, free Negro of Natchez, about the races at the Pharsalia Race Course at that city. Who was doing the swindling? In this case we do not know, but horse racing was regarded by Porter and his friends as the sport of gentlemen, and crookedness and uncouthness were usually made synonymous in his pages. It may also be assumed that whenever Porter's contributors depicted racing as practiced by the riffraff of the backwoods and riverfront, they implicitly compared the upper and lower classes to the disadvantage of the lower. They derived an ironic humor from the inferiority of the sport as indulged in by down-at-heel tavern loafers to the pastime as practiced by the exclusive jockey clubs of plantation owners with thoroughbreds and full wallets. The comparison of classes is made explicit in part by "Boots" when he describes a race meeting involving "rale scrub-ticky-tail hosses, what ain't felt the curry comb since they were fotch from the ole feals."[9] It is also plain in "A Quarter Race in Kentucky," by Thomas Kirkman, the owner of the famous thoroughbred racer

---

304–305, reprinted in J. M. Field, *The Drama in Pokerville* (Philadelphia, 1847), 108–11; and John Q. Anderson, "Folklore in the Writings of 'The Louisiana Swamp Doctor,'" *Southern Folklore Quarterly*, XIX (December, 1955), 243–51.

[8] By William C. Hall. Reprinted in Haliburton (ed.), *The Americans at Home*, III, 340–51.

[9] "Quarter Racing in Mississippi," *Spirit*, VIII (1838), 310; William Ransom Hogan and Edwin Adams Davis (eds.), *William Johnson's Natchez, the Ante-Bellum Diary of a Free Negro* (Baton Rouge, 1951), 757; Davis and Hogan, *The Barber of Natchez*, 207.

Peytona. For us the main interest of this sketch lies in other aspects than that of sporting, but we may note also that it is, among other things, a severe critique of racing as practiced by a most ungentlemanly tavern crowd of ringtailed roarers, gamblers, and loafers. The story concerns a match race at an upcountry meet and gets underway with a detailed description of the arrangements for judging, timing, and starting this obviously rigged contest. The description is given from the point of view of a cultivated traveler who has merely happened along and who circulates inconspicuously in the crowd. The man finally chosen to judge the race is portrayed in a vivid, ironic caricature:

"He was said to have caught a turkey-buzzard by the neck, the bird being deceived, and thinking he was looking another way; and several of the crowd said he was so cross-eyed he could *look at his own head!* It was objected to him that he could not keep his eyes on the score, as he did not see *straight*, and it was leaving the race to the accident of which of his optics obtained the true bearing when the horses were coming out. The objections were finally overruled, the crooked party contending that Nature had designed him for a quarter judge, as he could station one eye to watch when the foremost horse's toe struck the score, and could note the track of the horse that followed, at the same moment, with the other eye."

As for the jockeys, the narrator eyes them with moral sternness: "It is customary, I believe, to call such a 'feather,' but they seemed to me about the size of a big Christmas turkey gobbler, without feathers; and I was highly delighted with the precocity of the youths—they could swear with as much energy as men of six feet, and they used fourth-proof oaths with a volubility that would bother a congressional reporter."

The race takes place and ends in a hotly disputed draw (a real gentleman does not dispute the judge's decision, especially if it is rendered against him). But the contest itself is only incidental to the traveler's experiences among the rough characters in and around the tavern. He has made three or four bets with various people about the bar, but in one case the man who had volunteered to hold the stakes for the traveler and his rival bettor has disappeared. The rival wagerer holds the narrator responsible nonetheless, and by virtue of having a lot of bone and muscle, as well as friends in the crowd, forces the narrator to "shell out." The traveler goes off to look up his other bets, with equally dismal results. One man, whittling ostentatiously with a nine-inch dirk knife, declares, "I'm a man that always stands up to my fodder, rack or no rack; so, as you don't want the money, I'll negotiate to suit you exactly; I'll give you my *dubisary*: I don't know that I can pay it this year, unless the *crap* of hemp turns out well; but if I can't this year, I will next year probably; and I'll tell you exactly my principle—if a man waits with me like a gentleman, I'm sure to pay him when I'm ready; but if a man tries to bear down on me and make me pay whether or no, you see it is his own look out, and he'll see sights before he gets his money." The fact that this fellow has been drinking and offering large bets at the bar just previous to this declaration of financial independence does not help matters, but the luckless traveler has to make the best of it, and he accepts Wash's "dubisary," or promissory note. His final comment is, "I wish you would try Wall-Street with this paper, as I wish to cash it; but I'll run a mile before I wait for a quarter race again." [10]

The strength of this story lies in its close-packed, authentic detail, its ironic humor, and its complete absence of sentimentality. The traveler is a stranger in a crowd of rough, hard men, and he takes the consequences—that is essentially what happens, and there is no balm except his own quiet and pervasive sense of the ridiculous. Viewed historically "A Quarter Race in Kentucky" is a blend of the factual sporting epistle, the restrained style of the *Spectator* essay, and the oral tall tale of the frontier. Into the triple mold of these three forms—indeed, helping to create the mold—was poured much realistic detail concerning local character and setting as well as some manifestations of class snobbery. "A Quarter Race in Kentucky" was one of the first of many stories about the sports of ignorant whites; a number of these tales embodied most or all of these elements, and "A Quarter Race" differs from these other narratives only in the superior skill with which the amalgamation was effected.

Thus "A Race and a Frolic," by "Jeremiah Smith," is much like Kirkman's story in situation and incident but lacks its unity and sharply vivid humor. Moreover, Smith abandons the attitude of tough-minded realism by having a pious but sturdy gentleman rescue the narrator from the crowd in the nick of time. Another tale, "A Quarter Race in Alabama," by "Barkeloo Dempsey," makes livelier reading than Jeremiah Smith, chiefly because it is written as a dialect letter in explicit imitation of Pete Whetstone.[11]

Another story of racing is typical in its experimentation with the slang of the rural turf and might equally well have been classed among the pieces whose chief interest is the speech of the characters. Mention has been made of the race epistles of George Washington Harris and Charles F. M. Noland. Whenever the writer really warms to his job, as in the Pete Whetstone letters, they are not essentially different from "A Quarter Race in Kentucky" in their depiction of a motley crowd of rough characters collected around a doggery (grocery or tavern) where morality is a handicap and bets, oaths, fists, and knives fly thick and fast. The same is true of literally dozens of other sketches in the *Spirit*. One is left to wonder whether these writers were clamped too tightly in a mold or whether rural racing really existed as depicted. However, a recent survey of American sport in the decade of the thirties does not differ in its essentials from the picture as presented in the *Spirit*.[12]

II

Another sport—if we may call it such—in which the less admirable qualities of the poor-white backwoodsman tend to be stressed is fighting with fists, teeth, and knives. In most of the yarns in the *Spirit* about fights the bloody battles depicted start from the most trifling of causes, such as a prank, a disputed brag or bet, or an accidental push when two men meet on a gangplank.

[11] *Spirit*, VI (1836), 162; VIII (1838), 357.
[12] "Lexington (Miss.) Races and Wild Cats!" *Spirit*, VIII (1839), 377. Cf. *Porter's Spirit*, II (1857), 149; see also Robert E. Riegel, *Young America 1830–1840* (Norman, Oklahoma, 1949), 211–24.

"Ance Veazy's Fight With Reub. Sessions"

In a yarn which resembles Mark Twain's first published sketch a
fop on board a steamboat tries to have some fun by bullying
a loutish looking fellow on the wharf. For his trouble he gets a
knockdown punch between the eyes. This tale-type traveled into
many a country newspaper office besides the one where young Sam

Clemens was setting type, and like so many other themes, reappears in different guises.[13]

Most of the fights, however, in which one or more poor whites were engaged do not encourage us to root heartily for either side. One of the grimmest pieces in the *Spirit* concerns an encounter which took place merely because one ringtailed screamer accidentally nudged another off a narrow gangplank into the Arkansas River. The ducking calls forth a series of brags and challenges: "May I be run on a sawyer, and may my brains fall down into my boot heels as I am walking up a stony hill if I care you had a rough and tumble with the devil. You pushed me off the plank, and you must fight." The two gladiators strip and go at it, and soon one receives a blow with "iron-bound knuckles, that laid his cheekbone as bare, as though the flesh had been chopped off by an axe." The wounded man is soon knocked down but contemptuously refuses to cry "nough" and shouts, "Come on you white wired ————," to which the other and older man replies, "See here, stranger, stop thar. Don't talk of my mother. She's dead—God bless her! I'm a man from A to izzard—and you—you thin gutted wasp, I'll whip you now if I die for it!"

"With a shout from the bye-standers and passions made furious by hate and deep draughts of liquor, with a howl the combatants again went to work. Disengaging his right hand from the boa constrictor gripe of his opponent, the younger brute buried his long talon-like nails directly under the eye-lid of his victim, and the orb clotted with blood hung by a few tendons on his cheek! As soon as the elder man felt the torture, his face for an instant was as white as snow, and then a deep purple hue overspread his countenance. Lifting his adversary in the air as though he had been a child, he threw him to the earth, and clutching his throat with both hands, he squeezed it until his enemy's face became almost black. Suddenly he uttered a quick sharp cry, and put his hand to his side, and when he drew it away it was covered with

---

[13] "A Georgia Cracker," *Spirit*, XVII (1847), 471; Mark Twain, "The Dandy Frightening the Squatter," in Meine (ed.), *Tall Tales of the Southwest*, 445–48; Fred W. Lorch, "A Source for Mark Twain's 'The Dandy Frightening the Squatter,'" *American Literature*, III (November, 1931), 309–13.

blood! The younger villain while on his back, had drawn his knife, and stabbed him." [14]

The knife wielder then plunges into the river and makes his escape from the friends of the man he has stabbed. Halfway across he rises on a small island and utters a crowing brag which further angers the reader, who would like to see him get his deserts.

But at least twice he has tempted our sympathy, once when he was accidentally knocked into the water and again when he fought valiantly on after horrible punishment. The ultimate victim too has claims on our sympathy—first, when he makes a half-hearted attempt to refuse the other's hotheaded challenge and second, when he resents the insult to his mother. The latter passage is absurdly sentimental and the sketch has other lapses both lurid and mawkish. Yet it contains neither the hero nor the villain characteristic of sentimental narrative, and one feels that the writer was reporting this bloody and needless encounter as objectively as he could, within his subjective purpose of showing two frontier ruffians fighting outside of any code of fair play.

One may here realize just how frank and vivid Porter's correspondents could be in 1843, when so little narrative writing appeared that was not swathed in sentimental gauze. Even Longstreet's "The Fight" falls considerably short of this sketch—and although Poe had liked *Georgia Scenes* on the whole, he described "The Fight" as "involving some horrible and disgusting details of Southern barbarity." Perhaps the Arkansawyers were even rougher than the Georgians of that generation. Timothy Flint had said of them: "The people of this region are certainly more rough and untamed than those of the state of Missouri, or of more Northern and Western regions." And no one has yet called the men and women who settled Missouri lilies of the valley.[15]

The hard-hitting realism of the previous sketch was by no means unparalleled in the *Spirit*. Noland renders an equally stark, if slightly less gory, account of one of Dan Looney's battles. Dan

[14] "An Arkansas Fight," *Spirit*, XII (1843), 611, reprinted in Masterson, *Tall Tales of Arkansaw*, 172–74.

[15] Timothy Flint, *Recollections of the Last Ten Years* (Boston, 1826), 269–70; see also Chapter II, note 11.

licks a fellow by gouging his eye out; then Dan, Pete, and some others go nonchalantly off to a card game at Dan's cabin. "Dan and me yoked two new comers at Old Sledge. Six bits a game, and just as the chickens crowed for day—we had them for eight dollars and twenty-five cents." The terseness of the description and the abrupt change of mood show us what Noland intends that we think of these tavern loafers and gamblers. We may admire the physical prowess of men like Dan and Pete, but we are not expected to admit them to our table or our legislative halls any more than one would ask a prize fighter to run for Congress.[16]

For a bit of grim variety one may turn to Ben Wilson, the rough and reticent fisherman whose partner upset his canoe in order to drown him in the Mississippi. Ben managed to survive, and his curt comment was, "Joe?—he was a-missin' 'long with my bowie-knife!" But we have probably waded in blood deep enough— the reader is referred to the *Spirit* for further tales of gore and slaughter.[17] One should add that in American humor and folklore the savage battles of backwoods ruffians are made vehicles of boisterous humor only occasionally,[18] and purely humorous treatment of such themes is rare among the cultivated correspondents of Porter's magazine.

III

Rough, farcical humor is the rule, however, when the borderer frolics in the pages of the *Spirit*. The rich possibilities for comedy offered by the boisterous wedding parties, quilting bees, and dances tended to sweep the politer, better mannered writers off their literary feet and carry them far beyond conventional restraints in

---

[16] *Spirit*, X (1841), 558. Eventually Noland gave Pete some respectability and did indeed run him for the legislature, but he did not change his own general attitude that a backwoods bully was unfit for positions of responsibility.

[17] "Ben Wilson's Last Jug Race," by "John of York" [William C. Tobey], *Spirit*, XXI (1851), 157, reprinted in Thomas Chandler Haliburton (ed.), *Traits of American Humour* (3 vols.; London, 1852), III, 70–78. See also, for example, "Ance Veazy's Fight With Reub. Sessions," by "Azul of Mississippi," *Spirit*, XV (1845), 405, reprinted in Porter (ed.), *A Quarter Race in Kentucky*, 43–46; "Something Like a Fight . . . ," by "Falconbridge" [Jonathan Falconbridge Kelly], *Spirit*, XVI (1846), 403; "How Jim Blander Salted and Pickled the Quaker 'Friend,' " *Spirit*, XXII (1852), 51; "Full-Blooded Nag," *Spirit*, XXII (1853), 590.

[18] E. g., Botkin (ed.), *A Treasury of American Folklore*, 23.

their treatment of these matters. Then too the *Spirit* was a gentleman's magazine and a sporting journal; it was less hampered by the need for delicacy and reticence than the editors of *Godey's Lady's Book* or, let us say, the *Christian Examiner*. Porter's correspondents could and did make more of these wild celebrations, born of frontier isolation and the scarcity of milder amusements, than did the writers for the "family" periodicals.

Longstreet had introduced the backwoods dance as a topic of literature in *Georgia Scenes* (1835). Charles F. M. Noland, who is by now an old acquaintance, was one of the first to attempt to mine for the *Spirit* the humor inherent in a country frolic. Writing as "N." in 1837, he said "the way we 'racked back Davy,' and 'oh my roaring River,' till just afore day was amusing." They sent out a big Negro for a big jug and when he came back they "pounced upon the jug like a duck upon a June bug." Two and a half years later "Natt. Phillips" of Kentucky really set himself to describe in dialect a wedding frolic in his home state. The dialect narrator has a lively time at this party; he begins by catching his foot in a crack and falling headfirst into the lap of a pretty girl and her ugly, redheaded beau. Pulling himself out of this fix, he takes over the fiddling chore: "But I struck up 'Old Leather Britches,' accompanied by a lad with a big clivice, and a negro with an old coffee pot, one third full of gravel, and the way we plade was curious, and the way they danced was a little after the old-fashioned of cast off and right and left." Soon, however, he gets into a fight with the redhead and knocks him into a kettle of grease, then cuts open the forehead of his enemy by throwing a section of backbone from the kettle at him. The redhead is blinded by his own blood and Natt runs him out the door. Outside a friend of his is lying drunk on a log pile; for a joke two other roisterers blow up the fire under him and burn his breeches and coat tails. The redhead's girl transfers her affections to Natt against the background of the frolic, which lasts until morning. Then the hardy menfolk all go off on a deer hunt—which is reported much less entertainingly.[19]

[19] *Spirit*, VII (1837), 204. Cf. *Spirit*, VII (1837), 265; "Wedding and Deer Hunt in Kentucky," by "Natt. Phillips," *Spirit*, IX (1840), 583; "Bill Jinkins' Troubles on the First Night of His Marriage," *Spirit*, XVII (1847), 279.

A wedding frolic to which suspense is added by the fact that the parson is late is "Polly Peablossom's Wedding," by John B. Lamar. This piece subsequently gave its title to an anthology of southern humorous sketches.[20] Of more interest to the student of back-country realism is Pierce Butler's account, already referred to, of a wedding in Arkansas. The groom is a loutish, brutal fellow and the bride weeps at the prospect of being married to him. The wedding takes place, however, and a frolic ensues at which the guests play a boy-and-girl game called "Sister Phebe." The girls place each man in turn in a chair and then sing:

> How happy, how happy, how happy was we,
> When we sat under the juniper tree;
> Put this hat on your head to keep it warm,
> And take a good kiss, it will do you no harm.

Two girls then sit on the lap of the occupant of the chair. At least once they put their heads so close to his that he has trouble turning his head to kiss them. The bride goes sorrowfully to bed, but the clod of a groom decides that "Sister Phebe" is good enough for him at the moment. The bride's attendants get her up again and the frolic continues until morning. Even greater freedom of treatment and a much more eager groom are found in another account, in which the lucky man neighs and squeals like a horse. "As soon as 'Amen' was heard, he seized his newly made wife under his arm, and at one jump disappeared with her under the bearskin." About four months later the writer finds him the proud parent of a pair of twins.[21]

We have earlier surveyed the exchange of comments between "Sugartail" (George Washington Harris) and his friends in East Tennessee, a byplay which led to Harris' first whole-hearted attempt to depict backwoods life. That sketch itself, "The Knob Dance—a Tennessee Frolic," is cast in the form of a dialect letter and reveals to the full Harris' crispness and power in handling dialogue and in using descriptive metaphor. Dick the narrator and

[20] Rep.inted in T. A. Burke (ed.), *Polly Peablossom's Wedding; and Other Tales* (Philadelphia, 1851), 13–23.
[21] [Pierce Mason Butler], "Western Life and Manners," *Spirit*, XIV (1844), 25–26; "A Wedding Frolic in Arkansas," *Spirit*, XVIII (1848), 247.

Jule his girl go to a local frolic, where one may expect fun; "I said *fun*, and I say it agin, from a *kiss* that cracks like a wagin-whip up to a *fite* that rouses up all out-doors." All is confusion as the celebrators make ready for the dance:

"'Holler! why I was jist *whispering* to that gall on the bed— *who-a-whoopee!* now I'm beginning to *holler!* Did you hear *that*, Misses Spraggins, and be darned to your bar legs? You'd make a nice hemp-brake, you would.' 'Come here, Suse Thompson, and let me pin your dress behind? Your back looks adzactly like a blaze on a white oak!' 'My *back* aint nuffin to you, Mister Smarty!' 'Bill Jones, quit a smashin that ar cat's tail!' 'Well, let hir keep hir tail clar of my ant killers!' 'Het Goins, stop tumblin that bed and tie your *sock!*' 'Thankee marm, its a longer stockin than you've got—*look at it!*' 'Jim Clark has gone to the woods for fat pine, and Peggy Willet is along to take a lite for him—they've been gone a coon's age. Oh, here comes the lost "babes in the wood," and *no lite!*' "

The merrymakers get the fiddler good and drunk and then begin the dance. Around three o'clock in the morning one of the girls eggs two fellows into fighting over her; the brawl soon becomes general. The fight is a wild one and is described in bizarre detail. One man gets knocked into a meal barrel, and Dick himself fares little better: "Luck rayther run agin me that nite, fur I dident lick eny body but the fiddler, and had three fites—but Jule licked her gall, that's some comfort, and I suppose a feller cant always win!" Anyway he still has his Jule, whose legs "make a man swaller to-backer jist to look at 'em, and feel sorter like a June bug was crawling up his trowses and the waistband too tite for it to git out."

Roughly the same indecorous pattern as in "The Knob Dance" is followed in "A Quilting in 'Tucker's Hollow'" by "C. H. B.," who claims to have witnessed the scene in East Tennessee when he was traveling through. During the dance and supper one of the girls "sets her cap" for the narrator and clings to him tenaciously. A man gets pushed headfirst into a kettle of boiling soap and shortly thereafter the frolic breaks up in a brawl. The writer's tale then grows tall: a dozen or more of the fighters roll into the Big

Spring and choke it so badly that it dams up and overflows, flooding the entire valley. Two of the other brawlers have to be parted by a chain and team attached to each. It looks as if "C. H. B." intended to burlesque Harris' piece, although the intent cannot be proved.[22]

Two other sketches, studied by themselves, seem reasonably authentic descriptions, but when compared with "The Knob Dance" they seem indebted to that story. Both are rough, gay frolics ending in free-for-all fights; the second has additional resemblance to Harris' story in some of its dialogue: "La, sister Susan, if the een of the table cloth ain't hanging outer your coat behine jes like a cow's tail." "Hush, you ilmarmerly wrech, you. I always said mamma woodent half fotch you up. Chunk up that ar light wood, thar, and let me see who this is that I is jes drawed." Moreover, during the brawl one man falls into the soap kettle and two other combatants emerge blindly from the house and tumble into a spring even as Dick Harlan and one of his foes had fought their way out of the house and into a stump hole. A final daring fillip is provided when one of the girls catches her calico dress on a branch and her horse goes right on, so that she has to ride home in her red flannel shift. Approximately the same incident spices another account of a frolic at which one of the girls backs too close to the fire and loses her dress in the flames. She flies from the room—"If one of my modesty might speak of bare shins, and those bare shins a lady's, and that lady's shins rather of the *thinnish* order, spinning through the air in '2:32' time, why, sir, 'I could a tale unfold!'" Note here the evidence of a sporting interest and of some literary culture on the part of the author.[23]

At least three other writers about frolics may have cribbed a few details from Harris' story or one of the other pieces just discussed.[24] More important than these possible borrowings, however, is the general similarity of treatment—farcical, boisterous, crude,

---

[22] See Chapter III, note 43, also *Spirit*, XVI (1846), 436.

[23] "St. Valentine's Day in Coon Hollow," *Spirit*, XVII (1847), 37–38; "Commemorative Ball in Bates," *Spirit*, XVII (1847), 2, credited to the St. Louis *Reveille;* "The Wedding at Old Clem Duncan's," by "Jean Pierre," *Spirit*, XVII (1847), 202–203.

[24] "Abe Newham's 'Nupshals,'" *Spirit*, XVII (1848), 539; "Music on That Long Thing," by "Uncle Solon" [Solon Robinson], *Spirit*, XXI (1851), 79; "My First Ball on Goose Creek," *Porter's Spirit*, II (1857), 52.

"Chunkey's Fight With the Panthers"

suggestive—which is shown in nearly all of the stories based on frolics that appeared in Porter's journal. The manner in which his correspondents depicted the backwoods frolic seems to have crystalized into a tradition.

IV

The literary treatment of women, adultery, and the human anatomy is a pretty fair index to the measure of realism achieved in any branch of letters. We have already seen enough of how the writers for the *Spirit* depicted the poor whites' wives and girl friends to make a shrewd forecast of how these subjects were presented in accounts other than those having to do with frolics. Astonishingly free indeed was the treatment and broad the humor which was derived from situations that even today might not escape the blue pencil of a cautious publisher. One or two causes of this freedom may be induced. First, Porter's writers did not feel that they were writing literature; consequently they did not feel bound by the laws of formal literature. Second, these writers were depicting a class of backwoods people who dwelt beyond the pale of refined society. Porter's contributors did not feel the urge to identify these men and women with themselves or with their own wives and daughters. This same principle—that a writer may well show greater freedom, especially in sexual matters, where a lower, outcast social group is concerned—may be observed in Mark Twain's bold presentation of the Negro slave woman Roxy and her illegitimate son in *Pudd'nhead Wilson* as well as in the treatment of Judith Hutter in Cooper's *The Deerslayer* and of Bush's wife in *The Prairie*. By the same token, in Porter's magazine a member of a minority group, for instance a Dutchman, could say "By scheesus" (by Jesus), an oath not printed and rarely implied elsewhere in the *Spirit*.[25] For that matter, the principle operates in the bawdy plays of the old Roman comedy in which panders, prostitutes, and rakes constituted the *dramatis personae*, respectable persons being rarely depicted.

Third, the treatment of off-color subjects was distinctly masculine. Strong negative evidence for this statement may be found in the fact that contributors were not interested in the humdrum daily routine of the pioneer woman as she spun, sewed, cooked, washed, made soap, and frequently toiled in the corn or cotton patch alongside her man. Instead, the double standard operated in pronounced fashion. Along with the conventionally sentimental pieces praising woman for her purity and nobility, and her civilizing and refining effect on wicked man, we find the broad and frequently bawdy stories and anecdotes shortly to be reviewed.

[25] "Bill's 'Pete,'" *Spirit*, XVII (1847), 177–78, by "Thomas the Rhymer" [Thomas Dunn English].

There was no middle ground, but in either case the interest of Porter's writers in woman was a wholly sexual one, whether they were praising her to the skies as the shrine of chastity, purity, and refinement or telling tavern stories of illicit love and adultery.

A fourth reason for the liberal, not to say loose, treatment of women in the *Spirit* was the genuine roughness of backwoods life and the undoubted fact that it did demand a virility and hardihood in women which amazed and rather shocked eastern visitors to the frontier. A leading historian of the South cites a number of authentic examples of rough-hewn women of the backwoods, including a Confederate officer's amusing account of a profane, club-wielding landlady in the North Carolina lowlands. As often happens, a stub of fact sprouted a luxuriant growth of mythology; before the *Spirit* began printing much backwoods material there had come into being "Sal Fink, the Mississippi Screamer," "Sally Ann Thunder Ann Whirlwind Crockett," and other female ringtailed roarers. In the *Spirit* itself the most plausible females are the wife of William T. Thompson's Major Jones, Mary Jones, née Stallins, and her two sisters Kesiah and "Calline." This irrepressible trio love to play April Fool jokes on the Major, such as "sowin up the legs of my trowses, borein holes in the water gourd, so I wet my shirt bosom all over when I went to drink, and bendin' the handle of the tongs, and cuttin' the cow-hide bottoms of the cheers loose so I fell through 'em when I went to set down, and all such devilment." Their antics reach a climax when Kesiah throws a bundle of rags downstairs and yells to the Major that it's the baby. Yet Mary develops into a most dutiful wife and mother.[26]

But the essential mildness of Thompson's women is exceptional. More typical are an account of "The Maine Girls," reprinted in the *Spirit* from an Arkansas paper, and "The Girls of Arkansas," which may be a reply to the former article. The girls of the state of Maine are described as submitting only to cave-man tactics on

[26] Phillips, *Life and Labor in the Old South*, 350; Dorson (ed.), *Davy Crockett*, 20–21, 49–50; Botkin (ed.), *A Treasury of American Folklore*, 66; "Original Letter from the Georgia Major," *Spirit*, XIV (1844), 73, reprinted from William T. Thompson, *Major Jones's Courtship* (Madison, Georgia, 1843), where it appeared as Letter XXVIII.

the part of their lovers; "The Girls of Arkansas" is really an anecdote about one certain girl who told her ardent swain that the hour was late and he had better go. How did she know it was late? Because her mother was snoring. The astonished lover replies, "I swear I have been all this time thinking it was the puffs from an up-river boat, and was wondering what the deuce made it so long coming around the bend!" The girl went for him; he sloped and never came back.[27]

This story is one of several in which one object clearly is to puncture the tradition of the dainty and helpless female. With the "feminine fifties" well under way an item in the *Spirit* tells of a lady in a store who wants a pair of gloves "just the color of your drawers there," meaning the store drawers, which were painted gray. The answer of the embarrassed young man is, "My drawers, miss! why I don't wear any!" Whereupon "The young lady was carried home on a shutter." In yet another such account a Kentucky writer is lost in admiration of a beautiful girl as they both watch a hawk chase a smaller bird which, exhausted, finally alights on the bosom of the lady. She hands it to a servant with the command, "Polly, wring that thing's head off, and cook it for my supper." This gave the writer quite a turn. "I was assisted to my state-room in a raging fever, and did not recover for three weeks." [28]

Porter printed several tales in which the main incident was a man's being precipitated by one force or another into a ladies' dressing room. In one such piece a young man is engaged to a southern belle; her father suddenly pushes him into a room in which he finds the fair Ellen and her female guests "searching for fleas in their sacred linen." The young man survives this shock, but the engagement does not. This tale is a bit unusual in that it debunks the sentimental heroine of the upper class rather than girls of the lower class of southern society. And she could stand a bit of debunking—sloth, dirt, and inefficiency could be found all too often among the plantation mistresses of the Old South.[29]

---

[27] *Spirit*, XX (1850), 29; XX (1850), 56.
[28] *Spirit*, XXII (1852), 101; XVII (1847), 25.
[29] "My Uncle's Love Story," by "A. O'Brady," *Spirit*, XVIII (1848), 410. See also "A Backwoods Wedding," *Spirit*, XVII (1847), 387; Frederick Law Olmsted, *Journeys and Explorations in the Cotton Kingdom* (2 vols.; London, 1861), *passim*; Phillips, *Life and Labor in the Old South*, 334.

Further, these last three writers would hardly have been moved to burlesque a literary tradition without themselves being well read in that tradition. Once more we see how the education and culture that were among the advantages of a solid economic position could influence the writing done about the rougher element.

Not all the accounts of female mores in the backwoods were written as burlesque. There is no burlesque or satire in the vivid description by "Yazoo" of a den of prostitution and gambling in "Natchez under the hill," the red-light district of that famous old river town. With a fine eye for the pictorial this correspondent describes the four-piece orchestra, the Kentucky boatmen lounging against the walls, the girl dancers, and the gang around the roulette wheel in the back room. An appeal to the ear is not lacking; a Negro boy shakes a tambourine while one of the girls sings a song with the refrain, "The old woman she —— —— —— hid in the haymow." One of the girls asks the narrator to dance. When he refuses she says, "Then d——n you, treat me." He buys her a drink and goes into the back room, where the proprietor, a customer feigning drunkenness, and another gambler collaborate to cheat him out of five hundred dollars in a complicated swindle known, says the correspondent, as "my grandmother's trick." [30]

Yazoo was not the only member of the literate and presumably well-to-do class to fare ill at the hands of his social inferiors, including a female. An emigrant squatter family lost a dog which was picked up and sold to a gentleman whose name is given as "Coll." Coll. set out on a journey along the selfsame road taken by the emigrants. When accosted by the head of the squatter family he insists that the dog belongs to him, knowing nothing of the circumstances which had led to the sale. After an argument, Coll. and the squatter agree to bet one dollar on the dog's ownership and to let the sixteen-year-old daughter of the squatter, described as a "rosin-heel gal," hold the stakes. The emigrant proves his ownership of the dog by setting it on Coll. After the dog's fangs have torn off most of Coll.'s clothing the squatter's wife tries to interfere, but the daughter says to her father, "Let her shake him till he says it's your hound; I'll keep mammy back." Eventually

[30] "Reminiscence of Natchez 'Under-the-Hill,'" *Spirit*, XIII (1843), 523.

Coll. has to give in. Then "Here, dad," cries the "rosin-heel" gal, "here's yer two dollars, and, dod rot him, let the naked crittur go hum." [31]

Two other stories emphasize the charms of girls bathing *à la* September morn in lonely swimming holes: "You've read about nymphs, syrens, and so forth? They couldn't compare. Hair loose, and floating on the waves; arms, &c., &c., glistening in the water. Polly was white as snow. Sue was plump as a partridge in peatime, and sat in the waves like a bird in its nest. Troup was slim all over, except the upper works . . . . They splashed, and paddled, and chatted like mad." Thus chanted one rapt humorist from New Orleans. In another yarn the Peeping Tom, after treating himself to a similar sight, is discovered, caught, over-powered, and tied up by the girls before they bother to put on their clothes. They then whip him thoroughly and release him only by making him run the gauntlet stark naked. [32]

Other girls of the backwoods who had no difficulty in taking care of themselves include an inamorata of the rascally Simon Suggs who by her quick wit saves him from the clutches of the sheriff. Outside of the *Spirit* we may also find such sturdy specimens of liberal morality; witness George Washington Harris' story of the girl in the black silk dress who beat up the preacher for declaring that women who wore black silk were headed straight for hell. In these two sketches the girls are clearly a part of their rude backwoods environment, and in a number of other tales the embarrassing nature of the respective situations as well as the uncouthness of the females concerned arises directly from the crude circumstances forced upon the dweller in remote areas. "Going to Bed Before a Young Lady" is one such tale. The author-narrator, who is probably the "little giant" of Illinois, Stephen A. Douglas, stops overnight in a small cabin, and because of the cramped quarters and scarcity of accommodations he has to undress for bed before the sharp eyes of one of the girls. He does so, but with extreme embarrassment. According to Porter this story re-

[31] *Spirit*, XXI (1851), 451.
[32] "Ducks in Summer," *Spirit*, XVIII (1848), 169, by "Stahl" [George Michael Wharton], credited to the New Orleans *Delta;* "Fire in the Rear," *Spirit*, XXI (1851), 136.

minded Joseph M. Field of the St. Louis *Reveille* of a parallel anecdote, and Porter reprinted both together in *A Quarter Race in Kentucky* (pp. 52–59).[33] He did not republish a third tale occasioned by Douglas' yarn. "A New Correspondent" mentions "Going to Bed Before a Young Lady" in telling how he himself had to turn in in full view of the two daughters of a hospitable squatter named Bean. Reluctantly, or so he tells it, he took off all of his clothes except his shirt:

"'Why don't you wear drawers, stranger?' said the big Bean [i.e., the oldest daughter].

"'Or longer shirts,' echoed the little one from the chimney corner, as I dived into the bed." [34]

Besides tales in which a man was pushed into a ladies' dressing room, Porter used a few stories in which the tables are turned and a woman finds herself amid a crowd of men at an embarrassing moment. A couple of these smoking-room yarns have more narrative force than the others. Both are built around the vogue of the bustle. In one, by John S. Robb (Solitaire), a girl tries so hard to strap on a cushion as a makeshift substitute for the bustle that she suddenly tumbles naked through the loft into the midst of the assembled company. Another contribution, by Henry Clay Lewis (Madison Tensas) of Louisiana concerns a woman who let herself be tempted into a horse race and as a result was pitched nude into the middle of the congregation in church. The tables are turned back when a girl with no special squeamishness gets rid of an unwelcome suitor by inducing her other male friends to take him swimming and scare him with an outcry of "Indians" when all he has on is his short red shirt. The girl yells that the house is full of Indians; he runs away and is seen no more. Finally, a man and his wife suffer mutual embarrassment on account of her set of store teeth. She has concealed from him this aspect of her beauty, but

[33] "The Muscadine Story," *Spirit*, XIX (1849), 55, reprinted in Johnson J. Hooper, *The Widow Rugby's Husband* (Philadelphia, 1851), 52–63; "Bart Davis's Dance," in Harris, *Sut Lovingood*, 181–92; "Going to Bed Before a Young Lady," *Spirit*, XIV (1845), 617; *ibid.*, XV (1845), 9.

[34] "Lodging in Iowa," *Spirit*, XIX (1850), 612. Cf. "Wolf Shooting on the Turkisag," *Spirit*, VIII (1838), 81–83, 197–98.

at a peculiarly inopportune moment they slip from her mouth into his.[35]

If the reader expects adultery and the female anatomy to recur as topics in the *Spirit,* he is not to be disappointed. Neither Noland of Arkansas nor at least one of his imitators was averse to off-color jokes on these subjects; neither was Obe Oilstone. Take also the dialect letter of "Curnill Jenks" of Mississippi. The Colonel's epistle is, on the whole, a fine piece of descriptive writing. Having returned to his ancestral village, which he had left ten years before, he finds that "it aint a bit poorer, not a bit meaner, than it was ten years ago." It is still full of poverty and ague. "The principal vegetable productions of the country round is composed partly of bars an panters, snakes, skeeters, coons, possums, young babies, jimpson-weed, and a slite sprikklin of Injuns and mulattoes. The great peculiarity of the country is, that the children is mostly orphans an nobody knows where is their daddies." Moreover the ague makes folks "so yaller in the face that its amost impossible to tell a white man from a nigger, eksept by his manners, an in that case, the nigger very often has the advantage." This is surely not intended as a compliment to the Negro people but as an insult to the whites. Thus the prevailing immorality is mentioned not primarily for its own sake but as part of the general wretchedness of this poor-white settlement. One is reminded of equally run-down Arkansas river towns in works by T. B. Thorpe and Mark Twain.[36]

Illicit intercourse, frankly treated, is the central episode in a

[35] John S. Robb, "Nettle Bottom Ball," *Spirit,* XV (1845), 169, reprinted, XIX (1850), 592. Credited to the St. Louis *Reveille* and printed also in John S. Robb, *Streaks of Squatter Life and Far Western Scenes* (Philadelphia, 1846), 59–64. See also "How Sally Hooter Got Snake-Bit," *Spirit,* XX (1850), 89, credited to the New Orleans *Delta;* "A Tight Race, Considerin'," *Spirit,* XVI (1846), 505–506, published also in [Lewis], *Odd Leaves from the Life of a Louisiana "Swamp Doctor,"* 42–53; [William Tappan Thompson], "The Unclad Horseman," by "Major Joseph Jones," *Spirit,* XIX (1849), 441; "Deacon Smith's Bull, Or, Mike Fink in a Tight Place," *Spirit,* XXI (1851), 52, reprinted in Haliburton (ed.), *Traits of American Humour,* III, 79–87; "Ingins About," *Spirit,* XX (1851), 567; "Bob Bridges and 'Snaggle-teeth,'" *Spirit,* XVII (1847), 285. Cf. "A Client's Identity Illustrated," by "Bob Bumble," *Spirit,* XX (1850), 229.

[36] *Spirit,* XVI (1847), 606; XIX (1849), 62; XV (1845), 254; XXI (1851), 453; T. B. Thorpe, "Remembrances of the Mississippi," *Harper's* XII (December, 1855), 37; Mark Twain, *Huckleberry Finn,* Chapter XXI. Cf. Phillips, *Life and Labor in the Old South,* 340–41.

number of tales. In one story a talkative fellow who resembles
the digressive witness in "Cousin Sally Dilliard" asks the judge for
an action against his wife. The judge's questioning reveals that
she is thoroughly promiscuous. In another tale, contributed by
"Charlie," one of George Washington Harris' fun-loving friends,
a man comes home from prayer meeting and unwittingly gets into
bed with a young woman friend of his wife who is staying overnight. Polly, his wife, has him up in church for this blunder; the
man's defense is that he thought he was in bed with Polly. The
friend, whose name is Nancy, testifies that "she thought she was
Polly too, until next morning." [37]

And she did not faint, nor did she dissolve in tears.

An even broader yarn concerns a grand jury which is investigat-
ing charges of prostitution brought against an old woman and her
"gals." In answer to a question by the foreman, "Don't you know
that Mrs. F—— keeps a house of bad repute?" a witness replies
with a leer, "You, sir, can tell the Jury more, sir, as to that matter,
than I. I saw you there, as I was passing a few days ago." This
answer cuts short the investigation.[38]

Another story about a lecherous hypocrite has to do with a
Squire Funk who is caught one night by the local bully, Jake, and
his drunken gang. The Squire has been carrying on a flirtation
with Jake's good-looking wife, and at that very moment he has
an incriminating letter from her in his coat pocket. Jake and the
gang force the Squire to drink soda water until he is almost burst-
ing; then Jake brings out a pack of cards. The Squire, trying to
take the offer to play a card game as a joke, puts the cards in his
pocket. Jake, in relieving him of the deck, also pockets the fatal
letter without knowing it. The Squire is forced to drink still more
soda water, with unpleasant physical consequences; [39] but his real

[37] *Spirit*, VI (1836), 125, credited to the New York *Sun*; *Spirit*, XIX (1849), 157.

[38] "A Scene in a Grand Jury Room," *Spirit*, XV (1845), 471, by "Satchel."

[39] When the Squire tries to get the letter under cover of a handshake, ". . . he
got such a bustin' hug that everything went.—all aft was a wreck, I tell ye! . . . .
There he lay, explosion behind, a bowie knife before;—certain death staring him
in the face, both sides." Later he falls into a puddle, in agony, "esplodin' all the
while. . . . No one could tell which eend he was nastiest!" Omissions mine. In
"Squire Funk's Awful Mistake," *Spirit*, XV (1845), 360, credited to the St. Louis
Reveille.

worry is, of course, the letter, which he keeps trying to obtain by one ruse or another. The gang torment him further by shoving a coon into his pants and turning a dog loose after it. Not for quite awhile does Jake take pity on him, but when he does, he gives the Squire his own coat—with the letter in the pocket—to go home in. This tale is almost like one of Flaubert in its irony and in its complete lack of any sympathetic character, and yet the jovial brutality of the gang, more repellent because it is jovial, compels our sympathy for the unfortunate Squire. We feel that he has been punished quite enough and then some. Moreover, the situation is developed so as to provide considerable suspense without being unconvincingly prolonged. In addition the dialect form of the story is distinctive but not difficult. All in all, it is one of the best stories in which the theme of adultery is presented, and it deserves republication.

There are a few anecdotes and images in the *Spirit* which have no special feature to justify their off-color quality and therefore must be considered as simply in bad taste.[40] Yet Porter rejected many stories with some such comment as, "The details were quite too spicy for our columns," and at one time claimed that he had on hand fifty or more tales that were unprintable but were going the rounds, hand to hand, of his friends. Even so, his relative leniency toward smut and bawdiness strikes one as inconsistent with his statement that horse racing should be practiced in such a manner that the whole family could enjoy it.[41] We are again reminded of the clash between his formal allegiance to the code of the southern gentleman and his informal interest in writing by the rougher, sportier kind of gentleman about the still rougher folk that inhabited the mud-chinked shacks of the pine barrens, the canebrakes, and the prairie. One is tempted to question whether the inconsistency lay in the fact that a number of southern gentlemen had two sets of morals, one for public use and another for private, and that Porter was merely aping these gentry in adopting both sets. But this much-debated subject is properly one for the social historian.

[40] Such selections may be found in *Spirit*, XI (1842), 615; XV (1845), 369; XV (1846), 537–38; XVIII (1848), 541; XXII (1852), 508.
[41] Cf. the note appended to "A Mississippi Correspondent 'Down on His Luck!'" *Spirit*, XX (1850), 294; and *Spirit*, X (1840), 102.

V

Apart from lechery and adultery, the writers for the *Spirit* found a great deal of humor in other breaches of the moral code by gamblers, blacklegs, horse traders, roving Yankees, and just plain crackers. A very large class of tales, sketches, and anecdotes in the *Spirit* sound the "sour note in western humor," as Professor Cargill has put it. This sour note may be heard before and after the period of the *Spirit of the Times* and in the East as well as on the frontier. For example, Yankee slyness and cleverness at "doing" somebody in a trade were proverbial in and out of the *Spirit,* and American humor in general reflects the concept of "every man for himself," which on the Dixie frontier became Simon Suggs's motto that "It is good to be shifty in a new country." Jim Bowie and his family have been mentioned as land-fraud artists on a grand scale. Rampant speculation in land throughout the backwoods area certainly encouraged the feeling that sharp wits rather than strict honesty were what counted; in fact two of Suggs's escapades had to do with land speculation.[42] Nevertheless, in stories of swindling and swindlers the writers for Porter's journal were merely imparting the flavor of their own regions to material which was already the property of Americans in all parts of the country.

In addition to its regional coloration, one other shaping force must be noted in connection with the plentiful humor of sharp practices and shady dealing that one finds in the *Spirit.* This force is, once more, the superior social position of Porter's crew of correspondents. Surely the upper-class treatment of the stories which littered the desk of the "Senior Editor" had much to do with the fact that both the swindlers and the swindled are generally of the bottom layer of society. In just one of the better yarns does a citizen of substance appear, and he does so only to outfox a group of crooked gamblers at their own game.[43]

Gamblers, especially on the riverboats, play a large part in

[42] Oscar Cargill, *Intellectual America, Ideas on the March* (New York, 1941), xix, 399–405; "Simon Speculates," and "Simon Speculates Again," in Hooper, *Some Adventures of Captain Simon Suggs,* 30–41, 69–81. For Yankee swindlers see Dorson, *Jonathan Draws the Long Bow,* 78–94; Thomas D. Clark, *The Rampaging Frontier* (Indianapolis and New York, 1939), 301–20.

[43] George W. Bradbury, "An Original Angling Sketch," *Spirit,* IX (1840), 524.

these stories of sharpers and their victims. In fact, the reader may have noticed that a disproportionate share of all yarns in the *Spirit* have come from the Mississippi Delta, that highway of southwestern commerce and travel. Thus is additional weight lent to the hypothesis that folk-tales, lore, and legend tend to follow trade and travel routes in their dissemination.[44] In the story just cited the main character remarks that the blacklegs on the Mississippi are so many that "the true way to exterminate them is to let them prey upon each other." The arterial river attracted commerce and travel, the traders and travelers attracted the sharpers, and the sharpers generated, inspired, or attracted the tales eventually set down in writing by correspondents of the *Spirit*.

Most of the gambling yarns follow a very few set patterns and consequently lack variety. In some the sharper and his confederates fleece their victims successfully; in some they do not. Several tales of the latter variety will be reserved until we deal with the motif of "the biter bit." We may here look at three or four of the more interesting anecdotes of card games which take place in localities away from rather than on the river. In one such tale a big mountaineer discovers that a tin speaking tube runs along the wall from behind his opponent to a loft in which another sharper crouches. The man in the loft looks at the mountaineer's hand through a group of small holes punched in the floor and reports on its strength through the speaking tube. The incensed victim beats up one of the blacklegs and is given back his cash. Two other stories are constructed around the motif of a country boy who goes to the city and comes home to report sorrowfully to his father that he has lost his horse by the turn of a jack. The phrase "Where's your horse?" is found in both tales and one feels that the later story owes something to the first one.[45]

[44] Franz Boas, "The Growth of Indian Mythologies," *Journal of American Folklore*, IX (January–March, 1896), 1–11.

[45] The victim loses his money with no compensation of any kind in "A Game of Poker on the Mississippi," by "Satchel," *Spirit*, XVI (1846), 445; "The Game of Thimbles," *Spirit*, XV (1846), 528, credited to the Montgomery (Alabama) *Independent*. Cf. *Spirit*, XIV (1844), 493; "The Arkansas Turf," *Spirit*, IX (1839), 330; " 'War's Yure Hoss,' " *Spirit*, XIX (1849), 208, by "The Little 'Un" [Coddington C. Jackson], and reprinted in Haliburton (ed.), *Traits of American Humour*, I, 157–60. Cf. "How Simon Suggs 'Raised Jack,' " *Spirit*,

In addition to gambling one would expect the "sour note" stories in a sporting magazine to concern horses, horse trading, and the turf. And a sizable group of tales do concern the trick of shoeing a racer with lead in order to slow him down during the trial runs and removing the lead shoes just before the race, after the bets have been irrevocably placed. Another motif appears in "The Grey-Bay Mare," by Henry P. Leland. A man has washed his mare with a decoction of boiled walnut leaves in order to rid her of flies; this mixture turns her a weird bay color. The owner of her prospective rival in a match race seizes this opportunity to try to back out. He claims that his horse was to race "your grey mare." Eventually, however, he is held to his bargain and "the grey-bay mare" wins.[46]

Another horse story worth mention includes a vivid character portrayal of "Col. Pierch," who is plainly anything but a bona fide colonel. Instead he is a loquacious, drunken, swaggering bully who rides his own horse in a race and afterwards beats up a Jewish peddler who had innocently got in the way of his nag and caused him to lose the contest. Then he makes a stump speech, and finally tells the narrator in confidence that he has got back half his stake. "And mind, I don't say they're fraudulous to my certain knowledge, but I'm mighty afeered that Keeno or whoever locates, will find diffikilty in gettin *patterns* on them surtifikits he's got—left." Another yarn about a shifty fellow made one of the "Scraps" from the notebook of a droll Missouri lawyer. This tale is about a Yankee peddler who sells a clock to a reluctant backwoodsman by the hoary device of leaving it at that man's hut, ostensibly to lighten his wagon. When he passes that way again the wife discovers that she just can't get along without this contraption.[47]

This same lawyer contributed a story which once again calls attention to the poor white's supposed unfitness for political office

---

XIV (1845), 544, reprinted in Porter (ed.), *The Big Bear of Arkansas*, 62–79, and in Hooper, *Some Adventures of Captain Simon Suggs*, 7–29.

[46] "The Fight at Perry's Mill," *Spirit*, XXVIII (1858), 481–82, by "Thomas the Rhymer" [Thomas Dunn English]; "The Grey-Bay Mare," *Spirit*, XXV (1856), 616.

[47] "A Texas Quarter-Race," by "Luke Lightwood," *Porter's Spirit*, II (1857), 149; "Yankee Clock Pedlars in the West," *Spirit*, XVI (1846), 314.

by presenting two rival candidates, one of whom is charged with hog-stealing, the other with horse-stealing. The latter is smart enough to admit the charge and to tell in self-defense a wild story of how he rode a mad, wounded elk into an Indian camp and finally made his getaway aboard an Indian pony. "He was elected." [48]

The largest single group of "sour note" tales includes those built around the motif of "the biter bit" or "the cheater cheated." In this motif either one sharper out-swindles another or the victim, nominally an honest man, turns the tables on the swindler at his own game. The outcome in either pattern is not so much a triumph of honesty over crookedness as of one set of sharp wits over another. Little allegiance is paid to abstract moral scruples on either side.

A lively example is " 'Old Tuttle's' Last Quarter Race." The boys think they can come it over Old Tuttle by sneaking into his stable at night and substituting a broken-down old nag for the smart pacer that he is going to run the next day. But Old Tuttle has anticipated them and has "planted" another, worthless steed in place of his favorite.[49] Another story, "Dead Open and Shut," not only is written with zest but is remarkable for the fact that a Yankee is treated sympathetically and actually comes off victor, although this may be explained by his being contrasted with a cowardly Frenchman. One "General William Montgomery," a "quick-witted, low bred fellow," who was in fact well known locally as a swindler, accompanies a Frenchman and a big Yankee to Fort Smith, Arkansas, in a boat owned and operated by a friend of his. On the way Montgomery bets the Yankee five hundred dollars that the latter has in his bag the traditional wooden nutmegs and horn gun flints of the Yankee peddler. The "General" has previously planted some of both in the big fellow's bag and the Yankee loses his money. Montgomery then bullies the Frenchman into playing a game in which the General hides his hands behind him and makes the former guess whether they are open or shut. Natu-

[48] "Life in the Backwoods," *Spirit*, XVI (1846), 355–56. See also *Spirit*, XVIII (1848), 507; XIX (1849), 499; XIX (1849), 523.

[49] *Spirit*, XVI (1846), 205, signed "Buckeye" and reprinted in Porter (ed.), *A Quarter Race in Kentucky*, 117–21.

rally the General always wins, but finally the Frenchman gets the Yankee to play in his stead. The General posts the boatman with a loaded musket on the deck to cover his opponent, whereupon the Yankee asks for odds of two to one in his favor. Montgomery scornfully agrees and soon has planked down four thousand dollars to cover the Yankee's two thousand. The General puts his hands behind him and asks if they are open or shut. The Yankee plants his huge fist between the General's eyes and knocks him sprawling.

"Open, by gosh," cries the Yankee as he sees the other's hands flying through the air. He grabs the money, heaves the General ashore like a bag of meal, and shoves off. The General's accomplice tries to fire his musket—but the Yankee has replaced the flint in it with one of the horn "flints" supplied by the General. With his thumb to his nose the Yankee cries, "Don't get to playin' none of your 'dead open and shut' with a Yankee again," and he adds to the flourish of his fingers by giving his other arm the motion of turning a crank, and keeping time by moving his right foot up and down, as long as he is in sight.[50]

To the same company of sharp-witted gents belongs the Kentucky farmer who had lost two thousand dollars to a gambler. The farmer challenged the gambler to a shooting match at five hundred dollars a shot. After he had won four rounds and thus got his money back, the farmer said, "You stocked the cards on me, and to get even I had to stock the bullets on you." And he showed the gambler how he had cut in half the bullets which the gambler had been using in his gun and loosely stuck them together again.[51]

We shall pass over a couple of other good stories to look at those "biter bit" tales which involve card games. In submitting one such story "The Little 'Un" (Coddington C. Jackson) refers to two earlier versions and claims that the tale was an "old Joe" before either was thought of. His own version occurred, he says, on a Lake Ponchartrain steamboat:

[50] *Spirit*, XVI (1846), 400, credited to the Cincinnati *Casket*. For data on "General Montgomery" see Featherstonhaugh, *Excursion Through the Slave States*, II, 58–60. Cf. "Kicking a Yankee," *Spirit*, XV (1845), 263, reprinted in Porter (ed.), *A Quarter Race in Kentucky*, 161–64.

[51] *Spirit*, XXV (1855), 399. Cf. *Col. Crockett's Exploits and Adventures in Texas*, 238.

". . . four persons were playing poker when one of the party item'd to a person in *cohoot* with him (sitting opposite), that he had 'two pair,' letting two fingers appear on the right hand. After the 'Arkansas tooth pick' had taken them off, the injured person exclaimed—

" 'What the h——l'd you do that for?'

" 'Oh, you may thank your luck that you didn't have "four aces," or you'd have no fingers on that hand,' replied the other." [52]

The climax of this yarn is rough-hewn in more ways than one. Several other tales in which an intended victim outplays, outmanipulates, or outthinks the blacklegs may be lumped together in a note [53] over which we may jump to horse-trade stories of the "biter bit" variety. There are not many such tales in the *Spirit* despite Porter's interest in the turf. Most of those one does find follow the pattern set in Longstreet's "The Horse Swap," in which one party succeeds in trading off a horse with a hideous saddlesore but finds that he has received in exchange a nag who is blind and deaf. One such story in the *Spirit* is of additional interest by virtue of a horse dealer's brag about his wares: " 'Got an all-fired putty hoss tew hum,' he continued, 'fresh from 'Hio—slick as a new dollar—smart as young lightnin' arter a spankin—and will trot it like a bullgine down a greased sun-stroke.' " [54] The brag of the ringtailed screamer has been channeled to a different purpose. The effect is strictly farcical when we find that the animal on whom the dealer is heaping such praise is a sawhorse.

In view of our remarks about speculation and speculators we should not be surprised to find a few "sour note" stories in the *Spirit* that feature this activity and its practitioners. That more do not crop up in its pages is probably because speculation was chiefly an

[52] *Spirit*, XXII (1852), 43.
[53] "Doctor W. in a Tight Place," *Spirit*, XVI (1846), 439; Sol Smith, "A Friendly Game of Poker," *Spirit*, XV (1845), 144, reprinted in *The Theatrical Apprenticeship . . . of Sol Smith* (Philadelphia, 1847), 146–52; "Reminiscences of a Man About Town," *Spirit*, XII (1842), 243; "A Stronger Game Than the Thimbles," *Spirit*, IX (1839), 266–67, credited to the New Orleans *Picayune*; "Hog Skins vs. Whiskey," *Spirit*, XVIII (1849), 589; "Colonel Crickley's Horse," *Spirit*, XXII (1852), 76.
[54] "Catching a Weasel Asleep," *Spirit*, XIX (1849), 113, credited to the New Orleans *Crescent*. Cf. "Selling the Wrong Horse," *Spirit*, XVI (1846), 270.

upper- and middle-class activity. It is true that one could go into the business of booming and selling worthless land if one could command a few hundred paper dollars for claim fees and a little newspaper publicity, but the poor white of the backlands could rarely command even that. In the longest and most fully developed of these narratives about "fliers" in land, a seedy-looking squatter does appear, but he has been hired by land agents to act as caretaker of a city which is now merely the scene of a collapsed venture in paper and publicity:

". . . we found stakes marking tier on tier of streets, and on an old gum stump, some ten feet high, was stuck a white-washed board on which was scrawled with charcoal, BROADWAY, it was unnecessary for us to look for the PARK—it was around and about us . . . . Streets, alleys, lanes, and squares were pointed out; names from every city, and all lands, were scattered round this skeleton village, thick as the liquid mud which floated, streaked, or stood in pools on every hand."

The interior of the squatter's home is no less wretched than the general aspect of this city of Belleair. Several years later one of the party returns and finds nothing but wilderness on the site of this ambitious project.[55] Once again the description recalls Mark Twain's immortal composite of all the run-down villages of the southern backwoods, the town in which Huck Finn witnessed the shooting of Boggs by Colonel Sherburn. (The fact that Mark Twain's town still had a few people is incidental.)

VI

In addition to "sour note" tales in several keys, we find in the *Spirit* another large class of narratives in which the note sounded may have been merry or boisterous to the devotees of the magazine but seems discordant enough to us. This note is the practical joke, played in ways that are as rough as they are ingenious and varied.

---

[55] "A New Town in Arkansas," by "Concordia," *Spirit*, XII (1842), 295–96, reprinted in Masterson, *Tall Tales of Arkansaw*, 79–81. Masterson thinks "Concordia" is Robert Patterson, co-editor with Thorpe of the Concordia *Intelligencer*. Cf. "An Awful Place," *Spirit*, XV (1845), 60, reprinted in Haliburton (ed.), *Americans at Home*, II, 116–22.

If one writer and jokester is to be believed, his predecessors of a generation earlier were even cruder in their antics. This Tennessee prankster writes plaintively: "Twenty-five years ago it was not thought amiss to play a little innocent trick for your own amusement, or for the amusement of others. No one 'dubbed' you with the epithet of 'wag,' or thought you 'in the broad road to ruin;' but he who could bring the greatest fund of amusement to the circle in which he moved was ever considered a good fellow." He himself had played a "little innocent trick" in those good old times. On seeing a slave cleaning the entrails out of a pig, he had her take three or four feet of small intestine, blow it up, and tie the ends tightly enough to prevent the air from escaping. Then he put this "snake" in the bed of his sleeping friend, adding a fillip to the prank by passing it between the sleeper's legs. The results may be imagined.[56]

Yet this disappointed prankster need not have mourned so. The practical joker was in his heyday throughout the age of Jackson. Nor was he confined to the frontier; P. T. Barnum thought it was funny to send a member of his circus rushing homeward from a tour because of a false telegram that the family homestead was in ashes or that he was the father of twins. A group of wits in New York played a cruel joke on a vain and unstable poet named Mc-Donald Clark by leading him to think that a certain well-born lady was enamored of him and sending him to her door on a forged invitation. The men in the office of the *Spirit* themselves were wags of no small energy; they drove the short-tempered sporting writer Henry William Herbert (Frank Forester) almost to madness by dispatching him on false clues to run down an anonymous satirist who had offended him. On one occasion Porter himself was the victim of a group of jokers who published a fake story of his having gone off on a hunting trip. The Tall Son took this comparatively mild prank in good part, but his own corrective article showed his anxiousness to clear the matter up.[57]

Thus, although practical jokes formed the subject matter of

[56] "One of the Snake Stories," *Spirit*, XXI (1851), 64, credited to the Nashville *Gazette*. Cf. "How Uncle Jimmy Was Bitten by a Snake," *Spirit*, XXII (1853), 614.

[57] M. R. Werner, *Barnum* (New York, 1923), 184; Adkins, *Fitz-Greene Halleck*, 243; Judd (ed.), *The Life and Writings of Frank Forester*, I, 52.

many a frontier tale and anecdote, we may say only that perhaps the rough life of the backwoods merely encouraged and accentuated the general tendency toward practical joking, both in fact and as a subject for narrative. Certainly the spirit of the true frontier joker was as irrepressible as his taste was catholic. Some Texans who had been captured by the Mexicans during the raid into New Mexico in 1842 were being prodded along on their death march to Mexico City. Although they were being shot for not dragging their sick, half-starved bodies along fast enough, one of the captains could still play a prank by telling a certain man that a Mexican woman insisted on selling him a child. Again, at a log-rolling, when men were carrying a log by means of sticks shoved under it, one man might poke one end of a stick in manure, then push it under the log for his partner to grasp. Chasing a dog or a pig through the cabin of a poor white, wrecking everything in the path, was also a lot of fun. After all, the cabins of the southern backwoods were so ramshackle in build and crude in furnishing that fastidiousness was intolerable and impossible. In any case, the code of the mountaineers of North Carolina demanded that no one was ever to get angry at a joke played on him, no matter how rough it might be.[58]

These examples should show that the taste in humor of the genial Porter and his crew was more or less that of the times and therefore needs only a brief survey. Thus in the *Spirit* itself we find such pieces as that of the two farmers, each of whom was annoyed at the other's stock trespassing on his land. One of these farmers caught the other's sheep and having slit one hind leg of each animal, forced the other leg through the slit, thus creating a new species of three-legged sheep. The owner of the maimed animals bided his time and eventually caught his neighbor's hogs on the wrong side of the line; whereupon he slit their mouths from ear to ear. The hog raiser descended upon him, enraged, but the sheep farmer merely said, "The fact is, my friend, I didn't cut open them ar hog's mouths, but seein' my sheep running on three legs, they split their mouths a laughin!" [59]

[58] George Wilkins Kendall, *Narrative of the Texan Santa Fe Expedition* (2 vols.; New York, 1844), II, 98–101; Dick, *The Dixie Frontier*, 126–27; Wade, *Augustus Baldwin Longstreet*, 62–63; H. E. Taliaferro, *Fisher's River (North Carolina) Scenes and Characters* (New York, 1859), 111.
[59] "Yankee vs. Yankee," *Spirit*, I (September 1, 1832), 3.

This dry reply is a real tall tale, especially in the perfectly serious delivery. Cruelty to animals is likewise involved, although the actions on both sides are so utterly fantastic that this cruelty tends to be forgotten. Not quite the same is true of another yarn concerning a farmer "who was noted for his waggery." This man stopped at an inn from which the landlady had stepped for a moment and left a pot boiling on the stove. The farmer dropped the landlady's cat into the pot and traveled on. When he stopped by again on his return from town, the landlady served him a tasty dish of meat, and after he had partaken his fill, revealed to him its identity. The story closes with the remark, "The man was never known to boil a cat afterwards." [60] Humor of understatement lends punch to the last line, but readers in the 1950's may not be amused, being acclimated to the more remote cruelties of the hydrogen bomb.

One more example may suffice. "An Officer of the U.S. Army" wrote that an agent of the United States bank came to call on a certain old hunter in hopes of buying up some specie with worthless paper banknotes. Mac, the Negro slave of the hunter, caught a score of rats, cropped their ears and tails, and released them in a small log pen. The stranger was induced to fish for "amphibious trout," cast his line over the log, hauled in a rat, and was badly bitten.[61] This tale reveals how close is tall-tale humor to the practical joke, hoax, or "sell," though it is a bit unusual in its political, anti-bank implications.

Yes, practical joking was an art and a science to the hard-handed humorists of the 1840's and 1850's.[62] Of twenty-four tales in the *Sut Lovingood* yarns of George Washington Harris, at least sixteen may be considered practical jokes, and the collections of Robb, Field, Thompson, and others contain one prank after another. The tall tale itself may be thought of as a kind of practical joke. But really tall narrative is distinct enough in its backgrounds and techniques to call for separate treatment.

[60] "Boiled Cat," *Spirit*, XVII (1847), 467.
[61] "A Sporting Adventure in Arkansas," *Spirit*, XII (1843), 531.
[62] E. g., *Spirit*, XVI (1846), 415–16; XIV (1844), 279; *Porter's Spirit*, I (1856), 6–7.

CHAPTER SIX

Tall Tales in the Spirit

I

IT is a commonplace that one function of the tall tale is to befool a stranger. I have heard a resident of the rainy Willamette valley in Oregon assure a visitor from Washington, D.C., that "Out here we drain our tires daily." The yarn-spinner in Thorpe's "The Big Bear of Arkansas" obviously and methodically sets out to gull the newcomers to the Mississippi Delta. Submerging the smell of the lamp in that of the campfire, Professor Boatright has creatively retold some of the tough stories of the Texas plains by putting them into the mouths of a gang of cowboys who are trying to take in the tenderfoot of the outfit.[1]

Another commonplace, eloquently voiced by Mr. Van Wyck Brooks, among others, is that the West was in fact a region where marvelous and highly improbable things happened often and on a vast scale, that life itself was "tall." Hence the tall tale grew from a nucleus of events which were amazing but often true enough (Thus a certain hunter and his three sons were reported to have killed 2,000 birds in one season).[2] This theory of American tall-tale origins dovetails neatly into the view that the tall tale originated in an attempt to fool the newcomer. Westerners, upon finding that easterners and foreigners were not likely to believe their soberly factual accounts of life in the West, may have deliberately tried to gull the stay-at-homes.

But we cannot theorize for long on the origins of the oral tall tale. We are confined to the tall story as frozen in print in the

[1] Mody C. Boatright, *Tall Tales from Texas* (Dallas, 1934).
[2] Van Wyck Brooks, *The World of Washington Irving* (New York, 1944), 107–32, 379–83; *Spirit*, XXI (1851), 462.

"The Great Kalamazoo Hunt"

Spirit of the Times. True, many of the tales in the *Spirit* are transcriptions of yarns spun orally by local characters, but in very few cases can we be reasonably sure that the memory and ear of the writer enabled him to transcribe a tale uncolored by his own personality and by events exterior to that tale.

A further reservation must be made before we plunge into

our analysis. A recent work on some of the philosophical problems raised by modern physics suggests that for the terms "cause"
and "effect" one would do well to substitute the more accurate
phrase, "functional dependencies." [3] In a nonmathematical context one might take this suggestion to mean that instead of saying
that AB is the result of two processes, A and B, we should state
that A and B are always and inextricably bound up with AB whenever AB occurs, even though we cannot assume that certain elements in the denoted phenomenon (AB) are operative as causes
or that the object itself is necessarily an effect of A and B. In the
field of literary history it is even harder to prove the existence of
causal relationships than in physics; consequently we must explain
carefully what we mean when we say that this chapter is primarily
a study in the "origins" of tall-tale literature. In conventional
language, we shall try to show that the tall stories in the *Spirit*
reflect the action of a number of forces. Some of these interrelated
forces are: marvelous but real happenings in the backwoods areas,
the attempt to befool a stranger, and a local pride which is often
aggressively defensive. Other forces are the distinctive attitude
of the southern upper classes toward the bottom class, literary
attempts to imitate the oral tale, and Porter's own personal taste.

Not only are most of these elements interrelated in the various
tales, but the tales themselves seem to strengthen some of the
attitudes which they reflect. There is a process of mutual contribution and enhancement between tale and attitude. For example, a
large number of tales in the *Spirit* are functional dependencies
of the well-to-do southerner's beliefs about the poor white. The
older and less accurate approach would be to assume that these
beliefs were shaping forces in the tale; that is, these beliefs *caused*
certain aspects of the tale to be what they are and those aspects
were the *effects* of those beliefs. But we are entitled to make no
such simple assumption. We may say that the tall tale tended to
strengthen the cultured white's prejudices concerning the poor
white by grooving certain stereotypes that may or may not have
had much correspondence to external reality. We may also say
that these stereotypes conformed with and enhanced his previous

[3] Martin Johnson, *Time, Knowledge and the Nebulae* (London, 1946), 32–36.

notions about the down-at-heel set and stimulated him to note down or produce additional tall tales about these people. We cannot say which came first, tale or attitude; ultimates have no place in our analysis.

The oral tale itself may well be treated as an important functional element in the tales printed in the *Spirit*—in other words, most of the tales ushered into print by Porter are functional dependencies of the oral tale as well as of other factors. However in his book *Native American Humor*, Walter Blair has cogently discussed the technique of the oral tale and its adaptation to the literary short story by writers for the *Spirit* and for other outlets of publication. Among other comments he makes the point that there is no sharp line dividing the realistic article from the tall tale—a point we have tried to make earlier in our own way. Even so, the tall tale is a genre of its own, distinct from the merely realistic piece. The tall tale is not realism; it is a fantastic yarn rendered temporarily plausible by the supporting use of realistic detail. Therefore some of the tall tales in the *Spirit* have been forcibly segregated from the realistic pieces without regard to the fact that such epistles as Obe Oilstone's "Chase of the Spectral Fox" and Harris' "The Knob Dance" definitely incorporate elements of both kinds of writing.

There is little question that the attempt to bemuse an outsider manifested itself in many a tall tale. An anonymous writer for the *Picayune*, whose article was reprinted in the *Spirit*, declared that when men in the South saw the Englishman Frederick Marryat taking notes on American ways, they deliberately "sold" him; hence the inaccuracies of his *Diary in America*. Marryat on his part had prided himself on not being taken in by 'cute yarn-spinners and scolded Harriet Martineau for falling into their traps and thus repeating many inaccuracies. But the "Pic" man chortled that Marryat had been sucked in most properly by a fake gambling game held especially for his benefit, with stakes supposedly at five thousand dollars a point. One man "lost" thirty thousand, then with admirable composure went out for a drink.[4]

[4] "'Sawing' a Tourist," *Spirit*, XVI (1846), 88; Marryat, *Diary in America*, I, 9, 74, 233.

But if the British captain was sold, he was no more so than the New York visitor to North Carolina who was gulled in one of the many tall-tale nuggets to be found embedded in the dull ore of sporting epistles. A dog happens to tree a cat in the depths of the forest. The New Yorker wonders how a domestic animal happened to be out in the wilderness. Dick, one of the hunters, "gravely informed him that they were kept for the preservation of the woods."

" 'Preservation of the woods! come, master Dick, I am not so easily sold as all that comes to; how the devil can they preserve them, and from what?'

" 'From what? why the rats, to be sure; they grow very large if they are not disturbed, and gnaw the bark off young trees, and the roots of the large ones, which renders their hold on the ground so insecure that the slightest wind upsets them; in such a case, it is really dangerous to ride through them.'

"All this being said with a very serious countenance, and being in itself rather plausible, Nat, in spite of his disclaimer, would have been sold, had I been able to restrain my laughter." [5]

The cat concerned is a wildcat, of course. Later Mark, another hunter, assures Nat that cats foil the pursuing dogs by running in relays; one cat will circle awhile and then another will take its place. Dick "corrects" Mark and swears that the real reason why cats are never caught alive is that "They run ahead for some time, and then back off, hind feet foremost; the dogs, being obliged to do the same, or lose their track, make but little progress."

Here the writer claims to have been an authentic witness to an actual incident. If this claim is valid, the two hunters Dick and Mark speak amazingly literary English for Carolina backwoodsmen. On the other hand, the imaginative cleverness of their sell may be hampered by the recorder's lack of an ear for dialect speech, although the effect of the tall tale is not wholly destroyed.

Another claim to truth is made implicitly by a correspondent

[5] "Sporting at the South . . . ," *Spirit*, XVI (1846), 1–2. Cf. "A Wild-Cat Story," *Spirit*, XX (1850), 148; "Where Joe Meriwether Went To," *Spirit*, XX (1851), 607, reprinted in V. L. O. Chittick (ed.), *Ring-Tailed Roarers* (Caldwell, Idaho, 1941), 41–45.

who writes of a quick-witted landlord in his vicinity. A sow had
been killed and paid for and a newcomer to the inn chanced to
see the bill of sale and to misread "son" for "sow." The landlord
thereupon fed him a story about how cheaply human life is held
in the backwoods. The poorer people, he said "turn out the children in the morning with the cows—drive up the survivors at
night—count the missing—make out a bill—present it—we pay
the amount rather than make cost." He elaborates on this theme
until a thoroughly scared stranger leaves the inn in a hurry.[6]
This tale may well be an example of the humor of self-burlesque.
The dweller in the backwoods, knowing of the exaggerated ideas
held by outlanders about the roughness and wretchedness of back-
country life, takes his revenge by exaggerating these notions still
more, until the stranger's eyes pop out of his head in astonish-
ment and fear. We see this process of self-burlesque in operation
also in the gambling game arranged for Marryat.

Constance Rourke and others have suggested that self-carica-
ture as a defense may be at the bottom of most frontier tall talk.[7]
This explanation seems over-simplified as an account of the origin
of this type of humor. At the risk of tedium I repeat that there
is surely no single origin of tall-tale humor and the term "origin"
had better be discarded in favor of some such noncausal term as
"functional dependency."

In another selection the stranger was not exactly sold but was
bested in an abortive tall-tale contest. The writer indicates his
own social background by his opinion of the squatters of Arkansas:
"With all the laziness and degradation of the race, they are by no
means deficient in shrewdness and cunning." The correspondent
had reason to know this. He had offered one of these squatters a
drink and asked him

"if he had, in his journey, seen any hats floating upon the sur-
face of the bog, where their owners had sunk down over head and

[6] "Killing No Murder," by "An Old Correspondent," *Spirit*, XVIII (1848),
157.
[7] See also James R. Aswell (ed.), *Native American Humor* (New York and
London, 1947), xii; Mody C. Boatright, *Folk Laughter on the American Frontier*
(New York, 1949), 161.

ears. His reply was, that if I wanted to see that, I must go the other road.

" 'Where is that?' I asked, in the tender innocence of my heart.

" 'Why,' said he, with a leer and a grin of intense meaning, as if he enjoyed in anticipation the effect of the "coup" before it had parted, *'It is just six feet under the old one.'* " [8]

This type of tall-tale "duel" seems to have been a definitely established tradition and may have been an expression of the suspicious attitude held in the backwoods toward any stranger. If a newcomer could tell a tough yarn to beat that of the next fellow, he thereby proved to the men looking him over with narrowed eyes under coonskin that he was one of them, entitled to their confidence and respect. Thus the tall tale was sometimes a test of fitness, like a contest of marksmanship with the rifle. This tradition had enough solidity to provide one of the most effective episodes half a century later in Owen Wister's *The Virginian* (Chapter XVI).

A test is certainly given and passed in Major Bunkum's tall-tale set-to with a hairy stranger who rode into his camp in Texas one evening. The shaggy one asks him how he managed to cross the roaring Trinity River:

" 'Oh,' say I, 'mighty easy, you see, stranger, I'm powerfull on a perogue, and so I waited till I see a big log driften' near the shore, when I fastened it, sot my critter astraddle on it, got in the saddle, paddled over with the saddle bags, and steered with the mare's tail!'

" 'Yer didn't tho' by Ned!' says he, 'did yer?'

" 'Mighty apt to,' say I, 'but arter you've sucked in all that, and got yer breath agin', let's know how *yer* crossed.'

" 'Oh,' says he (settin' his pigs eyes on me), 'I've been ridin' all day with a consarned ager on, awfull dry; and afeard to drink at the perara water holes, so when I got to the river, I went in for a big drink, swallowed half a mile of water, and come over dry shod.'

[8] "An Arkansas 'Sell,' " *Spirit*, XXVI (1856), 230. Partially reprinted in Masterson (ed.), *Tall Tales of Arkansaw*, 237–38.

" 'Stranger,' says I, 'you're jest one huckleberry above my persimmon; light, and take some red-eye, I thought yer looked green, but I was barkin' up the wrong tree.' " [9]

The tall tale as a test of fitness is seen again in a lying match between backwoodsmen from two different areas, New England and Indiana. The Hoosier bests the Yankee eventually, thereby proving himself the better man, and the Yankee clears out.[10] We may not be far wrong in guessing that the contributor of this tale lived closer to the Wabash than to the Connecticut.

Another variation of the deliberate sell is the type of "tall tale" which turns out not to be tall; in other words, the listener or reader is sold in a different way. This kind of yarn usually culminates in a punch line which instantly destroys the hearer's or reader's expectations and lets him down with a psychological thump. Professor Boatright has called this negative climax the "less-than-to-be-expected" ending. One such tale was purportedly heard by a correspondent when he went into Jim Gregg's store in Pine Bluff, Arkansas, for some gunpowder. Jim launches into a tale about how "the old lady" served a customer the night before and left the cover off the powder keg. Jim says he opened the store this morning, not knowing the powder was exposed:

"I lit a segar and sot down on that box and smoked, and thought what a tramp I had had the day before, and then I took a look at my barked shin, and wonder'd whether it was of any use to let the old woman put any more soap and sugar on it, and then I tried to smell what she was cooking for breakfast, that smelt so nice, like 'ingins,' and by that time my segar was smoked eout, so I thought I'd walk over to Sam Hurlitt's and take a drink, to give me an appetite for breakfast. Without thinking I carelessly threw my 'stump' away, and as luck would have it, it went right into that powder-cag, *and before I could go over to Sam's and take a nip, and walk back, I'm dog-gone if the bloody stuff weren't*

[9] *Spirit*, XVIII (1848), 439, reprinted in Hammett, *Piney Woods Tavern*, 39–48, with considerable emendation.
[10] "The Hoosier and the Yankee," *Spirit*, XI (1841), 406. A Kentuckian out-talks a Frenchman in *Spirit*, X (1841), 601.

more'n half burnt eout. Ain't that enough to make a fellow look 'grumpy?' "

Considerable care has been taken by either the teller or the writer (or both) to build up suspense by the use of trivial, normally irrelevant detail. A story of the same kind, told with less artistry, concerns an Englishman hunting in Oregon who lost a valuable diamond ring. Later a member of his party shot an old bear. "And upon opening him, what should he find? Why, nothing but the ———— entrails!" [11]

Thus, whenever outlanders, American or foreign, figure in the tall tales of the *Spirit,* they are made the dupes of rustic yarn-spinners. When outlanders were not concerned, the tall-tale con-tributors turned another, harsher light on those same rustics, emphasizing their propensity to poverty, vice, improvidence, dis-honesty, and low cunning, and the tales verged on caricature rather than pure fantasy. "Jay R. Aitch, of Shandy Hall, Mo.," obviously a man of some culture, who contributed a number of sporting epistles and humorous sketches, included this bit of tall humor. A local hunter (said Jay R. Aitch) thought he heard the thrumming of a pheasant's wings during a ramble through the woods one day; but soon he came upon old Abe Wilson currying one of his half-starved horses, "and every time he drawed the curry-comb over his ribs, as it glanced from one to tuther, the in-side was so holler it sounded for all the world like a pheasant a-beatin' on a holler log!" Another writer claimed to have stopped one night at a Tennessee squatter's cabin at which the father told of his son's terrific attacks of fever and ague. The boy, it seems, had shaken himself right out of his breeches on one occasion; on an-other he had shaken himself into the fire. "The doctor fout the var-mint his darndest all day but he couldn't face him—he was badly whipped certain." So on the third day papa tried his hand at a cure—he lured the boy into the yard and switched the shakes right out

[11] "Bad Powder," *Spirit,* XX (1850), 367; "A Bear Story," *Spirit,* XX (1850), 330. Cf. "A Loafer," *Spirit,* VII (1838), 382; "The Sentimental Loafer," *Spirit,* XX (1850), 89, credited to the Albany *Dutchman.* See also Boatright, *Folk Laughter on the American Frontier,* 91.

"Cupping on the Sternum"

of him. The old woman crowned pa with the frying pan, but as for the boy, "He aint been troubled with the shakes since." Another yarn, which has affinities with the Arkansas Traveller motif, concerns a sullen, inhospitable squatter whose hogs are so poor they can't eat corn—the grains fall right out through their shrunken hides. In this same part of Arkansas the contributor claims to have shot a goose that was so poor it would not fall to the ground, "and I was obliged to get a stick and pull it down." [12]

Negroes are made the butt of one of the rare stories in the *Spirit* in which they are characterized at all. "Kentuck" writes, "To prove to you that a Negro's feet are as thick and as insensible as his head, I will relate a little anecdote." On making the rounds of his plantation one night the author states that he glanced into a slave hut in which the Negroes slept with their feet toward the fire in the center of the room. One Negro declares, "I smell foot a burnin!" and asks his neighbors whose foot it is, then finally discovers that it is his own and, satisfied, calmly goes to sleep again. The correspondent presents this incident as fact; however Professor Boatright has turned up a version of the same story involving a girl of the poor-white class.[13] The motif is thus revealed as the functional dependency of an upper-class attitude which regarded both poor whites and Negroes as belonging to an inferior class of beings, even though the southern gentleman differentiated sharply between all whites and all Negroes whenever outsiders questioned the "peculiar institution."

II

In connection with the absence from the *Spirit* of Negroes with "tall" characteristics, one is tempted to ask if the tall tale required too heroic a quality on the part of even its comic characters. Could the southern white afford to acknowledge the existence of a John Henry or his prototypes? I am not aware that he did. Another subject of historical interest, however, certainly does crop up in the tall tales in the *Spirit*, namely the great gold rush of 'forty-nine. The attitude reflected in the fairly large group of gold-rush tales is precisely that which one would expect from the socially well-established and financially comfortable landowners of the South and their journalistic allies. Such vested interests of the backwoods and semisettled areas might be expected to join skeptical north-

---

[12] "Horses vs. Iron," *Spirit*, XXIII (1853), 158; "Chills and Fever," *Spirit*, XXII (1852), 529, by "Esperance"; "A Trip to Possum Walk," *Spirit*, XVIII (1848), 241–42.
[13] *Spirit*, XVII (1847), 6. Cf. "Who Dat Fut A-Burnin'?" *Spirit*, XVII (1847), 94; Boatright, *Folk Laughter on the American Frontier*, 34.

erners in discouraging emigration to the Far West as an unsettling force which depopulated the lower classes, drained the older regions of free white labor, created unrest among the Negro slaves, and lowered the price of land. We need not be surprised to find that these tales tend to debunk the dazzling myths of untold riches and to poke fun at the eager gold-hunter. "Jimima Anne J——" writes an old flame in the East about how her "dear John" and she have been faring in the ore-heavy promised land. The two had set up a store at which one of their customers was an Indian who bought a hoe and paid for it with gold-bearing sand. Dear John went off with him, and when he came back, "He had great lumps of gold with him as big as his fist! They don't find such now, all the big pieces are picked out."

With their new-found wealth the pair obtained a fine farm and house, but John died of the "climate fever." Jimima, lonely for her former sweetheart, invites him out West in this semiliterate dialect letter.[14] But the real author is surely discouraging, not encouraging emigration to the gold fields. Earlier we have remarked that often when a humorous writer wanted to put over a point he would cause a thoroughly disreputable character to say exactly the opposite of what the author wished to convey. Thus, Petroleum Vesuvius Nasby, a rascally Copperhead preacher, is made to support the southern cause in such a stupid, hypocritical way that the Union sentiments of his creator, David Ross Locke, are plain to all but the blind. Even so does Chunkey, in his hurrahing for unlimited credit, reflect by his brash ignorance the real beliefs of his anticredit, hard-money author, the Democratic ex-Governor Alexander McNutt. In this letter from the gold fields Jimima is revealed as not only illiterate but capable of writing a mash note of most unmaidenly boldness. Thus, by the standards of the forties, she is definitely of the "wrong kind," an entirely disreputable person and not to be believed on any account.

A debunking attempt which is more baldly obvious is the suggestion of another writer that the surest way to make money in California is to raise poultry near the gold fields; since the gold occurs in coarse grains, the poultry will eat it "to triturate their

[14] "A Valentine," *Spirit*, XIX (1849), 13.

food," (i.e., as grit) and "the gizzard of a California chicken must contain a very considerable quantity of the precious metal." Another burlesque of the wild tales about the riches to be had in "Californy" assimilated some rich soil of its own by way of tall-tale material. The writer says that in this area one may find seven mountains of gold, all of them products of volcanic eruptions— streams of gold have flowed down their sides. Sweet potatoes growing near one of these mountains are three feet long and "as large as a man's leg." Profits from the diggings average thirty million dollars per hour; with what he has earned the writer offers to supply "our friend Obe Oilstone, Jun. with the funds necessary to carry out his bold and original idea of tunnelling through on a level from St. Louis to San Francisco, and making a railroad and ship canal in conjunction." In a postscript this writer, "Peter Zigzag," describes a huge cavern of diamonds so bright that the party can only examine it behind goggles made of thick buckskin colored green. By contrast there is the bitterly factual warning of a "New York Volunteer" who wrote from Mokaleme Diggings that "Thousands—aye, tens of thousands, are doomed to meet blank disappointment in visiting these mountains." [15] For all his interest in tall stories as such, Porter cannot be accused of encouraging migration to the gold fields. Rather, he co-operated with his southern friends in throwing cold water on prospective sufferers from the gold fever.

The attitudes of the backwoods planter are further reflected in the occasional tall stories which satirize the intemperance or the fighting propensities of the ungentlemanly classes. Fighting, we recall, is not often treated humorously in the *Spirit*. A much larger group of tall yarns than those dealing with drinking or brawling have to do with the poor white's lack of scruple and his sharpness of wit in tricking his neighbor. Most of these tales are tall versions of the "biter bit" motif. Money or the urge to drive a hard bargain is not always the motive in these tales. In one story a settler is chased up a tree by a bear which he catches and holds by

[15] "A Profitable Poultry Yard," *Spirit*, XVIII (1849), 570. Cf. "A True Story," *Spirit*, XIX (1849), 484; "Letter from a New York Volunteer," *Spirit*, XIX (1849), 336.

the front paws, not daring to let go. He shouts all night for his neighbor, who deliberately leaves him in this precarious position until the next morning. The treed hunter then asks his neighbor to trade places with him so he himself can have the pleasure of killing the bear. The neighbor consents; whereupon the erstwhile victim lets him hold the bear for several hours in his turn.[16]

Most of these stories, however, do concern money or a trade. In one a would-be horse-trader urges an auctioneer to sell his horse for him and do it quickly because the beast is dying. The auctioneer sells it so cheaply that the trader has to pay him fifty cents. Yet the trader saved something on the deal. He chortles afterward, "Cheap enough! I couldn't a gin him away at no price, and it would have cost two dollars and a half to bury him!" Another story, unusually well presented, presents a battle of wits between a Yankee and a Dutchman in which the Yankee makes the Hollander (or German) believe that the latter has killed a deer illegally. Another Dutchman exposes the Yankee and then claims half of the ten-dollar fine as his reward. The Yankee is sentenced to ten lashes instead and successfully insists that the first Dutchman receive half the "pay." The story is thus an American rendition of the old motif of "strokes shared," which may be found in the medieval romance *Sir Cleges* and many other early works.[17]

One effective "biter bit" yarn comes from an army officer of the so-called military or Fort Gibson cycle of correspondents. An old farmer known as Cut Legs suggests to the Devil that the two of them work a farm on shares. The Devil proposes that he take the roots of all crops while the farmer takes the tops. The farmer sows corn that year and takes everything. The Devil then wants to take the tops of the next crop. So of course the farmer plants potatoes the next year. Meanwhile a sow furnished by Cut Legs

---

[16] "The Drunkest Man Ever Seen," by "Timothy Baggs," *Spirit*, XVI (1846), 92; "Drivin' the Centre; or, Uncle Billy's Rifle Fight," *Porter's Spirit*, I (1857), 316; "A Western Bear Story," *Spirit*, VI (1836), 71, reprinted by the *Picayune* and re-extracted from that paper by the *Spirit*, XI (1841), 417.

[17] "A Horse Story," *Spirit*, XI (1841), 500–501, credited to the *Picayune*; "A Story of the Olden Times," *Spirit*, XII (1842), 77, credited to the *New England Review*; Walter Hoyt French and Charles Brockway Hale (eds.), *Middle English Metrical Romances* (New York, 1930), 877–95; John R. Reinhard, "Strokes Shared," *Journal of American Folklore*, XXXVI (1923), 380–400.

has littered and the hogs are full grown. The hogs are divided equally but they break out of their small respective pens and intermingle again. Cut Legs says that he had twisted the tails of all the pigs belonging to him; in consequence he gets all the pigs except for one lean old sow "who from want of strength and old age combined, had let the kink out of her tail!" One wonders if the officer-author knew Irving's "The Devil and Tom Walker" and if Stephen Vincent Benét knew the story of Cut Legs when he composed "The Devil and Daniel Webster." Much cleverer than the Devil were the backwoods thieves who stole a sawlog so smoothly and quietly that they left the two watchmen playing poker on the hollow shell of bark.[18]

III

In these stories and in many more the poor-white protagonist is presented in a patronizing manner. We find a few stories which are notable exceptions to this rule, but most of them have antecedents west of the Mississippi or north of the Ohio. In the tales of this small but interesting group the narrator is usually the hero. Further, these tales were all supposedly oral at one time, and the skill with which they are told is beyond that of the average tale in the *Spirit*. A definite correlation seems to exist between the author's point of view and the excellence of the tale-telling; whenever the narrator is presented as somewhat of a hero the tale is usually better told and possesses more epic sweep and breadth of the comic imagination than do most of the stories which more accurately embody the beliefs of the backwoods aristocracy.

For instance, there is the widely traveled yarn-spinner Sam Higgins, presented by "John Brown." Sam tells a tale of how the Michigan sand dunes drift so rapidly that they soon bury trees clear to the top; then the next day the wind changes and uncovers the trees to their roots again. One night Sam went to sleep in a

---

[18] "The Origin of the Twist in Pig's Tails," *Spirit*, XIV (1844), 109, by "G**" [Captain William Seaton Henry]; "Tough Stories," *Spirit*, XVIII (1848), 185, credited to the *Yankee Blade*. Cf. "Making Up for Lost Time," *Spirit*, IX (1839), 434, credited to the *Picayune;* "A Sale on Lake Erie," *Spirit*, XVI (1846), 253, by "Dunne Verrie Browne, Esq."; "India Rubber Pills," *Spirit*, XVI (1846), 325, by "Cheval," reprinted in Porter (ed.), *A Quarter Race in Kentucky*, 151–53; "The Yankee Joke," *Spirit*, XVIII (1848), 410.

sand bank and woke up the next morning in a tall tree top, thanks to a change in the wind. How did he get down? "Seeing that the wind was about to rise, I just waited till the sand drifted back again!" [19] This story (parallel in theme to one of Baron Munchausen) illustrates how the tallest incident in a tale may be prepared for or built up to by means of details and incidents that are fantastic enough but less so than the climactic event. This "apex" incident of the tall tale thus gains in effectiveness by the building up of a mood in which the reader is led to expect almost anything in the way of a "whopper."

In a tale told by Black Harris, Rocky Mountain guide and fur trapper, the same type of build-up is used. Event is piled on event and detail on detail, each taller than the last, until the apex, the tallest incident of all, is reached. First of all, the circumstances leading to Harris' telling the tale are carefully explained by the author, "Major Job Whetstone," whom we have met earlier. The Major claims to have taken part in a buffalo hunt with Harris and a number of companions. The camp is thrown into confusion by a tenderfoot who believes that Indians are attacking and raises the alarm, but the "redskins" turn out to be a pair of mule's ears sticking up from behind a rock.

Instead of settling down again for the night, the group decides to tell stories. We are informed that Job leads off with a story told just as it was written down for the "Pikeyoon" last spring. Then Black Harris spins his yarn, which is really a series of yarns. He tells about a wild ride aboard a mad buffalo and caps this incident with an even taller tale about fishing in the Arkansas River. He hooked one fish which was swallowed by another before he could lift it out; the second was swallowed by a third, and so on until he finally hauled in eight fish on that one hook, each fish inside the other. The largest and outermost "cat" was no less than seven feet long. Then comes his climax, or apex incident, a version of the famous "petrified man" story, well done but somewhat briefer than and inferior to the tangy version Harris is made to tell in Ruxton's *Life in the Far West*. It is not bad though; the quiet, pungent denouement occurs when Harris sees a man leaning on his

[19] "A Blow Out in Michigan," *Spirit*, XVI (1846), 285.

rifle and attempts to question him about the origin of this "putrified" region. He discovers that man and gun are both solid stone
and remarkably taciturn.[20]

Two other pieces are noteworthy in this small group of tales
which feature a skilled oral narrator as comic hero. One of these
was picked up in Texas by George Wilkins Kendall and deals with
a ranger who roasted a chunk of horseflesh over a fast-moving
prairie fire by running just ahead of the fringe of flames. The
other, from North Carolina, deals with a man who fires and then
traps the bullet in his gun; this is one of the few tales in the group
which comes from the Old South.[21]

IV

Major Job Whetstone mentioned a campfire yarn which was
told "just as he [another member of the party] rote it down for
the Pikeyoon last spring." This example of a yarn-spinner retelling
a tale from a printed source suggests that the "pure" or "uncor-
rupted" tradition of the oral tall tale was being influenced by
printed material as early as 1843, the date of this contribution.
True, direct influences are difficult to establish in the realm of the
folk tale; moreover, most of the newspapers and magazines in
which informal humorous tales were printed have long since fallen
prey to mildew and fire or lie forgotten in attics and unclassified
archives. Even so, students of nineteenth-century American folklore will do well to remember that such an influence of printed
upon oral folk humor did exist, and to take that influence into
consideration.

As a matter of fact, a fair-sized group of tall tales in the *Spirit*
reveal in one way or another that they were mainly products of
journalists or letter-writers who were trying to be funny in print
and were not utilizing any special material that they had received

---

[20] "Buffalo Hunting in Missouri," *Spirit*, XIII (1843), 365. Cf. "Tough
Stories," *Spirit*, XVII (1847), 105, credited to the *Yankee Blade* and reprinted in
Dorson, *Jonathan Draws the Long Bow*, 103–105.

[21] "Bill Dean, the Texas Ranger," *Spirit*, XVI (1846), 229, reprinted in
Porter (ed.), *A Quarter Race in Kentucky*, 122–24; "The Hardest Day's Work in
My Life," *Spirit*, XXI (1851), 506.

by word of mouth. Such men were simply trying to write humor-ously, and even though some of them wrote from back-country areas, their works are no different in method from the humorous writings of, let us say, Washington Irving or Oliver Wendell Holmes. In other words, these men were wholly literary in their endeavors. Whether their work was of high quality as humor or not is another question altogether.

In any case, the chief among these literary humorists of the frontier was John Phoenix (Captain George Horatio Derby, U.S.A.), about half of whose *Phoenixiana* was preprinted or re-printed in the *Spirit* in 1855 and 1856. But before him there had been "Trebla" (Albert C. Ainsworth) of New Orleans, who wrote many letters in which he dished out drama news, puns, society gossip, and vignettes of local sights and characters. Rarely, how-ever, did he use backwoods material or attempt to retell word-of-mouth tales in anything like their oral form. He did try desper-ately to be funny, and occasionally he succeeded. In one of his few efforts at tall-tale humor he said that the hair of the girls at a quadroon ball was so curly "that when some of these quartroons want to commit suicide they have only to let a few links of the 'tie-string' out, when their hair curls their head right off." In the same letter he quotes the New Orleans *Crescent City* thus: "The editor remarked that he had been introduced to a Frenchman with such long hair, that when the vessel he was in had been to sea three days, his locks were not 'clear' of the Custom House!" An-other forced effort is "A Quilting in 'Tucker's Hollow,'" which appeared during the year after Harris' "The Knob Dance" and is probably one of the burlesques of that tale.[22]

To the previously mentioned elements of which the tall tale is a functional dependency we must add the newspaper hoax. Let us define a hoax as an article in which the writer deliberately attempts to deceive the public, either for the fun of the deception or from an ulterior motive.[23] An example of an ulterior, pecuniary motive is that of Barnum in perpetrating his "Grand Buffalo Hunt," a

[22] *Spirit*, XI (1842), 573; XVI (1846), 436, by "C. H. B." For a story in which a New Orleans dandy catches his hair in a door and walks two blocks before he finds it out, see *Spirit*, VIII (1839), 403, credited to the *Picayune*.
[23] Cf. Curtis D. MacDougall, *Hoaxes* (New York, 1940), vi.

piece of fakery which seems to have taken in Porter himself.[24]
Some of the tall tales which we have been studying fit the definition of a hoax just given; in fact the humorous newspaper hoax is a
form of both the practical joke and the written tall tale. This conclusion is strengthened by the fact that more than one hoax in the
Spirit utilized frontier tall-tale material with an imaginative humor
comparable to the oral tales of pineland and prairie storytellers.

One of the cleverest hoaxes in the *Spirit* had originally appeared far from the frontier, in the *Massachusetts Ploughman*,
and was reprinted in the "Farmer's and Breeder's Department" of
Porter's journal. The teeth of this hoax had been drawn; that is,
a humorous comment had been added by the editor of the *Ploughman* warning the public of the sell. The article was entitled "Fancy
Manures" and indicates the broadness of Porter's editorial taste
(not to mention that of the editor in the "puritanical" Bay State).
The anonymous writer declared that all other kinds of guano were
insignificant in comparison with that of a certain species of sea
bird called "Deville," which lived on desolate arctic islands and
fed on "a species of fish similar in some respects to the electric eel,
the manure of which, in consequence of this pungent food would
exert a real living influence on vegetation, similar to that which a
galvanic battery appears to exert on the defunct animal economy,
and would therefore, be as much more efficacious than guano, as
that is more than common barnyard manure." Unfortunately this
bird is not especially productive: "It is said not to make a deposit
but once in three hundred and sixty-five days, and six hours, just
at the time when at the north pole the sun is seen sweeping a circle
on the horizon, with only his semi-diameter in view. The effluvia
arising from it at that time, is fatal to the olfactory nerve of
man." [25] The writer elaborates with imaginative coarseness on the
properties of this bird's fabulous deposits.

A more famous hoax in the *Spirit* was Derby's "Remarkable
Discoveries in Oregon and Washington Territories," printed originally in the San Francisco *Herald*. This yarn was undoubtedly

---

[24] E. g., see "On Dits in Sporting Circles," *Spirit*, XIII (1843), 306; also
see Werner, *Barnum*, 68–71.

[25] *Spirit*, XIV (1845), 573. Cf. "Street Chronology in New York," *Spirit*, VI
(1836), 33, credited to the New York *Mirror*.

written to poke fun at the accounts of remarkable scientific discoveries in the West and contains an elaborate description of the fossil remains of the "Guyascutus" and the "Prock," two remarkable if extinct animals. The article was credited in the *Spirit* to "The Natural History of Oregon./ By Dr. Herman Ellenbogen, M.D.," and may or may not have taken in the editorial staff at No. 1 Barclay Street completely.[26]

Two rollicking journalists familiar to southwestern readers concocted hoaxes on each other in which they used tall-tale material fresh from the frontier. In 1843 Sir William Drummond Stewart, a Scottish sporting gentleman, made the last of several hunting tours of the northern Rocky Mountains.[27] In his party was Matthew C. Field, a brother of Joseph M. Field, who wrote for the New Orleans *Picayune* and the St. Louis *Reveille* under the pseudonym of "Phazma." While Stewart's expedition was still out among the bears and boulders our old acquaintance, T. B. Thorpe, then co-editor of the Concordia (Louisiana) *Intelligencer,* wrote a series of articles for his paper purporting to come from the pen of a member of the expedition who called himself "P. O. F." The *Spirit* discovered the hoax in due time, indignantly denied that they had ever been fooled, and went right on running the letters. Porter bounced out of his seat thus:

"*Sold.*—Somebody has been quizzing the editors of the 'Picayune.' Hear them:—

"Our friend T. B. T. of the 'Concordia Intelligencer' gets up his letters from the Far West very well, even for a backwoodsman. At the North they do not appear to take the joke. 'The Spirit' has

[26] "Discovery of Two Remarkable Animals in the Rocky Mountains," *Spirit,* XXV (1856), 617. This hoax probably inspired Mark Twain's fake account of a fossil discovery, "The Petrified Man." See Gladys Bellamy, "Mark Twain's Indebtedness to John Phoenix," *American Literature,* XIII (March, 1941), 29–43.

[27] See Matthew C. Field's manuscript diary in the possession of the Missouri Historical Society; William Clark Kennerly, *Persimmon Hill* (Norman, Oklahoma, 1948), 143–67, 257–58; Dale L. Morgan, "Miles Goodyear and the Founding of Ogden," *Utah Historical Quarterly,* XXI (July, 1953), 195–218 and XXI (October, 1953), 307–29; Bernard DeVoto, *Across the Wide Missouri* (Boston, 1947), 363–65; Rickels, "Thomas Bangs Thorpe: His Life and Works," 138–50.

been 'done brown' by him. They are cut by a *saw* of which T. B. T. possesses the exclusive patent.

"So they don't take the joke at the North! Oh no! We republish another of the letters today, from the 'Intelligencer,' and hope 'the Pic.' will be able to publish some half as clever from its exclusive correspondent. No wonder they are horribly exasperated in 'the Pic.' office, that people in the North will not 'take the joke' of reading MAT. FIELD's dull letters, when THORPE's are to be had at the same price. We recollect no Northern editor who has been 'sold' so cheap!"

Porter was kinder to Field in a later comment that also reveals how several editors continued to use Thorpe's letters after they knew of their spurious nature—even as Porter was using them, although he at least hung out a warning flag for his readers.[28]

Thorpe's "Far West Letters" are a mixture of concrete description of life on the trail as he imagined it to be, burlesques of real and imaginary characters in the Stewart party, and tall tales written with a vivacious cleverness and a sweep that might earn these articles a considerable reputation were they more accessible. They contain such yarns as that of a mighty buffalo carcass attacked by a vulture and two wolves. These animals disturb the carcass so much that it rolls down a bank, killing the vulture and pinning the wolves to the ground with its horns.[29] This and other tales in the series are entertainingly discussed by Dr. Milton Rickels, who interprets them as burlesques of western travel accounts and of the lore of fabulous animals such as white steeds and evil bears. We shall content ourselves with merely presenting another of the yarns—one of the best, in our opinion.

According to "P. O. F.," he went out hunting one day, equipped for rough travel in a suit of fresh deerskin. He stayed away from camp overnight in wet weather and slept on the ground in two inches of water. The next day after his return to camp he was

[28] Cf. *Spirit*, XIII (1843), 426; "The Rival 'Saws' of Thorpe and Field," *Spirit*, XIII (1844), 546; and "Sir William Stewart's Expedition," *Spirit*, XIII (1843), 356.
[29] *Spirit*, XIII (1843), 356.

stricken with a strange and alarming paralysis. He felt on the verge of strangling and his fright and discomfort were not eased by the fact that one of the "friendly" Indians had his knife out and was making cutting motions in his direction. To complete his misery, the friends of "P. O. F." picked him up and laid him in a stream to "soak it out of him," upon which brutal treatment he gave himself up for lost. Soon, however, he felt much relieved and eventually learned that his deerskin suit, wetted by the shower, had dried and shrunk in the hot sun and the stiffening rawhide had encased him as in a vise of iron. The tale concludes with a disquisition on the remarkable properties of rawhide:

"An old hunter informed me that a whole party of white men, who were thus dressed, were caught by a sudden coming out of a hot sun, while eating their dinner; they were rendered helpless, before they were conscious of the reason, and sat staring at each other, with a buffalo steak in each hand, until they starved to death, their clothes not permitting them to move; and what made it more awful, after they were dead, damp weather came on— they melted down on the ground, and remained prostrate until the next sunshine--they then, as their skin clothing contracted by the heat, came up right again, in all imaginable positions, exhibiting one of the most melancholy spectacles that ever greeted the eye of humanity." [30]

Thorpe claimed that "Sir William pronounced them [the Far West letters] the most truthful of all that were written, never for a moment suspecting they were not from some member of his party." [31] This claim itself seems tall; however if Sir William had a sense of humor he surely enjoyed the hoax as much as we may Thorpe's adaptation of the tall tale.

But Matt Field, the journalist who actually did tramp the Rockies with Stewart, had a potent pen too, in his way, Porter notwithstanding. Toward the end of the trip he began to prepare from

[30] *Spirit*, XIII (1843), 421.
[31] Evert A. and George Duyckinck (eds.), *Cyclopaedia of American Literature* (rev. ed.; New York, 1866), II, 612–13. The manuscript of this biographical sketch is in the New York Public Library; it seems to be in Thorpe's handwriting and is labeled "M. S. from T. B. Thorpe—for C. Scribner, 145 Nassau St."

his journal a series of bona fide articles about the expedition and his adventures as a member of the party. All in all he wrote thirty-four articles for the *Picayune* and five for the *Reveille* before his sudden death from illness in December, 1844. Of these thirty-nine letters the *Spirit* republished only five. Luckily all of Field's articles are available for study in typescript.[32] They include soberly factual descriptions and incidents of life on the trail, authentic tall-tale material picked up from hunters and trappers themselves, humorous burlesques of sporting epistles, and burlesques of Thorpe and his hoax.

The progression of differences in Field's approach is interesting. Not until the seventeenth of his letters to the *Picayune* do we find anything but sober fact in his accounts. But in that letter, which appeared in the *Picayune* of November 26, 1843, several of the members of the expedition are caricatured in exactly the same style as Thorpe himself was using. Very likely Field had just become aware of Thorpe's hoax; he was certainly aware of it by the nineteenth letter less than one week later, in which he introduced an exaggerated portrait of Thorpe, making him a member of the expedition and calling him "The Concordia Intelligencer Man." This journalistic freak was "about four feet four in height, with a head like the decapitated upper part of a brass andiron." (Thorpe was indeed a short, stocky man and far from handsome, as his picture in Duyckinck's *Cyclopaedia* reveals.) Porter reprinted Field's caricature with gleeful commentary of his own.[33] Thus we have two journalists concurrently writing articles on the same subject, one doing a complete hoax, the other inserting among his factual material a hoax aimed at burlesquing the former writer.

But the humorous letters in Field's series were not confined to a caricature of Thorpe and his efforts. Selections in the *Spirit* include two versions by Field of the same event, a grim winter journey over the central Rockies by Black Harris and Milton L. Sublette, both famous trappers and traders. One of these accounts

[32] Anonymous, "Matthew C. Field: Stewart Expedition of 1843. New Orleans, 1843–1844 . . . . ," unpublished typescript in the American History Room, New York Public Library. Hereinafter referred to as the Field typescript.

[33] See note 28 above. The sketch appeared in the *Picayune*, December 2, 1843, according to the Field typescript.

is a tersely factual summary of the entire journey; the other is a humorous account stressing a single episode in which a favorite dog is eaten by the trappers to fend off death by starvation. An authentic tall tale of the frontier in Field's letters is Black Harris' story of the "putrified forest," the second version we have encountered in the *Spirit*. The journalist claims to have heard the tale from Harris' own lips, and well he may have.[34]

For our study the chief significance of this double hoax of Thorpe and Field is its clear demonstration of how multifarious and blurred are the "origins" of the tall tale. In these two series of letters, factual writing shades off into burlesque and burlesque into tall yarns from both the frontier and more cultivated soil. Moreover, the hoax is here seen to be closely related to the oral tall tale and to have a definite influence on frontier tall-tale humor. Thorpe himself had written such humor elsewhere. Such hoaxes as the rival saws of Thorpe and Field reveal that the tall tale, the journalistic epistle of fact or wit, and the literary caricature are often interrelated functional dependencies. In addition, the Thorpe-Field sequence, though often sinking into slapstick, holds interest on its own by being thoroughly readable. The oblivion in which these letters have lain deserves to be ended.

V

So far we have singled out for examination some of the tall tales with definite social, historical, or literary implications. There remains a large number of tales in which such implications are less clear, mostly hunting and fishing stories. One would, of course, expect to find tall hunting yarns and "fish tales" in a sporting magazine. Perhaps the leader of this group in point of interest is the tale about Captain Martin Scott, the mighty coon hunter. An imperfect redaction of this story was published in 1925; scholars have mentioned it since but no one has resurrected any version which preserved much of the flavor of the lost original. The version in the *Spirit* is taken bodily from the *American Turf Register and*

---

[34] "A Perilous Winter Journey," *Spirit*, XIV (1844), 62; "Death of a Dog," *Spirit*, XIII (1844), 548–49. In the Field typescript the humorous letter is recorded as having appeared in the *Picayune*, November 27, 1843 and the soberer account in the *Picayune*, March 14, 1844. Field's tale of the petrified forest appeared in the St. Louis *Reveille*, November 18, 1844.

Sporting Magazine and is in the form of a letter to the editor.[35] It bears the dateline "Little Rock, Arks., Aug. 29, 1832," and is signed simply "An Arkansas Hunter," but the author may have been a military man. The opening affords a good example of how many oral yarns got into print:

"Mr. Editor: In one of the numbers of your Sporting Magazine, you mention some well authenticated facts of Captain Martin Scott's skill in the use of firearms." The correspondent then offers "an anecdote which I have heard . . . which, though *improbable*, is so much to the point that I have been tempted to send it on to you." The writer is careful to be specific about the personnel and locale of the story; it took place when Captain Scott, then Lieutenant Scott, was in "the old rifle regiment," then stationed at Fort Smith, on the Arkansas River, under the command of Major Bradford. Scott could shoot a swallow on the wing on a misty day, but another lieutenant at the post, named Van Swearengen, was as notoriously bad a shot as Scott was good:

"It appears that a dog had treed a racoon in a very tall cotton wood, and after barking loud and long to no purpose, the coon expostulated with him, and endeavoured to convince him of the absurdity of spending his time and labour at the foot of the tree, and assured him that he had not the most distant idea of coming down the tree, and begs him as a fellow creature to leave him to the enjoyment of his rights. The dog replied naturally, but I fear not, in the same conciliatory style of the coon, but threatened him with the advent of some one that would bring him down. At this moment a cracking in the cane indicated the approach of some individual; the coon asked the dog who it was? The dog replied with some exultation, that it was Lieutenant Van Swearengen—the coon laughed, and he laughed with a strong expression of scorn about his mouth: 'Lieutenant Van Swearengen, indeed, he may shoot and be d——nd.' Van Swearengen made five or six ineffectual shots, and left the coon, to the great discomfiture of the dog, still unscathed, and laughing on the top of the tree. The dog smothered his chagrin by barking louder and louder, and the coon laughed

[35] "The Dog and the Racoon—*A fable*," *American Turf Register and Sporting Magazine*, IV (October, 1832), 81–82, reprinted in *Spirit*, I (October 13, 1832). Cf. Don C. Seitz, *Uncommon Americans* (Indianapolis, 1925), 43–44.

louder and louder, until the merriment of the one, and the mortification of the other, was arrested by the approach of some other person. The coon inquired who it was, the dog answered with quickness that it was Scott—who? asked the coon, evidently agitated! why, Martin Scott, by G——d. The coon cried in the anguish of despair, that he was a *gone coon;* rolled up the white of his eyes, folded his paws on his breast, and tumbled out of the tree at the mercy of the dog, without making the least struggle for that life which he had, but a few minutes before, so vauntingly declared and believed was in no kind of danger."

Into this yarn have gone all the ingredients of a good tall tale —a creative but controlled imagination, concrete and convincing detail, and a sense of form and structure. The narrator gently leads one into the tall portion of the yarn by way of a succession of details which grow more and more fantastic until they culminate in a climax of the preposterous. All is told apparently with utter seriousness, as though the teller were unconscious that he was saying anything humorous.

This yarn is also a good example of how a tall tale may attach itself to an authentic, living personage. A Captain Martin Scott really did exist, and he undoubtedly furnished the core figure of this tale. Born and raised in Vermont, the real Martin Scott was commissioned a second lieutenant of rifles in 1818 and a first lieutenant in 1819. In 1821 he was transferred to the Fifth Infantry, and the above version of the coon yarn is thus pretty well dated. A number of friends and acquaintances attest to his fabulous marksmanship—'twas said he could throw up two potatoes at once and hit them both with one shot—his love of hunting, horses, and dogs, his fondness for exact sporting etiquette and terminology, his gallantry in action, and his personal vanity, which got him into at least one duel. The climax to a long and eventful career in Uncle Sam's uniform was his death in action at the battle of Molino del Rey, September 8, 1847.[36]

[36] Marryat, *Diary in America,* II, 101–12; Randolph B. Marcy, *The Prairie Traveler* (new ed.; New York, 1861), 171–72; *id., Thirty Years of Army Life on the Border* (New York, 1874), 424–42; Marcus Hansen, *Old Fort Snelling 1819–1858* (Iowa City, 1918), 59–62.

Like the life of Crockett, then, the career of Martin Scott seems to have been eventful enough in fact. Moreover, a somewhat condensed version of the coon story floated into the Boone and Crockett legends and was printed in one of the Crockett almanacs in the middle or late 1830's. In 1838 a related version told on a Mississippi steamboat found its way into the *Spirit*. Jim Doggett in "The Big Bear of Arkansas" compared the "unhuntable bar" to Cap'n Scott's coon. Five years later a tree in Louisiana, when blown open with gunpowder, proved to be chock-full of dead coons, which occasioned the remark, "Cap'n Scott's coon story was some;—but that war fiction. I can prove every word of this by Jim Stokes." A North Carolina writer tells the story, substitutes a deer for a coon, and lets him off alive. Someone assured Captain Marryat that the expression "a gone coon" owed its origin to the Scott story. In short, the tale attained quite a circulation in the Southwest and, partly through the *Spirit*, in the nation at large.[37]

There were other stories of fabulous coon hunts and hunters,[38] but we must replace them in our files in order to have a look at some of the other hunting yarns sent in by numerous willing contributors. Some of these were full-fledged stories; others were primarily factual narrative epistles brightened by the inclusion of tall-tale material. A number of hunting stories owed something to Baron Munchausen; for instance, those built around the theme of the "wonderful hunt." A single example may suffice, since the pattern of events in this type of tale is quite regularized. "My grandfather," who "was considered a man of truth and integrity," went hunting one day. He fired at a deer and found that the ball had killed it, passed through the head of a sturgeon in a nearby stream, and ricocheted through the body of a fox. In addition it had split the limb of a tree. The limb had sprung shut again, catching by the legs two pigeons, and come to rest in a bee-tree, from which "a yellow juice was running down from a small hole—a ball hole—

[37] Blair, *Native American Humor*, 95; Dorson (ed.), *Davy Crockett, American Comic Legend*, 111–12; "A Good Shot," *Spirit*, VIII (1838), 40; "Cale Lyman's Coon Story," *Spirit*, XVI (1846), 389, credited to the *Louisiana Journal*; "Capt. Scott's Coon Story Outdone," *Spirit*, XVI (1846), 145.

[38] E.g., "A Thundering Coon Hunt," by "H. P. L." [Henry P. Leland], *Porter's Spirit*, I (1856), 106; "Major Brown's Coon Story," by "Hazel Green, Esq.," *Porter's Spirit*, III (1857), 247.

he put his finger to it, then to his tongue, and found that it was honey." Variations on this pattern are often ingenious but usually minor.[39]

Baron Munchausen once told another tale about how he rammed his arm down the throat of a charging wolf, seized it by the tail, and turned it inside out with a jerk. Two writers for the *Spirit* both substitute a panther for the wolf, but the story remains essentially the same. Munchausen is given some of the credit explicitly for one version. Another pair of yarns by the imaginative Baron have relatives in the *Spirit*, although these American cousins are first of all backwoods stories in setting, tone, and atmosphere. One has to do with a bitch that whelps as she runs. Each pup comes back with game in its mouth. The other story is about the hound that ran its legs off until it was merely a short-legged terrier. In the American version the motif is associated with a pony and with buffalo. Joe Dunklin, an old hunter, tells how he was chased by a maddened buffalo herd that pursued him until they had run themselves to death except for one bull, and he ran his legs clean off. Dick, Joe's faithful pony, himself ran his hoofs off. Later, in another race, Dick ran off the rest of his legs—"run 'em off smack up to his body." Yet, Joe averred, he stayed in the race. How? "He rolled, gentlemen, just as nat'ral as a saw-log on an inclined plane." And Joe mounted his remarkable pony and rode away.[40]

Fish stories seem to be a product of all modern times and cultures—wherever there are fish to be caught and fishermen to tell lies about them. The *Spirit* reprinted one item about two boys having caught six barrels of catfish and a bear in one afternoon. An

[39] William Rose (ed.), *The Travels of Baron Munchausen* (London, 1823), 34–36. Cf. " 'Tall' Shooting," *Spirit*, XI (1841), 205; also "Shooting Extraordinary," *Spirit*, VI (1837), 405; "An Extensive Shooting Story," *Spirit*, XI (1841), 289, by "A Subscriber, of East Baton Rouge"; "Another Fish Story," *Spirit*, XVI (1846), 510; "Tough Yarns," *Spirit*, XXII (1852), 309.

[40] "A Tough 'Un," *Spirit*, XVII (1847), 263. See also "Fighting the Tiger," *Spirit*, XVI (1846), 58, credited to the St. Louis *Reveille* and reprinted in Clark, *The Rampaging Frontier*, 213–15; "Joe Dunklin's Pony," by "Zeb Doolittle," *Spirit*, XVII (1848), 545; "The Greatest Dog Story Yet," *Spirit*, XVII (1847), 67; "That Wonderful Little Dog Nip," *Porter's Spirit*, I (1856), 130, by "Young 'Un [George Philip Burnham]; Rose (ed.), *The Travels of Baron Munchausen*, 31–36, 41–42.

editorial writer added, "The river is so full of them (we suppose he means bears), that we have seen old barking hounds picking them out at low water, and running away with them by hundreds." [41]

The writer further added that he didn't believe any part of the story. What would he have said could he have seen an authentic present-day photograph in the Portland *Oregonian* of men, women, and children scooping live smelt out of the Sandy River with buckets, butterfly nets, and old socks? Thousands of residents of the Pacific Northwest have "fished" successfully for smelt in this fashion during the brief period every two or three years when the smelt are running. Yet who would blame an eastern editor for not believing a story about this run, even when reinforced by photographs?

Fish stories, then, even of the tall variety, are not necessarily characteristic of the frontier; this statement holds true for flavor and atmosphere as well as for incident, with a few exceptions. Of these exceptions the best one is "The Mysterious Pilot," in which a catfish races a bear who is hooked to a steamboat and pulls it right along. "Straggler," the author, achieved a sustained narrative of imaginative sweep and gusto that he did not match again in the *Spirit*. [42]

Bear stories, because of the nature of the quarry itself, are more likely to be products of the backwoods than are fish stories. We have noticed how many factual epistles have to do with bear hunts. One may well expect some of these epistles to slide across the line dividing the mundane, factual epistle from the tall tale. Such a story is "How Bob Partridge 'Done the Bear.'" Bob swears he disabled his quarry by sticking a plug of tobacco in each of its eyes. This tale is such a little ways inside tall territory that one hesitates to say that it is not true. Thorpe's "The Big Bear of Arkansas," while rich in tall-tale humor, does not present the bear itself as altogether unbelievable; what gives the story its epic breadth and

---

[41] *Spirit*, VI (1836), 208, credited to the St. Francisville (Louisiana) *Journal*.
[42] *Spirit*, XVII (1847), 51, credited to the Murfreesboro (Tennessee) *Telegraph*. Cf. "The Way Billy Harris Drove the Drum-Fish to Market," *Spirit*, XX (1850), 219–20, credited to the *St. Mary's Beacon* (state unnamed), and reprinted in Haliburton (ed.), *Traits of American Humour*, I, 262–72.

dramatic conflict is the vital personality of the narrator and his somewhat awed feeling that "that bar was an unhuntable bar, and died when his time come." A bit taller, however, is the swimming bear which, when a hunter in a skiff tried to run him down, climbed into the boat, rode to shore, grinned amiably at the exasperated and unarmed huntsman, and ambled off. Perhaps a bit higher even than this "bar" is the one that deliberately picked the flint out of Ike Hamblin's rifle and calmly thumbed his nose when Ike tried in vain to shoot him.[43]

Thus, in bear stories as in other types of narrative we find several gradations of reality from the mundane to the fanciful. Other animals also figured in the tall tales recorded by the confraternity of the *Spirit*. In connection with dialect we wondered at a certain remarkable dog who was often squeezed by a bear until she "wasn't any larger than my arm and at least nine or ten feet long." Yet this hardy beast always recovered. A "strict member of the church" told a naval correspondent of the *Spirit* about a cat which had fallen into his well. How did she get out? "She commenced running round the circumference of the well, increasing her speed at each circuit, until she acquired such velocity that the centrifugal force threw her at least six feet above the top of the well!"[44]

Amazing animals called for amazing hunters to catch them. There was the rough-and-ready fellow who killed his deer by jumping on its back and screwing a gimlet into its forehead. There was the man who crashed through the brush in pursuit of his deer

---

[43] *Spirit*, XVII (1848), 548; "A Bear Story," *Spirit*, XXIV (1854), 464, credited to the Albany *Register*. Cf. "A Rather Tough Texas 'Bar' Story," *Spirit*, XXV (1855), 37; see also "Mike Hooter's Fight with the 'Bar,'" *Spirit*, XIX (1849), 452, credited to the New Orleans *Delta*, reprinted in Haliburton (ed.), *Traits of American Humour*, III, 22–29, and in Burke (ed.), *Polly Peablossom's Wedding*, 49–54. Cf. "A Bear Story and No Mistake," *Spirit*, X (1840), 391, reprinted in Henry William Herbert (ed.), *Sporting Scenes and Sundry Sketches, . . . of J. Cypress, Jr.* [William P. Hawes], I, 47–54, and in Porter (ed.), *A Quarter Race in Kentucky*, 188–96; also "Col. Crockett in a Quandary," *Spirit*, VI (1836), 214, reprinted in Haliburton (ed.), *Traits of American Humour*, I, 135–36.

[44] "A Backwoods Sheriff and His Dog," *Spirit*, VIII (1838), 175. Another dog story is "Old Bob Joyner," *Spirit*, XXI (1851), 426. See also "Two Stories That Are Hard to Beat," by "An Officer of the U.S. Navy," *Spirit*, XVI (1846), 223. Cf. "A 'Mud Turkle' Story," *Spirit*, XVI (1846), 342, by "De Grachia" [Matt Flournoy Ward].

oblivious of the fact that his eye had been ripped out by a branch and was "hanging on a bush and winking at me." There was also the man who used to catch rabbits by hiding in a hole with a she-rabbit tied to his hat. The device worked well until another hunter potted the decoy and nearly got its master.[45]

VI

Another kind of animal tale has been a favorite of mankind since Eden. Because of the peculiar fascination and horror which snakes arouse in man, one may expect to find a number of graphic and compelling snake stories in the *Spirit*. And snake yarns do form one of the most numerous groups of tales in Porter's journal, although most of these stories fall into certain well-defined motifs or tale-types. One story, appended to a soberly informative article on the life and habits of the rattlesnake, is the tale of the "living fang." The yarn concerns a pair of boots that had been worn by a man who was struck in the heel and killed by the bite of a rattler. The next two wearers of these boots died mysteriously, but it was finally discovered that one of the snake's fangs had re-mained embedded in the boot heel and the live venom still con-tained in this fang had caused the extra fatalities. This tale had deceived Crevecoeur in the eighteenth century, and it was an ancient yarn even then.[46]

Another clearly discernible tale-type is one in which a snake strikes a hoe handle that swells from the venom until it finally bursts the metal ring or socket of the blade. The flying pieces of metal sometimes kill one or more people. We have mentioned earlier the various yarns about the man who squats on his heels and is "snake-bit" by his spurs. Yet another theme recognizable through various permutations and combinations is that of a monster snake living in a deep and remote cave. Related to this type is the bizarre yarn of a West Indian snake so huge and sluggish that it is disabled by a Negro who, at the bidding of his master, allows

[45] *Spirit*, XVI (1846), 369; XXIII (1854), 556, credited to the St. Louis *Republican*; *Spirit*, XXII (1852), 422.

[46] *Spirit*, XXII (1852), 425; James R. Masterson, "The Tale of the Living Fang," *American Literature*, XI (1939), 66–73.

himself to be sucked part-way into its mouth and then cuts the muscles of its jaw.[47]

Another of those correspondents who went from fact to fancy in their hunting epistles brightened his narrative with two tall snake tales, one about a serpent which had hypnotized two crows, the other about a powerful blacksnake that surrendered to him and became as much a pet as any dog. A yarn about a blacksnake which swallowed "two squirrels, five birds, and two young negroes" appeared in a Mississippi paper and was deliberately out-topped by the *Picayune*, which reprinted the tale and then ran a story of its own about a snake in whose stomach was found "an unfinished mile of the Nashville Railroad, three stray horses, Cioffi's trombone, three packages of tickets in the Grand Lottery, a Dutch music grinder with his barrel organ, a plan of the city of Uncle Sam, lost since 1837, and a pair of old peg bottomed boots which the owner is respectfully requested to prove and take away." The *Picayune* added, "When you can tell of a bigger snake story we'll try again." One may take for granted that the second story if not the first originated in the fertile mind of one of the "Pic's" staff writers, who thus supplies further evidence that not all tall tales came to birth as oral yarns of the unliterate "folk." [48]

Reluctantly we leave some more marvelous serpents undisturbed in their dens in order to proceed on our tour of the fantastic forest of the tall tale. A certain yarn about the otter, in addition to being a pretty fair tall story, is another example of the freedom exercised by the writers of the *Spirit* in their subject matter and treatment. A Mississippi correspondent claimed to have witnessed a fight between two otters, one of whom was an "outraged husband," the other a "gay lothario." The adulterer was then tried by an otter court whose behavior was most sober and decorous: "When-

---

[47] *Spirit*, IX (1839), 511; XVI (1846), 289, credited to the *Louisiana Chronicle*; "Notes from Cale Lie-Man's Knapsack," *Spirit*, XVI (1847), 619, by "The Middle Aged 'Un"; *Spirit*, XVII (1847), 497; II (September 7, 1833), by "Delta." See also Josiah Gregg, "Commerce of the Prairies, Part II," in Reuben Gold Thwaites (ed.), *Early Western Travels* (32 vols.; Cleveland, 1905), XX, 58.

[48] *Spirit*, XX (1850), 266; IX (1840), 524, credited to the *Picayune*. Cf. *Spirit*, XXIV (1854), 293, credited to the St. Louis *Herald*; *Spirit*, XXII (1852), 380, credited to the Hamburg (South Carolina) *Republican*.

ever a knotty question presented itself, they did not puzzle and pother with it, but without more ado walked off and took a general slide; the gravest looking member leading down and the rest following in regular order. After which, they would walk out, lick themselves dry, reform the judicial circle, and proceed with the case." The male defendant was found guilty and sentenced to be gelded, which operation was performed on the spot; the female was then tried, convicted, and punished by being ducked unmercifully. The court at last dispersed, leaving the maimed Lothario to his misery. By adding that he shot the culprit out of pity the narrator adds a final touch of realism to this preposterous yarn.[49]

Certain domestic animals, particularly barnyard fowl, also inhabited the tall world created by Porter's exchanges and correspondents. Had these same fowl encountered any of the giant insects that made dangerous this world of fantasy, a battle royal would have resulted. The *Spirit* yields at least two versions of a familiar tale-type concerning giant mosquitoes. Attacked by these huge hummers, a man crawls under an old boiler or large kettle. The gallinippers puncture the metal shell with their bills, but he clinches the bills like nails with a hammer. So of course the mosquitoes fly away, boiler and all.[50]

The mosquitoes of Arkansas in particular seem to have acquired a name among Porter's contributors; Thorpe tells a tall mosquito tale by way of build-up to the main yarn in "The Big Bear of Arkansas," and Henry P. Leland records a story of Arkansas mosquitoes which are as large as the snipe of other areas. Arkansas hornets also seem to have been impressive in their own pointed fashion. Noland once heard a tale about a Scotsman settled in the state who stirred up a nest of them. The angry *hymenoptera* "bat" everything in sight—the man's pony, his brother-in-law's pony, his wife and children, "and they bat the coulter of my plough

---

[49] "Extraordinary Otter Story," *Spirit*, XVII (1848), 537, by "Trismegistus."
[50] "A Tough Goose," *Spirit*, VI (1836), 134; "The Toughest Gamecock on Record!" *Spirit*, XVIII (1848), 116, by "Dick Dashall," reprinted in *Spirit*, XIX (1849), 496; "Random Shots from a Western Fort," by "an Officer of the U.S. Army," *Spirit*, XVIII (1848), 55. See also *Spirit*, VI (1836), 9; XXIII (1853), 1. A well-told southern version of this mosquito yarn is in Zora Neale Hurston, *Mules and Men* (Philadelphia, 1935), 149-51.

that was made of the best Juniata iron, till it swelled up and burst the beam." [51] The kinship of this tale to that of the rattler that bit the hoe handle is obvious. Finally, another of the really tall insect stories has to do with southern weevils. A ship comes into New York from a southern port, loaded with corn. The consignee hurries down to the dock, gloating over what a splendid profit he expects to make on the cargo:

"Captain—Splendid h——l! ha! ha! (in derision) why the weevils from that corn crawled all over the ship, out on the yard arms, and up to the mast heads.

"Consignee (aghast)—Weevils!

"Captain—Yes sir, and when the ship was on a wind, you could see the d——d things a floatin' out in the air half a mile to lee-ward. Fact, sir!" [52]

This story by a writer living in the North resembles most of the tales by southern contributors in its showing how an ignorant dweller in the settled regions is sold. But the story is rather atypi-cal in the implication that there is at least one thing wrong with the South as a whole, namely the prevalence of bugs in that sec-tion. The other insect stories just given are more typical in that they turn this well-known defect of all warm, wet regions into material for aggressively defensive boasting. We see this same kind of boasting in the "rich soil" stories contributed to the *Spirit;* in fact "The Big Bear of Arkansas" includes a panegyric on the fertility of Arkansas "sile" as well as the whopper about Arkansas mosquitoes. Similar bragging about his home county of Coosa, in Alabama, is done by "Col. Jeemes Hummy": "The land is so rich up there that my little boy drapped a cotton seed on the yarth last Summer, and stomped his foot on it, and it grew up so des-parate fast that he wor carried right up among the branches, and had to be tuck down with a twenty-two feet ladder." [53]

[51] "Arkansas Snipe," *Spirit*, XXV (1855), 492; "Pete's Return to the Old 'Diggings,'" *Spirit*, IX (1839), 498.
[52] "Corn and Weevils," *Spirit*, XVIII (1848), 433. The story bears a New York dateline.
[53] "Curnel Jeemes Hummy's First and Last Speech in the Alabama Legyslaytr," *Spirit*, XVII (1847), 335. Cf. *Spirit*, XVII (1847), 78.

The prolific Noland also mentioned a tale about a bee-tree so large that three men chopped away on it from Monday morning to Saturday night, "when we found that three men had commenced the same time we did, on the other side, and had been at work all the time we had; so we compromised, and each filled our wagon chuck full, with fine honey-comb, when a puff of wind blew the tree down, and ke-whop it went into the Merrimack River; and if there is any truth in me, that river was pure metheglin for six weeks and three days!" [54]

Such "rich land" stories were one incentive to western emigration. An unidentified correspondent wrote rather patronizingly of some would-be settlers:

"Some were coming west because their children multiplied faster than their means of support, and Uncle Jonathan had 'writ' to 'un' that 'pumkins' grew so big out west that they made a stable for the cow out of one half, and fed her through the winter on the other half, and the only difficulty in raising garden 'sarce' was, that it grew so long that they pulled them through on the other side—and that the ground itself was so fat, that it would do very well to grease wagons and make candles, and on a pinch, it made tolerable good gravies." [55]

This writer, whatever his locality, does not sound like a sectional-minded boaster but like a man who has been somewhat disillusioned with the frontier as he actually found it.

But we are straying off the tracks of strange and unnatural animals. In contrast to the specimens we have observed so far, which are bona fide species with their actual traits exaggerated in degree though rarely in kind, we must now consider such original and completely fantastic species as the Guyascutus, which has a strength so great that he can never be kept in any menagerie. "As he is covered all over with scales, which I found by actual measurement to be a foot in thickness, he cannot be killed with a rifle, unless one can shoot him in the middle of the left fore foot, where there is a soft place leading up through the leg to his heart." This

[54] *Spirit*, XXII (1853), 591.
[55] "Reasons for Going West," *Spirit*, VII (1837), 182.

creature also carries a bag for his prey which, some claim, is made of skin. Others swear that it is made of vulcanized India rubber. A creature with a similar name, the Guyasticutus, is the key object in a swindle worked by some traveling showmen. They advertise this beast and entice a large crowd of paying spectators into the tent, then set up a hue and cry that this ferocious animal is on the loose. The crowd pours out of the tent in panic and by the time they have recovered their wits enough to call at the booth for their money the scoundrels have absconded, heading toward the next town and the next crop of victims.[56]

One should also try to catch a glimpse of the Haggletopelter, a marvelous beast resembling the Side Hill Gouger in that it has two short legs on one side and two long on the other. The Haggletopelter is thus built especially for running around side hills. A hunter finally bagged one by heading it off and forcing it to run the other way; whereupon it rolled over and over, helpless. Then there is the Wangdoodle, a sad creature, subject of an illiterate sermonizer whose oft-repeated refrain is, "And they shall gnaw a file, and flee unto the mountains of Hepsidam, where the lion roareth and the wangdoodle mourneth for his first born." [57]

So much for stories of fantastic animals. The writer of this study cannot help believing that most of the yarns about them found in the *Spirit* are "literary" productions, that is, pieces originally written for publication, not told for word-of-mouth circulation. One reason for this opinion is the fact that such unnatural natural history is an old literary tradition dating back to and before John Lyly's *Euphues* and *Euphues and His England*. Another reason is the comparative lateness of all these yarns in the *Spirit* (the earliest of those cited is dated January 4, 1851). A third reason is that most of them appeared after John Phoenix' hoax

[56] "Forest Scenes and Sketches, Adventure with a Guyascutus," by "A. Strecher, U.S.A.," *Spirit*, XXVII (1857), 278; "The Guyasticutus," *Spirit*, XX (1851), 548, credited to Mayne Read [Reid], "War Life." Cf. Botkin (ed.), *A Treasury of American Folklore*, 638–50.

[57] *Spirit*, XXVI (1856), 392; "The American Wangdoodle," bylined "Otto Ernest Fungsbrieton," *Spirit*, XXVIII (1858), 458, published also, in part, in Samuel P. Avery (ed.), *The Harp of a Thousand Strings* (New York, 1858), 224–26, as "Where the Lion Roareth and the Wang-Doodle Mourneth." This tale has been ascribed to William P. Brannan.

about the fossil Guyascutus and Prock, and may well have been influenced by that tale. The broad exaggeration in all these tales, however, certainly reflects the spirit of the frontier.

As we edge cautiously through the forest of realistic fantasy, stepping softly for fear of the Guyascutus and keeping a sharp eye out for the Haggletopelter, we are likely to suffer from a different aspect of this realm, namely the weather. Fantastically cold, hot, or dry weather as discussed in the *Spirit* seems to have been the monopoly of no single locality. One report alleges that in Salt River, Missouri, the weather has been so cold that all the possums had their tails frozen off. In another contribution an old sea captain is made to state, "Why, when I was off the coast last year, I had my thermometer hung up on a nail in the cabin, and it was so almighty cold one night, it broke the nail off!" Another story of unnatural cold at sea came from a ship in San Francisco Bay. A naval officer aboard the vessel enlivened a long and rambling factual epistle by telling how a sailor claimed he'd "got so fur to ther southard, that d——n me if the compass didn't freeze stiff, an' pinted right straight south all the time." [58]

A pair of tall ones about dry weather may have come from the supposedly tame and prosaic East. Two old farmers are discussing the great drought of 1825. One says, "I drove my brindle heifer round the pasture, round and round . . . fifty times before I could find water enough to wet her nose and then before we got near it, a large bull-frog sizzled it all up at a swallow." The other farmer replies that that was nothing to the dry times in the western part of New York. "Why, I remember as if twas yesterday, that I used to have to drive my cattle forty or fifty miles for water, and ford two rivers into the bargain, and then found none, positively Sir! Oh, it was the mercifullest time for no water!" [59] We might easily have placed this last yarn in the category of "let-down" or less-than-to-be-expected stories.

[58] *Spirit*, VI (1836), 99, credited to the *Evening Star;* "Scene from an 'Unwritten' Drama," *Spirit*, VI (1836), 1; "Letters from California," *Spirit*, XVII (1848), 603.

[59] "Positively! Sir!" *Spirit*, VI (1836), 68. See "Letter from 'N. of Arkansas' [Noland]," *Spirit*, XX (1850), 385, about a summer in which a snow fell in August. The sun then came out so hot that it cooked a brown crust on the snow.

VII

From the world of nature gone berserk in fantasy it is only a step into the world of the supernatural. The *Spirit* was concerned primarily with the things—mainly the sport and humor—of this world, and the category of stories dealing with the supernatural is small. Yet those few stories are nearly all well-developed narratives of some length. Three are ghost tales; one of which is ironically entitled "A Fish Story" and concerns two fishermen who hook a porpoise but lose him after a wild fight. The next year a "Devil Fish" drags the same pair off to sea in their skiff. They never return, but the old Negroes of the vicinity say they often see the ghosts of two fishermen in a phantom canoe on stormy nights. Another tale likewise concerns a phantom boatman. The third ghost tale seems full of Old World folk motifs. A stage driver tells how he once picked up a passenger who had only one eye, located in the middle of his forehead. The passenger suddenly whisked him through the air to a strange island on which a fire burns continuously. The one-eyed personage orders the stage driver to enter the fire and procure a jug therein; he declares that this fire will burn spirits like himself but will not harm human flesh. The stage driver enters the fire and gets three buttons, each of which will make a wish come true. He wishes himself at home —and surprises his wife with her illicit lover. He wishes the lover in Halifax, then—rather foolishly—offers the third button to his wife, who promptly wishes him dead. As the skeletons in the realm of the dead lay their bony hands upon him he wakes up and finds it is all a dream.[60]

The one-eyed spirit (who resembles the Cyclops), the island, the enchanted fire, the three magic wish-buttons, and the dream motif may recall the lore of medieval Europe, but the sardonic humor of this story is certainly not un-American. The pervasive humor of American and particularly of backwoods lore in the *Spirit* may be one reason why most of the yarns about supernatural

[60] "A Fish Story," by "J. A. Stuart, Esq., late Editor of the Charleston Mercury," *Spirit*, XVI (1846), 342; "The Haunted Bayou," *Spirit*, XVII (1847), 255; "The One-Eyed Man," *Spirit*, XVII (1847), 240–41, credited to the Cincinnati *News*.

beings have to do with the Devil or one of his incarnations. The Devil seems by his very nature to offer more possibilities for humor, especially of the sardonic variety, than other kinds of supernatural being (Mephistopheles, in Goethe's *Faust,* is often and perhaps essentially a comic character). In another category we have reviewed the story of Cut Legs, the farmer who outsmarted the Devil himself. A tale of roughly the same type features a doughty backwoodsman who offers the Evil One a pipe of tobacco—only he fills the Devil's pipe with gunpowder. The Devil merely says, "D——n strong backy, Morgan," but he has lost face and molests this mortal no further.

In one of the best of all the yarns buried in the *Spirit* the Devil appears to the protagonist as a fox. The contributor begins by telling how he and his friends were driven ashore by a storm while duck hunting off Long Island (the devil tales, like the weather tales in the *Spirit,* are not confined to the South and Southwest). In other words, this story commences as a factual hunting epistle. The frustrated duck hunters put up at the habitation of Uncle Jimmy, who entertains them with a tale: "I heered it from Garrit Hawkins, down to Spronk, who said he had it stret from Squire Randall, over to Shinnecock Pint, who said it happened to his grandfather's unkill, so he'd ought to know . . . . Now boys, you must spose as how I'm Unkil Jake, and he's a tellin' the story."

Uncle Jake, it seems, is a six-foot, seven-inch giant whom the Indians call "Catawampow"—Shinnecock for thunder-cloud. He also has a seven-foot beard, "but that must a bin airly in the morning, afore he'd trimmed it." Anyhow, one day in front of his home Jake encounters the biggest old red fox he'd ever laid eyes on. The fox could talk too. " 'Look a here, Jakey,' sez he, 'I'm that ere chap you run so tether day, when you had that ere haound 'long . . . so I cum out airly this mornin' to gin ye a fair chance without the dog.' " After a bit of terse, rapid-fire dialogue they shake on the bargain, and the race—or chase—is on. They run for awhile and then sit down together for a breathing spell. Jake gives the fox a drink of his whisky but the fox finds it too strong:

" 'D——n your whiskey!' sez he, hoppin round like a hen with her head cut off.

" 'Who larned you to cuss?' sez I.

" 'The devil,' sez he.

" 'D'ye know him?' sez I.

" 'Like a book,' sez he.

" 'Then step your puttiest,' sez I; and with that I ups and arter 'im like mad."

After another wild chase the fox takes to the water. The two swim clear across Long Island Sound and into New Haven Harbor. In the harbor a steamboat confuses the fox; he circles back and is caught and knifed in the stomach by his pursuer. Whereupon "He guv a roarin screech, kicked his hind legs into the air, and then duv like a flash. That was the last I ever see of that ere old red." Jake paddles ashore, flops down, and sleeps for six weeks. Awakening at last, he returns to where he had left his horses, wagon, and dog. The animals are dead; the horses' bones bleached white, and their tails are "jest whar they'd whisked off the last fly!" "Then thar was th' old hound's bones too, jest as I'd left 'im, with the yowl a comin out of his jaws that he'd sot up when I'd told 'im to stay to hum. They hadn't *none* on 'em dared to stir!" [61]

Once more we have a sustained narrative in which the vividly concrete and factual merge with the tall and the main incident is supported by a number of definitely fanciful details that are not, however, quite so tall. The tale is also an example of the boxlike structure, of dialect tale within a "straight" framework. It differs from several which we have considered in that there is no initial attempt to lull the reader once the main narrative has begun—the fact that the fox can speak announces at once that this yarn is a fanciful one, and the reader must accept it as such if at all. Then, too, we are offered a second climax, as it were, in the additional tall details which are supplied only after the main part of the story, the race with the fox, is over and done with. The unidentified writer also shows unusual aptness in rendering vigorous, sparkling dialogue.

Another tale hums with overtones of *Faust*, of Irving's "The Devil and Tom Walker," and of Chaucer's "The Friar's Tale,"

[61] "Uncle Jimmy's Story," by "The Broker," *Spirit*, XVIII (1848), 205–206.

and prefigures Benét's "The Devil and Daniel Webster." In this contribution the Evil One claims the fulfillment of a ten-year contract with a surly fisherman and suddenly sinks into the ground with him while two horrified neighbors look and listen. Finally Matt Field, he of the "Far West" hoax, did a satirical piece in which the Devil is represented as a Quaker, "buttoned up tight in a drab coat with pearl buttons, a right handsome affair, and he had a broad-brimmed hat of the same color on his head." Some suspense is generated when the Devil gambles with an angel, and a bit of "sour note" humor is induced when the angel beats Satan's three sixes (the highest total obtainable with three dice) by throwing "Two sixes and a seven!" The biter has been bitten, the Devil cheated again at his own game, and by a symbol of piety too! [62]

VIII

A properly balanced feast of material drawn from the *Spirit* must include some strong English ale in the form of tall stories from the not-so-tight little isle. A small but significant class of yarns were clipped from the British papers by Porter's busy scissors. England, like America, had its yarn-spinning travelers and swaggering bullies from wilder regions; even polite fiction reflected these bits of color in the gray, amorphous mass of Victorian culture. In Mrs. Gaskell's *Cranford*, Mr. Peter assured the Honorable Mrs. Jamieson that in the high Himalayas he had fired one day at a flying creature and unfortunately brought down a cherub. Then there was Major Goliah O'Grady Gahagan, Thackeray's blustering guardsman from India who swore in the best frontier manner that "I have been in more pitched battles, led more forlorn hopes, had more success among the fair sex, drunk harder, read more, and been a handsomer man than any officer now serving her Majesty." Thus it is not surprising that American tall tales found a ready reception in Britain, and some competition.

An item in the *Spirit* which is attributed to a "London Paper" runs: "Our transatlantic brethren are famous for their ingenuity.

---

[62] "A Legend of Glen Cove," *Spirit*, XV (1845), 69–70, by "Frank Elliott"; "The Three Sixes—a Pilot's Dream," by "Phazma." [M. C. Field], *Spirit*, XV (1845), 420, credited to the St. Louis *Reveille*.

But we think we can cope with them in anything, only we don't trumpet forth our abilities as they do. There is at present at Cockerham a tailor, who is so quick at his trade, that he has constantly beside him a bowl of water to cool his needle." A column entitled "Yankeeisms," extracted from *Bell's Life in London*—the original model of the *Spirit*—includes no less than four tall tales. The best told of these concerns an absent-minded carpenter who fastened his own legs to a decaying chair and made a new pair for himself, "never awaking to a sense of his error until the crazy piece of furniture sneezed, opened the door, and walked quietly and deliberately out of the room." A wonderful hunt tale turns up in a story about a fantastic, Merlinesque character who is right out of Celtic folklore. In the vehicle of the *Spirit* such tales circulated throughout the United States and the territories, particularly in the West and South. Moreover, lots of other tall tales told by Brother Jonathan were brought back to John Bull by his wandering sons and daughters.[63]

These tales of foreign nurture circulated among the sensitive American book-buying class, which read these English books on America chiefly to criticize and refute—but did read them. Doubly corrupted by being Anglicized and printed, these yarns were fed back all the way to the frontier by the *Spirit* and other agencies, and not only induced the self-conscious folk of the backlands to caricature themselves in self-defense but surely influenced the supposedly "pure" oral tales still springing into being on riverboats, in taprooms, and around buffalo-chip fires. Much study of this depurifying "feed-back" process is yet needed.

One aim of this chapter has been to show that the ingredients of the tall tales in the *Spirit* are diffused and intermingled, and may be defined only in terms which allow the greatest flexibility. In addition, when referring to the *Spirit*, one can hardly speak of a "pure" or oral tale; the mere fact of these tales being circulated in

---

[63] "Jonathan Outdone," *Spirit*, VIII (1838), 304; *Spirit*, VIII (1838), 283; "A Comic Story," *Spirit*, XXI (1851), 20, credited to *Notes and Queries*. See also Charles Dickens, *Martin Chuzzlewit*, especially Chapters XVII, XXI, and XXXIII; Marryat, *Diary in America*, I, 74, 233; *id.*, *Diary in America. Part Second*, II, 131–33; Martineau, *Society in America*, II, 210; Featherstonhaugh, *Excursion Through the Slave States*, II, 27–29, 97–98, 125–31. Relevant is Clarence Gohdes, *American Literature in Nineteenth-Century England* (New York, 1944), 71–98.

print by a sporting magazine constitutes a set of conditioning factors imposed between the present-day reader and the tales as told in their natural habitat. Some of these tales may not have arisen out of the mouths of backwoodsmen at all; they may have received their being as newspaper hoaxes or as imitations of authentic oral tales.

We have also attempted to strengthen the hypothesis that a number of the tall tales as well as the realistic pieces in the *Spirit* are in large part functional dependencies of the literate, well-to-do southerner's attitude toward the poor white, whom he patronized as an entertainer of infinite diversity and humor, but to whom he accorded a social status far below that of his own class. Much of the humor of these tales was derived by these gentleman writers and their journalistic allies from the ignorance, vice, poverty, and low cunning of the squatter class—in short, from the very traits that most clearly differentiated the poor whites from the master class, in the eyes of the latter. Since the *Spirit*, however, was a sporting magazine, a large category of tall tales had to do primarily with animals—objects of the hunt—and other aspects of unnatural natural history. These tales do not necessarily reveal this upper-class attitude.

Again, the tall tales, like the realistic pieces, illustrate the growth of the factual sporting epistle into something beyond itself. Finally, the best of the tall stories maintain an atmosphere of realism and an air of scrupulous accuracy in supporting narratives which are in essence thoroughly fantastic. Utterly uncontrolled fantasy was not the rule among the really accomplished yarn-spinners; the best tellers and writers of tales seem to have developed and practiced a discipline which had its own laws. By the middle of the 1840's at least, the combined efforts of tall-tale tellers and writers had developed in the *Spirit* and in a few regional newspapers a form of printed narrative as distinctive as the short story, which Poe was propagating about the same time in more genteel periodicals.

CHAPTER SEVEN

Disintegration

I

IN 1843 Porter's optimistic temperament and bad business judgment, revealed in his enthusiastic expenditures on several side projects, led him to the verge of bankruptcy and brought John Richards, a wholesale printer, into the proprietorship of the *Spirit*. Porter apparently remained the chief architect of editorial policy; at least, the magazine shows no appreciable change after Richards ousted him from the business and printing departments. Up to 1856 one finds no reliable indications of any difficulty in connection with circulation or finances, apart from an editorial assertion in 1855 that "Gentlemen connected with the Turf, and admirers of Field and Rural Sports generally, . . . are proverbially liberal, ... it is believed that they have too much pride to suffer a journal devoted to them and their amusements to languish for want of that liberality . . ." This bit of class-conscious puffery is a little too emphatic to reflect complete confidence.[1]

"The Editor's Annual Salutatory," in February of that year, contained the announcement that "In consequence of the Immense Outlay expended on its [the *Spirit*'s] production, the entire Free List is strictly suspended, with the exception of the public press." And yet the *Spirit* apparently flourished for another four years and lasted one more. Moreover, Porter had put his heart and mind into the building of the magazine, which was the realization of an ideal of many years' standing. In view of all this, we may well feel as surprised as his brother-in-law, Francis Brinley, was when in the

[1] *Spirit*, XXV (1855), 1. Several expensive mezzotint engravings in this issue may have indicated either a satisfactory circulation or an attempt to boost a falling one by offering added inducements to present and prospective subscribers.

late summer of 1856 Porter abruptly quitted the *Spirit of the Times* and his name appeared on the masthead of a new weekly publication entitled *Porter's Spirit of the Times*. Brinley declared, "Up to this time no intimation had fallen from him that he could be induced to sever his connection with it [the old *Spirit*], yet most unexpectedly to his friends, on the 26th of September he permitted his name to be associated with the publication of another weekly Sporting Journal." Strangely enough too, his long-standing employees and friends, Edward E. Jones and Dick Hays, stayed with the older magazine.[2]

Data as to any specific reason for Porter's sudden break with Richards and the *Spirit* (which we shall hereafter refer to as the old *Spirit*) are lacking. The only clues found so far suggest merely that Porter was losing some of the enthusiasm and interest which had sustained him for so long. A possible cause of this loss were the deaths, one by one, of his last three living brothers, George, Thomas Olcott, and Frank, in 1849, 1852, and 1855 respectively. Frank Porter died in February, 1855, and with his death William became the sole surviving male member of the Porter family. Brinley testifies as to the great affection the Porter brothers had had for each other and asserts that, while William still showed "flashes of humor," "from the day of the 'Doctor's' [Thomas Olcott Porter's] death, he was unlike his former self; even his interest in the 'Old Spirit' was much diminished."

Brinley also adds, significantly, that by 1855 William suffered considerably from the gout. This raises the possibility that Porter had suffered a physical decline as a result of intemperance or at least high living. This conjecture is supported by a tight-lipped comment of the theoretically bone-dry Greeley or an associate concerning Uncle Horace's old employer: "He was a free liver, and his excesses in this regard probably hastened his death." A New York doctor remarked after Porter's death that "He was, at one time, the most agreeable companion I ever met with." Did he, then, grow less agreeable as time went on? His old friend, "Acorn"

[2] *Spirit*, XXVI (1856), 1; Brinley, *Life of William T. Porter*, 266. Brinley is incorrect as to the date of the first issue of *Porter's Spirit*, which appeared on September 6, not September 26.

(James Oakes, a Boston journalist), wrote that "He, it is true, had his weaknesses, but they were those that did injustice to himself only—no wrong to others." All right, Porter liked his bottle. But the factual knots are wanting with which to tie this to his breaking camp and throwing in with a new outfit.[3]

One of course suspects that this switch may have been the result of a sharp difference with Richards over policy. But suspicion without evidence is a wagon with only one wheel. Whatever his reasons, Porter did make the break and went into an editorial partnership with George Wilkes, co-founder and editor of the *National Police Gazette.* Wilkes seems to have been a dynamic and rather unscrupulous personality. He had edited the *Flash,* the *Whip,* and the *Subterranean,* all "ephemeral organs of the city's political and sporting underworld." He had attacked gangsters and corrupt police officials so vigorously that he had been arrested six times and shot at twice, and even served a thirty-day sentence in the Tombs—from which experience he wrote a pamphlet exposing the miserable conditions in that institution. One writer claims that this sheet helped to oust the incumbent mayor in the next election. In 1845 Wilkes, with Enoch Camp, a lawyer, founded the *Police Gazette.* "During Wilkes' regime it was a robust, rowdy scandal sheet, objectionable to vicious and decent men alike." He and Camp sold that journal in 1857.

In the same year that he helped to found the *Police Gazette* Wilkes showed an interest in the West by writing a short *History of Oregon, Geographical and Political,* which was inaccurate and misleading, but in which he may have been the first writer to advocate a national railroad from the Atlantic to the Pacific. Four years later he actually went out West, accompanying the colorful ex-saloon keeper and later Senator David Colbreth Broderick to California. He returned to the East shortly before he went into partnership with Porter. Despite his western experience Wilkes

[3] Obituary of William T. Porter, New York *Daily Tribune* (July 20, 1858), 7; cf. Greeley's unheaded jingle in the *Lantern,* I (July 1, 1852), 258. See also "Reminiscences of the 'Spirit' Family," *Spirit,* XXIX (1859), 27–28, by "Nicholas Spicer," [Dr. Alban S. Payne of New York City]. Cf. the same gentleman as quoted in Pond, *Life and Adventures of Ned Buntline,* 39; and see "William T. Porter," by "Acorn," *Spirit,* XXVIII (1858), 289.

seems to have written nothing for the new magazine that could be called frontier in style or in theme, although he did compose a few sentimental pieces. Sports and politics seem to have been his main interests. Perhaps his activities concerning the turf were what drew Porter and Wilkes together—Wilkes, it seems, did his bit for progress by introducing pari-mutuel betting into the United States.[4]

Porter's Spirit of the Times was a sixteen-page tabloid which at first showed no great difference in appearance and content from the old *Spirit*. Porter was to handle all matters relating to the sporting and editorial departments and Wilkes was to take care of the business office, according to the masthead. The editors emphasized that the new magazine was really the old, somewhat improved and under a different name, and would pursue the same policy. Moreover, from the first issue, the names of a number of the most frequent correspondents of the old *Spirit* crop up in the new journal. "N. of Arkansas" (Noland), "Frank Forester" (Henry William Herbert), "Acorn" (James Oakes), "Azul," "Hal, a Dacotah" (Henry Hastings Sibley), "Jeems Pipes" (Stephen C. Massett), and "H. P. L." (Henry P. Leland) are a few of the familiar pseudonyms. Some of the most interesting sketches of Leland in particular appeared in *Porter's Spirit*.[5] In addition, the the new periodical printed pieces by several new correspondents.

Turf news abounds in the tabloid-size pages, and hunting and fishing items are collected in a department headed "Fur, Fin, and Feather." Most important, a glance at the reference notes to chapters Four, Five, and Six of this study will reveal that a fair sprinkling of humorous, realistic and tall-tale contributions appeared in *Porter's Spirit*, especially in 1856 and 1857.

As to circulation, the editors later claimed that the new journal had begun with twelve thousand purchasers, and one statement mentions that the paper had reached forty thousand as early as the

---

[4] Clarence B. Bagley, "George Wilkes," *Washington Historical Quarterly*, V (January, 1914), 3–11; Walter Davenport, "The Nickel Shocker," *Collier's*, LXXXI (March 10, 1928), 26–27, 28–40; George Wilkes, "The Dying Minstrel," *Porter's Spirit*, V (1858), 242. The *Dictionary of American Biography* supplies basic information on the lives of Wilkes and Broderick.

[5] Editorial, *Porter's Spirit*, I (1856), 8, 10. Samples of Leland's writing in *Porter's Spirit* are "Stick to Your Old Friends," I (1856), 3–4; "That Cock-Fight at Sand Patch," I (1856), 39; "A Thundering Coon-Hunt," I (1856), 106.

eighth issue. Such claims, of course, must be regarded with a squint.[6]

Noland, writing one of his last Pete Whetstone letters, pledged a toast to the "new 'Spirit.' " As time wore on, however, certain of the other correspondents who, like Noland, had also remained loyal to the old *Spirit* showed little enthusiasm for the new periodical. "Falconer" expressed his disgust with a certain article in *Porter's Spirit,* declaring, "One thing is to my mind most positive—Mr. Porter never penned that article; his antecedents are those of a gentleman." [7] Another correspondent, "Jonathan Oldbuck," vented his dissatisfaction with *Porter's Spirit* and said:

"At the time of Mr. Porter's leaving the old 'Spirit' (for what reason I never asked, and really did not care to know), he addressed me personally, in common, I suppose, with the multitude of his friends and personal acquaintances throughout the country, and asked for such co-operation as I could give to aid in the establishment of 'Porter's Spirit' on a 'safe and proper basis.' Of course this request was cheerfully complied with, and the more willingly as I then supposed that the old 'Spirit' was to be embodied in the new, and I sent on the names of the first list of subscribers which the new paper had from this region." [8]

The writer then accuses *Porter's Spirit* of arrogance and petty jealousy, and expresses his belief that "Mr. Porter was but a nominal man in the concern." He further adds that as a sporting paper the new *Spirit* is "a splendid failure" and calls it more of a "Police Gazette." His final charge is that its news coverage is poor and that it includes too many "sectionalisms and sectional political questions."

"Jonathan Oldbuck" was writing in September, 1858. Porter had died on the eighteenth of the previous month. But for most of that year the Tall Son of York had ceased to exercise any func-

---

[6] *Porter's Spirit,* V (1858), 9; I (1856), 128; Brinley, *Life of William T. Porter,* 266.

[7] "Peter [*sic*] Whetstone's Reception of the Spirit," *Porter's Spirit,* I (1856), 140; "Falconer 'Wrathy,' " *Spirit,* XXVII (1858), 594.

[8] *Spirit,* XXVIII (1858), 361.

tions for the magazine bearing his name, except to write an occasional article—usually the obituary of one of his old friends among the gentlemen of the turf. In fact, his main interest just before his final illness seems to have been the preparation of a biography of another deceased friend, Henry William Herbert.[9]

Consequently, the control of editorial policy of *Porter's Spirit* fell more and more under the hand of Wilkes. In 1858 the names of the older correspondents gradually disappear from its pages, and although they are replaced by new names, articles from the back country of a humorous, realistic, or tall nature dwindle greatly in number. One is not surprised at the verdict of George Harvey Genzmer in the *Dictionary of American Biography* that, "Though the *Spirit* remained primarily a sporting paper, it soon began to reflect its owner's relish for politics, and its political articles were influential." Porter's day, the day of the gentleman, was done, and in the rise of Wilkes is symbolized the final triumph of a new type, a type which in the person of James Gordon Bennett and men like him had risen in the 1830's simultaneously with the *Spirit*—the parvenu yellow journalist.

In short, *Porter's Spirit* ceases to interest us after 1858, except for a legal squabble between Wilkes and a rival editor over the use of Porter's name. This contest reveals the editorial prestige acquired by the Tall Son of York over thirty years. One Abraham C. Dayton had purchased a share of *Porter's Spirit,* or claimed that he had, and in September, 1859, Wilkes broke with the concern and announced his intention of starting a new paper under the name already in use, *Porter's Spirit of the Times.* Dayton secured a court injunction restraining Wilkes from using the name of Porter on any publication whatsoever, whereupon Wilkes commenced publication, on September 10, 1859, of a journal entitled *Wilkes' Spirit of the Times,* a political and sporting weekly which survived, despite changes of management, until 1902. Under Dayton and perhaps other editors *Porter's Spirit of the Times* survived until

[9] Brinley, *Life of William T. Porter,* 266–67; obituary of Porter, New York *Times* (July 20, 1858), 4, also quoted in *The Knickerbocker* LII (September, 1858), 310–11. One of the obituary notices done by Porter is "The Late Col. Wade Hampton," *Porter's Spirit,* IV (1858), 5.

August, 1861. Thus for twenty-one months there were three "Spirits" on the stands—a confusing situation.[10]

All of these events took place in a context of increasing sectional tension as North and South drifted rapidly apart. Wilkes survived as a magazine editor by abandoning the lukewarm, pro-southern attitude of William T. Porter and taking a firm, vocal pro-northern stand more in accord with his personal antislavery views. Wilkes's northern sympathies tended to exclude any interest in the southern back country and to alienate contributors from that region. How did the old *Spirit* fare?

II

When Porter "seceded" from the old *Spirit,* he was immediately replaced as editor by Edward E. Jones, who had worked for the paper since 1846 and perhaps done much of the editorial work for several years. At first no special difference is noticeable between the magazine under Richards and Porter and that under Richards and Jones, whom another member of the "press gang" found a "genial Southern gentleman of the old school" and "an entertaining and informing writer on turf topics." A year after Porter had left, the old *Spirit* derided the claim of Wilkes and Porter that the latter pair had captured nearly all the correspondents of the older journal: "How much truth there was in this last assertion our readers know well." [11] And in fact several prolific sporting correspondents, such as "Nemo," "Thomas the Rhymer" (Thomas Dunn English), "Guillermo," and "Bob" remain steady contributors, while a few of those who began to contribute to *Porter's Spirit* also continue to have letters or articles printed by the rival, "parent" magazine. These players on both sides of the fence include Noland, "Observer," "Acorn" (James Oakes), "H. P. L." (Henry P. Leland), "A Young Turfman," and the English correspondent "Carl Ben-

[10] "Abraham C. Dayton Against George Wilkes," *Spirit,* XXIX (1859), 372; Carvel Collins, "The *Spirit of the Times,*" *Papers of the Bibliographical Society of America,* XL (Second Quarter, 1946), 164–68.

[11] *Spirit,* XXIX (1859), 1; Fred E. Pond in Poore, *Biographical Sketch of John Stuart Skinner,* 2–3; "To Our Correspondents, Subscribers, and Exchanges," *Spirit,* XXVII (1857), 361.

son." Through the efforts of these and other contributors factual epistles on hunting and fishing continue to pour in, as they had poured for awhile into *Porter's Spirit*.

Nonetheless, a list of regular correspondents printed early in February, 1857, indicates a definite decline in the coverage of the South and West by the old *Spirit*. This list reveals that New York is far and away the best-covered state, having eighteen correspondents as compared with nine from Kentucky, which has the next largest number. Six of the southern states have several correspondents apiece; Louisiana leads the deep South with seven, but six of these are in New Orleans. And Mississippi and Arkansas, either of which, apart from Louisiana, contributed more local color material perhaps than any other state when Porter edited the *Spirit*, are represented collectively by only one correspondent under the new dispensation. This contributor, "A Young Turfman," from Natchez, seldom tried at any time to write humor or character sketches but usually confined himself to unimaginative sporting commentary. North Carolina, once well represented in Porter's columns, is now without a steady correspondent. So is Florida, while South Carolina and Texas have only one each. Clearly the loss of Porter with his friends and contacts was a heavy one.[12]

True, a certain number of the tales and sketches analyzed or cited in this study appeared in the *Spirit* after Porter had left the magazine. But a goodly percentage of these were of the literary variety, such as the writings of George Derby and Frederick Swartwout Cozzens, whose *Sparrowgrass Papers* (1855) played its part, as Professor Pattee has said, in making native American humor respectable during the feminine fifties. Further, much of the local color and humor that still found its way into the magazine did so by way of extracts from books that had already appeared, such as H. E. Taliaferro's *Fisher's River (North Carolina) Scenes and Characters*, and Samuel Adams Hammett's *Piney Woods Tavern*—books that had appeared without the aid of prepublication in the *Spirit* because the *Spirit* itself had helped to arouse

[12] "The Editor's Remarks," *Spirit*, XXVII (1857), 1. Cf. *Spirit*, XXIX (1859), 1.

enough interest in back-country life and lore that backwoods authors found their own outlets without going to the *Spirit* office, as Hooper and Thorpe had found it useful to do in the old days.

Yet it would be wrong to assume that original contributions of backwoods humor and realism died out of the old *Spirit* while the magazine lasted. Even in the final two years we find a number of such articles, sometimes by new and talented correspondents such as "Hazel Green, Esq." and "Spinning Bait." Meanwhile the editors are still extracting some pretty fair yarns from local newspapers.[13] One cannot say that the loss of Porter was a fatal blow to the magazine. A more likely hypothesis is that the national rupture of civil war killed this northern magazine—a magazine that favored the southern gentry and strove to reconcile the well-to-do sporting elements of both North and South. To sharpen this thesis still more, we may observe that the *Spirit* had consciously or unconsciously identified itself with the southern agrarian aristocracy throughout the thirty-year career of the journal. When that class found itself overshadowed by the rising industrial power of the North and eventually became desperate, the cause of the *Spirit* likewise became desperate. In fact, in its last days the *Spirit* was pursuing on a nonpolitical level a course of conservatism and reconciliation parallel to that followed during the latter part of his life by John C. Calhoun and during the fifties by the many southern moderates who tried to cool the fire-eaters.

This policy may be seen in some of the statements of the editors and proprietors after the death of John Richards, the "Governor," in January, 1859. Richards was apparently succeeded as proprietor by a three-way partnership of Jones, Thorpe, and Hays.[14] Near

[13] E. g., [Thomas Dunn English]; "The Fight at Perry's Mill," *Spirit*, XXVIII (1858), 481–82; "Aunt Judy's Recollections of Old Times in Kentucky," by "Hazel Green, Esq.," *Spirit*, XXIX (1859), 196; "How Sam Collins Got Broke Playing Agin a Hand Organ," *Spirit*, XXX (1860), 21, credited to the Montgomery *Mail*; "Quarter Racing in Copiah," by "Spinning Bait," *Spirit*, XXX (1860), 491; "Bear Hunt in Louisiana," *Spirit*, XXX (1860), 396; "Old Ben Winnie, of Arkansas," *Spirit*, XXXI (1861), 49, by "Persimmon, Jr."

[14] "Death of John Richards, Esq.," *Spirit*, XXVIII (1859), 606; "A New Volume of the 'Spirit,'" *Spirit*, XXIX (1859), 1; "The Late John Richards, Esq.," *Spirit*, XXIX (1859), 2. The masthead of the *Spirit*, beginning with Volume XXIX (1859), reads "Jones, Thorpe and Hays, Proprietors," and the first editorial of the new volume is signed "Edward E. Jones" and "Richard Hays."

the end of 1859 an angry editorial attacked northern newspaper-men and clergymen for sneering at "Southern strength and brav-ery" and scored "the determination of the 'agitators' to leave noth-ing untried that will engender ill feelings between the North and the South." The paper also printed a long attack on Dion Bouci-cault's play *The Octoroon*, calling it "A Disgrace to the North, a Libel on the South." At the opening of what was to be the last volume, the editors declared that "the public men of the South have from the beginning of our national existence had a pre-ponderating influence," and affirmed that the reason lay in the ad-diction of the southerners to such "manly sports" as the chase and the turf. The same editorial boasted that the *Spirit* had for years chronicled what was going on "among the refined and wealthy in the way of amusement," and "for the last twenty years it has been the organ of what may be justly termed the true aristocracy of the country." The editors also asserted that in giving detailed news of the turf and field, ". . . we have insensibly yet positively built up a public opinion that is fast becoming reformatory in its effects, and doing more to create healthy bodies, and consequently clear and comprehensive minds, than all the mistaken, but no doubt honest moralists, in our midst." [15] From these statements emerge two antagonistic poles, the impartial avoidance of the main political question of the time and sympathy with the southern upper class. This two-horned dilemma was the same one that Porter had at-tempted to solve for twenty-five years.

In spite of, or perhaps because of, its attempt to hold its pro-southern readers, the *Spirit* began sending up veiled distress signals early in 1861. A bold statement of a plan to add four new pages to the size of the paper and to supply new type was preceded by this ominous announcement: "To accomplish our wishes, par-ticularly in the face of the present political and financial troubles which afflict the country, we reluctantly go out of our usual course, by asking those who know themselves to be indebted to us to remit, at the earliest possible opportunity, the amount by mail. Though the

[15] "Sneers at Southern Strength and Bravery," *Spirit*, XXIX (1860), 566; "The Octoroon," *Spirit*, XXIX (1859), 529; "Salutatory—XXXI Volume," *Spirit*, XXXI (1861), 1.

sums are small to individuals, the aggregate is large and important to us." A few months later a lengthy appeal was made to friends of the magazine to solicit new subscriptions. Meanwhile, however, the editors were beginning to desert the sinking ship. Hays sold out to Jones and Thorpe late in 1860. In March of the following year Thorpe announced the sale of his interest in the paper to Jones, who thus became the sole editor and proprietor. In the same issue Jones pleaded again with delinquent subscribers to pay their fees, declaring: "More than $50,000 are due us; and we need only a tithe of that amount to make us 'easy in our boots.' " He also announced that "We intend hereafter to devote much more space than formerly to the English Turf, and to the Trotting Turf." [16] And well he might, since racing in America must have been nearly at a standstill on the eve of war. The sport of the southern gentry was declining with the power of the gentry themselves, and a self-appointed organ of that sport and that class was likewise on the decline.

Fort Sumter was fired upon on April 12, 1861. The death-blow to the *Spirit* came when the government of the dismembered Union stopped mail service to its wartime enemy, the Confederate States of America. On June 22, 1861, Jones brought out the last issue of the *Spirit* with the statement that publication of the paper would have to be "suspended" for awhile—he hoped "but for a few weeks." He declared that the suspension resulted, "not from want of patronage," but because, "Business in New York is nearly dead, and money is very scarce. By order of the U.S. Government we are deprived of Mail communication with our Southern friends, thus rendering it impossible for the undersigned to do justice to them or to his advertising patrons, many of whose favors are bestowed in consequence of the extensive circulation and high character 'The Spirit' enjoys in the Confederate States." Correspondents are urged to maintain their communications and agents to proceed with their collections. The editor bravely continues, "We trust all our friends will be prepared to pay their little bills when presented,

---

[16] "To Our Friends," *Spirit*, XXX (1860), 585; "An Especial Notice!" *Spirit*, XXX (1861), 609; "Extend Our Circulation," *Spirit*, XXXI (1861), 17; *Spirit*, XXX (1860), 513; XXXI (1861), 65.

or at least a portion, that we may be enabled to square up our accounts." [17]

Jones's appeal for business as usual with "our friends" must be construed as applying in part to correspondents and agents in the country of Jefferson Davis. In other words, Jones was technically committing treason in attempting to carry on peaceful business dealings with citizens of a nation at war with his own country.

The old *Spirit,* then, became a direct as well as an indirect casualty of the Civil War. Wilkes, however, carried his paper through the storm of sectional strife by shaping its character to weather the blast; *Wilkes' Spirit of the Times* was as much a political as a sporting journal, and its politics speedily became anti-slavery politics. In contrast, the editors of the old *Spirit,* having no real choice in view of their large southern circulation, stood to their guns and struggled to maintain their self-identification with a losing agrarian aristocracy. They were finally mowed down in the field of journalism as were the sons of the Confederacy on the battlefield.

III

But as far as backwoods writing is concerned, the *Spirit* had done its job. By 1861 the popularity of southern backwoods humor was assured. Even by the early 1850's the interest in back-country humor and realism was widening. This expanding interest is demonstrated by the increased number of anthologies of this material published at home and abroad. In the forties Porter's two volumes had been the only such collections. But in 1851 came T. A. Burke's collection of backwoods humor entitled *Polly Peablossom's Wedding,* and in 1852 appeared Thomas Chandler Haliburton's three-volume *Traits of American Humour,* followed two years later by a second three-volume work under his editorship, *Americans at Home.* In the late fifties came William E. Burton's *Cyclopaedia of Wit and Humor* (1858), Samuel P. Avery's *The Harp of a Thousand Strings* (1858), which took its title from a sketch originally appearing in the *Spirit,* and the anonymous

[17] "Important Notice," *Spirit,* XXXI (1861), 305, by "E. E. Jones."

American Wit and Humor (1859).[18] All these volumes contained a goodly proportion of southern and western humor, and all had drawn considerably upon the *Spirit* or upon Porter's two pioneer collections.

Several collections of backwoods humor by individual authors who had not contributed first to the *Spirit* appeared in the fifties, along with works by such contributors as Thorpe, Hooper, Thompson, the Field brothers, Robb, Hammett, Durivage, Burnham, Sol Smith, Baldwin, Kelly, and Leland.[19] The popularity, moreover, of works of backwoods humor by individual authors was demonstrably great and was not appreciably hurt by the Civil War. Longstreet's *Georgia Scenes* was brought out in separate editions in 1860, 1884, 1894, and 1897. Thompson's *Major Jones's Courtship* was re-edited in 1872; his *Chronicles of Pineville* was still in print in 1880 and his *Major Jones's Sketches of Travel* in 1893. Baldwin's *Flush Times in Alabama and Mississippi* was re-edited in 1876. George Washington Harris may not have brought out a collection of his sketches until 1867, but in that year *Sut Lovingood* appeared and the perennial popularity of these yarns warranted a new edition in 1954.[20]

The popularity of backwoods writing during and after the Civil War raises the question, Why did the *Spirit* fail, since it published a good deal of backwoods material up to its last issues? The answer, which has been implicit in this study, is that it was the social attitude of the *Spirit*, not its literary policy, that finally broke the magazine. In order to obtain this backwoods writing as well as comprehensive coverage of the turf, Porter had to gain the confidence of planters and journalists of the slaveholding class. This he did, but both he and they were anxious to shelve political issues

[18] Cited by Masterson, *Tall Tales of Arkansaw*, 318.

[19] Among such works were Marcus Byrne, *The Life and Adventures of an Arkansas Doctor* (1851); Joseph Beckham Cobb, *Mississippi Scenes* (1851); J. R. Montesano, *Redstick, or Scenes in the South* (1856); H. E. Taliaferro, *Fisher's River (North Carolina) Scenes and Characters* (1859). The contributions of Joseph G. Baldwin to the *Spirit* have never been identified, although Walter Blair cites Porter as having stated once that Baldwin contributed. See *Native American Humor*, 85n.

[20] Brom Weber (ed.), *Sut Lovingood By George Washington Harris* (New York, 1954).

during a period when compromise with the North and a preservation of the Union on the old basis seemed possible. The burning issues of slavery and the threat of northern industrial dominance over southern agriculture appear rarely, and usually only by implication, in the humor and realism of the *Spirit*.

In short, this early realism was achieved at the cost of narrowing the themes of this type of writing. Although the North and South went to war over the issues just named, northerners could read and laugh over these southern sketches without being consciously disturbed by any conflict between their own social beliefs and those underlying these productions. Many northerners were in full agreement with the southern writers that the bottom class of whites everywhere were a set of drunken, lazy, disreputable loafers and roisterers, amusing for their humor, quaintly picturesque, and at times showing flashes of shrewdness and courage, but of no account as social philosophers or political leaders. Add a certain nostalgia for the rural way of life that was passing in the North even more rapidly than in the South, and it is not hard to see why southern backwoods literature lived on despite sectional warfare.

Porter himself had gone far beyond most pro-southern Yankees in explicitly adopting the code of the southern gentleman. His successors not only accepted this code but identified its safety with the preservation of southern rights and privileges in politics. The onset of war cut the *Spirit* off from the South and destroyed the magazine. Thus the social attitude which built the *Spirit* also broke it, and would have done so even had Jones made a last-minute switch to a pro-northern line—which he probably never once thought of doing. A gentleman has principles.

Bibliographical Note

The *Spirit of the Times* justified its title so thoroughly that almost anything written between 1830 and 1861 in or about the South and West has bearing on this periodical. Any bibliographical discussion of materials relating to Porter and his magazine must therefore be highly selective, and the works actually cited in the notes to this study represent only a portion of the relevant material examined.

Manuscript material relating to Porter and the *Spirit* is not, however, extensive. Seven of the very informative letters from Porter to Carey and Hart may be found in the New York Historical Society Library, four in the Manuscript Room of the New York Public Library, and one in the Henry Carey Baird Papers, Historical Society of Pennsylvania (although that one, of January 18, 1845, is the most interesting of all, containing, as it does, much information about the genesis of and contributors to *The Big Bear of Arkansas*). One letter to Porter from the actor Dan Marble, February 20, 1844, is also in the Henry Carey Baird Papers, and one letter to Porter from Horace Greeley, June 1, 1839, may be found in the New York Public Library.

Some of the letters of Thomas Bangs Thorpe contain information on his relations with Porter and the *Spirit*. Twenty-one of these letters are in the New York Historical Society Library; twelve are in the Henry Carey Baird Papers. One of Thorpe's letters is in the Manuscript Room of the New York Public Library, which also has the manuscript autobiographical sketch of Thorpe written for the Duyckincks' *Cyclopaedia of American Literature*.

The letters of Henry William Herbert (Frank Forester) in the Duyckinck Collection, Manuscript Room, New York Public Library, contain bits of data on Herbert's relations with Porter and his magazine. One such letter, to Evert Duyckinck, May 13, 1847, reveals Herbert's intention of starting a magazine with the help of Duyckinck and some of Porter's contributors. A copy of a letter from Augustus B. Longstreet to James B. Longacre, September 1, 1842, gives facts and figures on the active sale of *Georgia Scenes* below the Mason-Dixon line. This copy is in the possession of Professor William Charvat of Ohio State University. The whereabouts of the original is not known.

The unpublished "Carey & Hart Record Books" for 1845 and 1846, in the library of the Historical Society of Pennsylvania, furnish considerable information on the costs of publication and number of copies printed of Porter's two anthologies and of Hooper's *Some Adventures of Captain Simon Suggs.*

The main printed source for a study of the *Spirit* must, of course, be that magazine itself. Of the rare issues available in Volumes I–V (1831–1835 inclusive), the author has consulted twenty-nine, fourteen of which are in the library of the American Antiquarian Society, Worcester, Massachusetts, seven in the Rare Book Room of the New York Public Library, seven in the library of Yale University, and one in the Harvard University Library. Dates and running titles of these issues are given in Norris Yates, "The *Spirit of the Times:* Its Early History and Some of Its Contributors," *Papers of the Bibliographical Society of America,* XLVIII (Second Quarter, 1954), 117–48. Clarence S. Brigham, "Letter to the Editor," *Papers of the Bibliographical Society of America,* XLVIII (Third Quarter, 1954), 300–301, corrects and supplements the previous article by means of an early file of the *Spirit* and the *Traveller* which has just come into the possession of the American Antiquarian Society. This file includes issues of the *Spirit* from December 10, 1831, to November 7, 1832, and of the *Traveller* (which soon merged with the *Spirit*) from December 1, 1832, to September 14, 1833.

A file of the *Spirit,* VI–XXXI (February, 1836–June, 1861), is available on microfilm in the New York Public Library and has been the chief single source for this study. Partial files of Volumes VI–XXXI are accessible in a number of repositories, as indicated by Winifred Gregory (ed.), *Union List of Serials* (2d ed.; New York: H. W. Wilson, 1943). A private file of these volumes, that of Franklin J. Meine of Chicago, has recently come into the possession of the University of Illinois library.

Further bibliographical data on the magazine may be found in the *Constellation*, IV (April 20, 1833, and August 31, 1833). Aspects of Porter's editorial policy and tactics are discussed in Lawrence H. Houtchens, "The *Spirit of the Times* and A 'New Work by Boz,'" *Publications of the Modern Language Association of America*, LXVII (March, 1952), 94–100; Carvel Collins, *The American Sporting Gallery. Portraits of American Horses from 1839—Spirit of the Times—1844 With a Commentary* . . . (Cambridge, Massachusetts: Harvard University Press, 1949); *id.*, "An Extra Issue of the *Spirit of the Times*," *Papers of the Bibliographical Society of America*, XLVIII (Second Quarter, 1954), 198. Convenient bibliographical summaries that must, however, be used with caution, are those in Frank Luther Mott, *A History of American Magazines 1741–1850* (Cambridge, Massachusetts: Harvard University Press, 1939), and Robert W. Henderson, *Early American Sport; a Check-List of Books by American and Foreign Authors Published in America Prior to 1860, Including Sporting Songs* (2d ed.; New York: A. S. Barnes, 1953). Data on *Porter's Spirit of the Times* and *Wilkes' Spirit of the Times* may be found in Carvel Collins, "The *Spirit of the Times*," *Papers of the Bibliographical Society of America*, XL (Second Quarter, 1946), 164–68, *id.*, "An Extra Issue of the *Spirit of the Times*," *Papers of the Bibliographical Society of America*, XLVIII (Second Quarter, 1954), 198, and in Lindley Eberstadt, "The Passing of a Noble 'Spirit,'" *Papers of the Bibliographical Society of America*, XLIV (Fourth Quarter, 1950), 372–73.

Tributes and obituary notices which contain bits of information on Porter include [Francis A. Durivage], *Ballou's Pictorial*, XI (August 16, 1856), 108; "Acorn" [James Oakes], *Spirit*, XXVIII (1858), 289; anonymous, *Porter's Spirit*, IV (1858), 328; anonymous, New York *Daily Tribune* (July 20, 1858), 7; anonymous, New York *Times* (July 20, 1858), 4; anonymous, "The Editor's Table," *Knickerbocker*, LII (September, 1858), 310–11; Col. Thomas Picton, "Reminiscences of a Sporting Journalist," *Spirit of the Times,* CIII (1882), 225–26. Other biographical sources include Francis Brinley, *Life of William T. Porter* (New York: D. Appleton, 1860)—inaccurate and incomplete, but containing much material not found elsewhere; Horace Greeley, *Recollections of a Busy Life* (New York: The Tribune Association, 1873); James Parton, *The Life of Horace Greeley* (Boston: James R. Osgood, 1872); Stephen C. Massett, *"Drifting About,"* or What *"Jeems Pipes of Pipesville"* Saw-and-Did (New York: Carleton, 1863); David W. Judd (ed.), *The Life and Writings of Frank Forester* (2 vols.; New York: Orange, Judd, 1882); Fred E. Pond, *Life and Adventures of Ned Buntline* (New York: Cadmus Book Shop, 1919); Fayette Copeland, *Kendall of the Picayune* (Norman, Oklahoma: University of Oklahoma Press, 1943); Nelson F. Adkins, *Fitz-Greene Halleck, an Early Knickerbocker Wit and Poet* (New Haven: Yale University Press, 1930); *id.,* "William Trotter Porter," in Dumas Malone (ed.), *Dictionary of American Biography,* XV (New York, 1935), 107–108.

Porter's editing jobs outside the *Spirit* are *The Big Bear of Arkansas, and Other Sketches, Illustrative of Characters and Incidents in the South and Southwest* (Philadelphia: Carey and Hart, 1845); *A Quarter Race in Kentucky, and Other Sketches, Illustrative of Scenes, Characters, and Incidents Throughout "The Universal Yankee Nation"* (Philadelphia: Carey and Hart, 1846); *Instructions to Young Sportsmen . . . By Lieut. Col. P. Hawker . . . To Which is Added the Hunting and Shooting of North America, with Descriptions of the Animals and Birds . . .* (Philadelphia: Lea and Blanchard, 1846). Some information on Porter's dealings with specific contributors to his paper may be obtained from Eugene Current-Garcia, " 'Mr. Spirit' and *The Big Bear of Arkansas,*" *American Literature,* XXVII (November, 1955), 332–46; Donald Day, "The Life of George Washington Harris," *Tennessee Historical Quarterly,* VI (March, 1947), 3–38; *id.,* "The Life and Works of George Washington Harris," unpublished Ph. D. dissertation (Chicago, 1942); W. Stanley Hoole, *Alias Simon Suggs, the Life and Times of Johnson Jones Hooper* (University, Alabama: University of Alabama Press, 1952); Milton Henry Rickels, "Thomas Bangs Thorpe: His Life and Works," unpublished Ph. D. dissertation (Louisiana State, 1953); James Raymond Masterson, *Tall Tales of Arkansaw* (Boston: Chapman and Grimes, 1942) (for data on the contributions of Noland and other Arkansas authors to the *Spirit*).

For sources of specific information on most of the writing which appeared in the *Spirit* and for general background, the reader is referred to the notes. Brief general surveys of the magazine itself have appeared with increasing frequency as the entire field of backwoods humor, realism, and folklore has come under the closer scrutiny of serious scholars. William Peterfield Trent (ed.), *Southern Writers, Selections in Prose and Verse* (New York: Macmillan, 1905), 271n., is, I believe, the first to cite the *Spirit* as a favorite medium of publication for humorous writers. V. L. O. Chittick, *Thomas Chandler Haliburton, . . . a Study in Provincial Toryism* (New York: Columbia University Press, 1924), 537–39, discusses the *Spirit* briefly and incidentally; Jennette Tandy, *Crackerbox Philosophers in American Humor and Satire* (New York: Columbia University Press, 1925), 71–74, supplies the first really useful survey of Porter and his work. Napier Wilt (ed.), *Some American Humorists* (New York: Thomas Nelson and Sons, 1929), x, gives the *Spirit of the Times* and the *Boston Carpet-Bag* special credit for publishing tales of the "comic illiterate."

Franklin J. Meine in his extremely useful edition of *Tall Tales of the Southwest . . . 1830–1860* (New York: Alfred A. Knopf, 1930), xxiv–xxix, indicates the importance of the *Spirit* as a source of frontier material, and reprints some of the best tales in Porter's journal. Constance Rourke, *American Humor* (New York: Harcourt, Brace, 1931), 79, 307, 310, likewise shows her awareness of the *Spirit* and its value as a source of regional writing. Bernard DeVoto, *Mark Twain's America* (Boston: Little Brown, 1932), 95–98, 174, and *passim*, not only notes the importance of the *Spirit* but discusses a number of parallels between sketches in that magazine and the work of Mark Twain. Carle Brooks Spotts, "The Development of Fiction on the Missouri Frontier," [fourth installment] *Missouri Historical Review*, XXIX (January, 1935), 100–108, discusses the part played by the *Spirit* in promoting the literature of a certain area. Arthur Palmer Hudson (ed.), *Humor of the Old Deep South* (New York: Macmillan, 1936), not only discusses the magazine in his introduction but reprints twenty-eight sketches and tales from its pages. Walter Blair, *Native American Humor* (New York: American Book Company, 1937), 62–101, presents a shrewd analysis of southwestern humor which includes a discussion of the spreading and mutation of tales in Porter's magazine. Blair also reprints several items from the *Spirit*. John Rickards Betts, "Sporting Journalism in Nineteenth Century America," *American Quarterly*, V (Spring, 1953), 41, provides a convenient summary of the *Spirit* as a sporting journal. Two valuable and recent surveys of frontier humor which emphasize the role of the *Spirit* are Franklin J. Meine, "American Folk Literature," *Amateur Book Collector*, I (January, 1951), 3–4, and Daniel G. Hoffman, *Paul Bunyan, Last of the Frontier Demigods* (Philadelphia: University of Pennsylvania Press, 1952), 65–73. A general discussion of southern comic realism which is useful although it does not especially stress the part played by the *Spirit* is Shields McIlwaine, *The Southern Poor-White from Lubberland to Tobacco Road* (Norman, Oklahoma: University of Oklahoma Press, 1939), 40–74.

A number of present-day anthologists, in addition to those already cited, have reprinted material from the *Spirit*, often adding comments of their own. Most extensive in his use of Porter's magazine has been Thomas D. Clark, *The Rampaging Frontier* (Indianapolis and New York: Bobbs-Merrill, 1939). Others include V. L. O. Chittick (ed.), *Ring-Tailed Roarers* (Caldwell, Idaho: Caxton Printers, 1941); Masterson, *Tall Tales of Arkansaw*; B. A. Botkin (ed.), *A Treasury of American Folklore* (New York: Crown, 1944); *id.*, *A Treasury of Southern Folklore* (New York: Crown, 1949); Richard M. Dorson, *Jonathan Draws the Long Bow* (Cambridge, Massachusetts: Harvard University Press, 1946); James R. Aswell (ed.), *Native American Humor* (New York and London: Harper, 1947); Ben C. Clough (ed.), *The American Imagination at Work, Tall Tales and Folk Tales* (New York: Alfred A. Knopf, 1947).

Writers for the Spirit

Index